Praise for *I Am Hutterite*

"A beautifully crafted memoir of a simple, faithful life. I read it with the intense conviction of the many years I spent in judgment of people serving the same God in a different way than I. Reading *I Am Hutterite* allowed a personal glimpse into a private world, leaving me with the impression that Mary-Ann Kirkby and her beloved Hutterites are the same kind of different as me."

> — Ron Hall
> coauthor of *Same Kind of Different As Me*

"Mary Ann Kirkby, in her outstanding book, *I Am Hutterite*, shares her own true story of moving out of the Hutterite culture in Canada as a youth, adjusting to the freedoms of eclectic culture today, but then reclaiming some of the outstanding character traits and faith and courage of the Hutterite culture she originally came from. I strongly endorse this book to understand another family of our own brothers and sisters both past and present."

> — Paul Meier, MD
> author of more than 80 books and founder of the national chain of Meier Clinics

"A superb memoir that takes us into the hidden heart of a prairie Hutterite colony. In a style both sparing and supple, Mary-Ann Kirkby conjures up both the warmth and simplicity of Hutterite life and the pain of leaving it. This has the makings of a prairie classic."

> — Award Jury,
> *Saskatchewan Book Awards*

"Honest, strong, clear, direct, it opens the door on what has been for so many of us a completely closed world. . . . If you've ever wondered about the life of a colony, and what it would mean to hold everything in common in this context, I encourage you to read this book. It's a beautifully sad story of one family who held onto faith, while at the same time choosing to stand for their own dignity and worth in a way that the colony could not understand. There is no hatred in this book, only a pervasive sense of loss, longing, and love, as well as an enduring respect for the freedom of what it means to truly live in faith."

— *Winnipeg Free Press*

I Am Hutterite

I Am Hutterite

The Fascinating True Story of a Young Woman's
Journey to Reclaim Her Heritage

MARY-ANN KIRKBY

THOMAS NELSON
Since 1798

NASHVILLE   DALLAS   MEXICO CITY   RIO DE JANEIRO

Published in Nashville, Tennessee, by Thomas Nelson. Thomas Nelson is a registered trademark of Thomas Nelson, Inc.

Thomas Nelson books may be purchased in bulk for educational, business, fund-raising, or sales promotional use. For information, please e-mail SpecialMarkets@ThomasNelson.com.

Scripture quotations are from the King James Version of the Bible.

Library of Congress Cataloging-in-Publication Data

Kirkby, Mary-Ann.
    I am Hutterite : the fascinating true story of a young woman's journey to reclaim her heritage / Mary-Ann Kirkby.—[Updated ed.].
      p. cm.
    Includes bibliographical references.
    ISBN 978-0-8499-4810-7 (hardcover)
    1. Kirkby, Mary-Ann—Childhood and youth. 2. Hutterite Brethren—Manitoba—Biography. 3. Hutterite Brethren—Manitoba—Social life and customs. I. Title.
F1035.H97K57 2010
289.7092—dc22
[B]   2009053304

Printed in the United States of America

10 11 12 13 14 WC 5 4 3 2 1

To my beloved parents, Ronald and Mary Dornn.

Thank you for teaching me the value of courage,

the importance of faith, and the power of forgiveness.

Contents

Foreword by Arvel Gray   xi

A Short History of the Hutterites   xv

Prologue   xix

Chapter 1 *"Der G'hört Mein!": "He's Mine!"*   1

Chapter 2 *Die Hochzeit: The Wedding*   17

Chapter 3 *"Du Sei Der Gute": "You Be the Good One"*   37

Chapter 4 *Tea Bags and Sugar Lumps*   53

Chapter 5 *Renie*   69

Chapter 6 *Die Teacherin: The Teacher*   87

Chapter 7 *Secret Flowerpot*   107

Chapter 8 *Weglaufen: Running Away*   127

Chapter 9 *Our Year at Dahl's Farm*   143

Chapter 10 *Rogers' Farm*   173

Chapter 11 *A Place of Our Own in Plum Coulee/Winkler*   199

Epilogue   227

Afterword   231

Acknowledgments   233

Family Tree   236

Hutterisch: Hutterite Language Glossary   239

Bibliography   243

Hutterite Sucre Pie   245

Foreword

I FIRST MET Mary-Ann Kirkby in 1999 when she spoke at a women's conference that I helped to organize, called Women Connecting Women. Her description of life on a Hutterite colony held us spellbound, as did her bittersweet recounting of leaving the colony and integrating into a new culture. Most compelling was the point of view of her story: the voice of an eager, joyful, but sometimes confused and frightened ten-year-old girl seeking acceptance. "To the outside world," she said, "we were Hutterites and we were different." Even as a journalist, she kept her past hidden, reluctant to reveal her cultural heritage and open up the old scars of prejudice and suspicion.

The delegates were so moved by her story that they encouraged her to write more.

And so she did.

Her manuscript has been seven years in the making, but like an archaeological dig, this was not a story to be hurried. I joined her in a hunt for a history that was several layers deep, where fragments would reveal themselves in their own good time. Often, when we hit a dead end or a snag, someone would unexpectedly come forward with a photograph or letter that had been tucked away in a bottom cupboard or offer up a memory from long ago.

Occasionally, Mary-Ann would take me to a Hutterite colony. I had often seen the Hutterites shopping in local big-box stores, sitting in a reception room at a hospital, or selling fresh produce at the farmer's market. Their unassuming demeanor and old-fashioned way of dress made me believe they were a shy and retiring people, but I quickly learned that on their home turf, their lives were as colorful and complex as those in the "English" world. In the big community kitchen at the Fairholme colony, I envied the head cook's fully stocked larder and industrial appliances, yet we were able to commiserate about the difficulty of keeping menus varied and which recipe for date squares provided the best flavor. Sometimes, we would time our visits for afternoon *Lunschen* at New Rosedale, and while we waited for the teakettle to boil, we would devour a plate of freshly baked buns and discuss education and politics. Each time I met with wise elders content with a life well lived, or saw their young people's artwork or heard their exquisite choirs, I began to understand why Mary-Ann's decision to share her story carried a heavy burden: her narrative would not only unravel her past; it would provide unique insight into the hearts and minds of Hutterite people.

Confronting the past has not always been easy for Mary-Ann, but in the end, her reward is a better understanding of who she is today. Her achingly poignant narrative is a balm to anyone who has faced ridicule and rejection, underscoring that who we are comes not from the clothes we wear or the songs we sing or the company we keep, but from a place deep within our souls.

I once believed that when the book was complete, the work would be over, but I now know the real opportunity for transformation lies ahead. When Jacob Hutter forged the Hutterite Church, his vision included a world without violence, where all things were shared; my hope is that this book will remind us that we are all part of the human family and that true harmony can be achieved with love, acceptance, and compassion in the absence of fear and judgment.

— A. G.

Arvel Gray is a Winnipeg-based writer/broadcaster and executive director of Waking the World, a project dedicated to uniting the voices of women globally.

::

A Short History of the Hutterites

And all that believed were together, and had
all things in common; and sold their
possessions and goods, and parted them to all
men, as every man had need.

—ACTS 2:44–45

THE HUTTERITE FAITH was born in the sixteenth
century when Jacob Hutter, an Austrian hatmaker, led a
fledgling group of Anabaptists to a new kind of Christian
community. On a dusty path in Moravia in 1528, a handful of refugees from Switzerland, Germany, Italy, and
Austria put a rugged blanket on the ground and on it
placed all of their possessions, including everything they
were carrying in their pockets. Thus began our history.

Inspired by the early church in Jerusalem, they mod-
eled their faith on the second chapter of Acts, verses

44–45, in the Bible: "And all that believed were together, and had all things in common; and sold their possessions and goods, and parted them to all men, as every man had need." Hutter's passionate vision of a society where property was shared and people worked together for the common good gave birth to the Hutterite Church and way of life, but his belief in community life, adult baptism, and pacifism provoked hatred and intolerance from the state and the predominant religions, forcing Hutterites to flee across Europe for nearly four hundred years.

In 1536, Hutter was burned at the stake in Innsbruck, Austria, for refusing to denounce his faith, as were many of our other forefathers. Still some survived and, in 1770, found refuge in the Russian Ukraine until their military exemption status was rescinded and they escaped to the United States.

The Hutterites arrived in New York on July 5, 1874, on the *Hammonia*, which had sailed from Russia. Battered but not defeated, they were determined to pool their resources and start over. My great-grandfather Jakob Maendel was among them. The first Hutterite Colony on North American soil was established in 1874 on the banks of the Missouri River near Yankton, South Dakota. It has special historic significance to all Hutterites today and is still in operation.

During World War I, entire Hutterite communities moved to Canada to avoid persecution as conscientious objectors. After the war, realizing their value as land and livestock farmers, the American government invited them to return to the United States. One-third of them willingly did, but the rest remained in Canada and established new colonies throughout western Canada, including my home colonies of New Rosedale and Fairholme in Manitoba.

The Hutterite commitment to the common ownership of goods sets them apart from the Amish and the Mennonites and distinguishes them as the finest and most successful example of community life in the modern world. Today their population sits at approximately forty-five thousand on four hundred colonies in the northwestern United States and Canadian prairies.

Prologue

IN JULY 2002, I was approached by a journalist friend to write a magazine article about Hutterite gardens. Manitoba is home to more than a hundred Hutterite colonies, but I knew exactly which one I wanted to visit. Selling the story idea to the head gardener at Fairholme Colony took a little work. Judy Maendel wasn't convinced hers had enough of a wow factor to merit a story.

"Oh, heavens, we only have a small garden this year." She sighs over the phone. "Why don't you try New Rosedale or James Valley? Their gardens are so big they're selling vegetables to the public." I really want to see Fairholme's, I insist.

Big, uneven, white clouds resembling a child's drawing fill the open prairie sky as I pile my five-year-old son, Levi, into the car for the journey. I do not need directions. I know the way as certainly as I know the sound of my son's voice. The rich, earthy smells of a Manitoba summer dance through the open car window as I head west on the Trans-Canada. On either side of the highway, yellow fields of canola stretch as far as the eye can see.

"Once upon a time . . ." begins the tape deck with the Robin Hood story Levi has chosen for himself.

Once upon a time, indeed! I tumble down memory lane, and in my mind I can almost hear the kitchen bell on the colony ringing, calling the women to work. A tractor hitched with a trailer idles impatiently near a sandy path that winds its way down to the garden on the banks of the Assiniboine River. I see my mother with the other women piling onto the flatbed, each with a three-gallon, stainless-steel pail in which they collect the day's bounty. Their distinct garments speak of safety, of duty, and of motherhood. On each head is a *Tiechel*, a black kerchief with white polka dots the size of garden peas. I see Judy's mother, Sara, the head gardener, among the women, and I know that in a few hours, they will return home for afternoon *Lunschen*, three o'clock lunch, with flushed faces and stained fingers, carrying ruby strawberries to the bevy of eager children awaiting them. In their simple kitchens they plop the sweet fruit into bowls, anointing them with fresh cream and a sprinkle of sugar. Their young ones with rested eyes and hungry mouths crowd around the table and eat until their stomachs are ready to burst. Soon the bell will ring again and the women must return to work. The bulk of the strawberries are sitting in the cool basement of the large community kitchen, waiting to be transformed into pies and cakes and jars of delicious jams . . .

Fairholme Colony, says the sign an hour's drive from Winnipeg. A dusty gravel road lined on both sides with mature oak trees escorts us into the heart of Fairholme, where colorful flower gardens give the neat rows of aging homes a festive flair.

My son and I make our way to Judy's house. Her sister, Selma, the head cook, is waiting for us. So are a group of curious, barefoot children. The girls are in identical black bonnets, their suntanned faces giving off a healthy radiance. "I really feel sorry for your dress," says Selma. I walk toward her in a fitted dress I purchased weeks ago from a major department store. "It's too tight!" She motions to a nearby residence. "Let's go see Tamara." We are scarcely through the door of the nearby house before Selma says, "Mary-Ann needs something to wear. She's uncomfortable." A young woman with the face of an angel rises from her sewing machine and offers me an outfit from her closet. It has a rosy pattern and a roomy, full-gathered skirt. The waistband is loose and forgiving, and the fabric soft and cool against my skin. A whiff of dried cotton and sunshine escapes from the opened closet, and I am transported back to the summers of my childhood. The children who follow us delight in seeing me in a Hutterite outfit. "*Bin ich schön?* Do I look beautiful?" I tease them in Hutterisch, their mother tongue, a 450-year-old Germanic dialect from the province of Carinthia in Austria. The children giggle and nod. I wink at my son, who's giggling too.

When Judy appears, we all squeeze into my small car for the short ride to the garden. "This car is full of Hutterites," reports Levi from the backseat, to a round of laughter.

At our destination we shed our shoes for a leisurely stroll. "It's a beautiful garden," Judy admits as she leads the way. Our miniature tour guides soon lose themselves in the pea patch, with Levi in tow. The "small" fifteen-acre garden is lush and green, thanks to the community's irrigation system. Rows and rows of vegetables are framed by a painter's palette of wildflowers and tall prairie grasses. "We only have enough for ourselves this year," she explains, referring to the approximately ninety community members the garden will serve.

Late afternoon finds me lingering in the community kitchen, where preparations for the supper meal are underway. The women laugh easily as they move between the oven, the fryer, and boiling pots of vegetables. I find it hard to pull myself away. I locate Levi twirling on the colony's wooden merry-go-round; he isn't any more eager to leave than I. On our way to the car, we cross paths with another of the locals. "Mary-Ann!" exclaims Thelma, taking me in. "You look so nice when you're not wearing all that paint on your face." I laugh at her candor. One doesn't have to read minds around here.

I fill the backseat of my car with a bouquet of wildflowers and pussy willows—favorites of my mother—and we drive to a small, fenced graveyard on the outer edge of Fairholme. Time seems to stand still as I lead my son to a small gravestone that reads, "Reynold Dornn, 1963–1965, Resting in Peace with Jesus."

"Levi," I begin, searching for the right words, "there is a little boy buried here. His name is Renie, and he is my brother." As we crouch down over the small grave, Levi closes his eyes and begins to pray. "Dear Jesus, thank you for taking care of Mommy's brother even though he's under the ground. Please help him to rose again." I tear up at his unexpected overture.

Thirty-three years ago, when I was a wide-eyed, ten-year-old girl, my parents made the painful decision to leave Fairholme Colony with seven children and little else. This community was once my home, and although I have been back for brief visits many times, here in this simple graveyard lies a stark reminder of where we have come from, a precious part of ourselves that we left behind.

Hand in hand we make our way back to the car. I am lost in thought when Levi forces me out of my reverie. "Mommy," he asks, a look of wonder on his round, little face, "are you a Hutterite?" My son's innocent question sends me on a journey into the inner recesses of the heart, where our deepest secrets are kept and the truth is stored.

This book is my journey to reclaim my past, a past I kept hidden for many years, unwilling to subject myself to ingrained taunts and prejudices. What I know with certainty today is that our humanity is what we have in common, but our cultural heritage is the special gift each of us is given at birth. Until we embrace who we are and really value the power it is meant to bring to our lives, we cannot realize our true potential. My story begins where most good stories begin, with my mother, the incomparable Mary Maendel.

— Mary-Ann Kirkby

Mary Maendel, age 18,
New Rosedale Colony.

ONE

"Der G'hört Mein!"

"He's mine!"

New Rosedale Hutterite Colony, Western Canada
November 1952

MY MOTHER, MARY Maendel, rose early Sunday morning and gently pushed back the feather quilt on her side of the bed, careful not to wake her niece, Sarah, who lay motionless beside her. No one stirred in the alcove just a few feet away, where her other nieces, Lena, Katie, Susie, and Judy, were still enveloped in

1

sleep. She collected her clothing from a nearby chair and slipped on her cropped white shirt, or *Pfaht*; her vest, or *Mieder*; an ankle-length, gathered skirt, or *Kittel*; and a pleated apron called a *Fittig*. Then she quietly proceeded downstairs.

Yesterday was cleaning day on the colony, and the floors and furniture had been thoroughly washed down and wiped. But in a culture where cleanliness and godliness were revered virtues, Mary was determined that today, one of the most important days of her life, the house would be spotless. A bar of homemade lard soap called *Specksaften*, resembling a square of butter, slowly melted into her pail of hot water, filling it with sudsy bubbles. Down on her hands and knees, she began washing the floors, her deft, young hands moving easily around the *Schlofbänk*, or sleeping benches, filled with children deep in slumber. The soundless movement of her washrag kept time with their breathing, and the house soon responded with the sharp scent of wet wood and wax.

By 7:00 a.m. she had finished her chores. Outside, the wind was tossing the lifeless branches of the old oak trees that separated the colony's neat semicircle of homes from the barns and machine shop.

Through the front window she could see lines of adults and children scurrying over to the community kitchen for breakfast. Bearded men wearing black, homespun jackets and trousers, and women in ankle-length patterned skirts and vests, some still knotting identical polka-dot kerchiefs under their chins, strode purposefully and in single file toward a large central building that drew them together three times a day for sustenance. Young girls in *Mützen* (bonnets) and long, flowered dresses, and boisterous boys looking like miniature versions of their parents trailed after them, drawn, it appeared, by some invisible string. To Mary, the scene was as familiar as the sunrise, but to an outsider the setting and period costumes, adopted from sixteenth-century peasants, would have seemed staged, as if the players were on a film set where a centuries-old story was about to unfold.

Peering through the window, Mary could have been taken for an actor waiting for her cue, but this was not a movie. This was life on the New Rosedale Hutterite Colony in southern Manitoba, and the one hundred men, women, and children who lived there were the cast of characters whose lives echoed those of their European ancestors of nearly five hundred years ago.

"Mein Himmel, eilt's! Good heavens, hurry up!" shouted Mary's brother-in-law, Paul Hofer, who was hastening his brood of children scattered throughout the house. Mary's sister, Sana, was the head cook, and she had been up since dawn over in the community kitchen, boiling choice cuts of beef for today's special noon meal and supervising the breakfast of boiled eggs, hot buttered toast, and plates of *Schmuggi*—soft, homemade cheese sprinkled with caraway seeds.

The thirteen Hofer children brushed past Mary to join the procession, and she shivered as a gust of crisp November air blew through the open front door. On an ordinary day she should have gone with them, but today was an exception. Today was her wedding day. After the morning *Lehr* church service, she would be making her formal vows of marriage, elevating her status from *Diene*, a young woman, to *Weib*, a wife, and increasing her worth and workload in the community.

The twenty-one-year-old started up the narrow wooden staircase to her bedroom, grateful for the seven years of shelter her sister had provided but eager to leave the overburdened household for a place of her own.

Until age thirteen, Mary had lived at the Old Rosedale Hutterite Colony sixty miles to the northeast, where her father, the well-respected Joseph Maendel, was the manager of the largest and most successful colony in Manitoba. It was to him that many other colonies had come for financial assistance. Old Rosedale's prosperity was rooted in its diversity and in its management.

Joseph Maendel had been a shrewd administrator, ensuring that the colony made an enviable profit from its field crops and livestock. In 1931, a devastating drought year for most prairie farmers, Old Rosedale's income was a princely $60,000 from grain and other enterprises. These included 900 hogs, 250 geese, several hundred cattle and sheep, and an apiary that produced 40,000 pounds of honey a year.

His devoted wife, Katrina, was the head gardener and special cook for the sick, but when she died suddenly of a gallstone attack at age forty-five, she left a husband and colony in shock, and sixteen children, including one-year-old Mary, without a mother.

A devastated Joseph Maendel poured out his grief in a letter to his sister-in-law at the James Valley Colony.

> Oh dear sister-in-law, it was very, very sad for us to be hit like this. We stared in disbelief as our desperately needed and precious mother lay dead in front of our eyes.
>
> Her sister Rebecca cried out loud, "Oh Almighty God, how can you take a mother like that out of this house!" But nothing helped. Our dear mother was in eternity with God. I told our daughters and all the children, "Let's diligently pray to God so that no other calamity should befall us." How sad it would be if I, their father, couldn't be with them anymore either. We hope and beg and pray that the Almighty God will have mercy on all widows and widowers and their orphans.

A year after his wife's death, Joseph Maendel began to write to mature, eligible women and widows from other colonies to secure a mother for his younger children. After a handful of rejections,

Rachel Gross, a widow with six children from the Maxwell Hutterite Colony, agreed to marry him, enlarging his family to twenty-two. Despite her best efforts, mild-mannered Rachel simply wasn't able to adequately nurture so many children, and Mary, left in the care of her older sisters, clung to her father, who gave what parental love and grounding he could.

Two years later the blended family was dealt a dreaded blow when fifty-year-old Joseph was diagnosed with intestinal cancer and underwent major surgery in Winnipeg. He was a steadying influence during times of turbulence at Old Rosedale, and his illness threatened the political stability he had worked so tirelessly to forge within the community. As the ravages of the disease drained his energies, *Marilein*, or "Little Mary," was often turned away from his bedside. One warm afternoon in September, as she was out playing in the bluffs of trees that surrounded the colony, she felt a sudden compulsion to go home and found the adults in an upheaval. "Where have you been?" they cried. "We've been looking everywhere for you!" Her father had wanted to say goodbye to her, but she had come too late. Overcome, the young girl buried her hands in her face and cried.

At age five, Mary was essentially an orphan. In succession, her three adult sisters—Sana, Anna, and Katrina—married, and each time was like losing her mother all over again as she was shuffled off to the care of the next sister. She escaped from her loss during the day when she could run and play in the vast open areas of the colony, and in the late afternoons when she would take a little stick and join the other children in rounding up the community's geese from the riverbank. Each of the ten families at Old Rosedale was in charge of seven geese, and Mary loved to shoo the Maendel geese home so they could lay their eggs in the wooden nests her father had built around their house. She knew each of them by name and could tell exactly which ones belonged to her family.

During the day she was always occupied, but at night, alone in her bed, she couldn't suppress the ache of loneliness that lingered in the pit of her stomach. She longed for her mother and tried to envision her face, to remember the smell of her skin and the safety of her arms. Under her covers, she practiced saying *Muetter*, or "Mother," out loud to the darkness. But then the tears would start, and every time she cried like that, she'd see a vision of her mother, Katrina, at the end of the bed, holding a lighted candle. Every night Katrina would come to her daughter this way, but the small child became so frightened she couldn't fall asleep. It was only after she willed herself to stop yearning for her mother that the haunting visitations ended.

After Joseph Maendel's untimely death, a change in leadership ignited years of smoldering conflicts within the community. His oldest sons had hoped one of them would replace their father as colony manager, but when they were outvoted by the Waldner and Hofer families, the bitterness escalated until the two factions could no longer live together. In the summer of 1944, Mary's brothers decided to leave Old Rosedale to establish a new colony in southern Manitoba. They named it New Rosedale and took most of their extended families and supporters with them. Thirteen-year-old Mary and her two teenage brothers, Darius and Eddie, became part of their sister Sana's household.

It was from the relative safety of Sana's house that Mary first laid eyes on Ronald Dornn. "*Der g'hört mein!* He's mine!" she wisecracked to her teenage nieces as they peered out of an upstairs window. She was eighteen years old and had a quick wit and a devilish sense of humor. "We'll tell him you said that!" the girls teased, but she knew they lacked the courage to follow through on their threat. Down below, the wiry frame of a handsome stranger emerged from the colony vehicle onto the sandy soil of the Assiniboine River valley. It was obvious from his square, black hat, lovingly referred to as the "washtub," that he was from the Lehrerleut in Alberta, one of three distinct sects of Hutterites in North America.

The cultural and religious differences between the three groups were minor, confined more to dress code than religious principles. To an outsider the discrepancies would hardly be discernible, but to the Hutterites they were so significant that intermarriage between the groups was rare. The Dariusleut in Saskatchewan were committed to simple buttons on their shirts and jackets, but the Schmiedeleut in Manitoba, which included New Rosedale, considered buttons too flashy, and opted for invisible hooks, eyes, and snaps. The Lehrerleut were the most conservative, insisting the zipper of a man's pants be at the side rather than the front, in case some unmindful man forgot to zip up. All three groups did agree on one thing: pockets on the back of a man's pants were far too worldly. Store-bought pants with "ass pockets" were strictly off-limits.

The new visitor from the Lehrerleut created significant excitement in the community, and people looking out of their large picture windows wanted to know which colony in Alberta he was from, how long he was staying, and why he was here. To the great surprise of no one, Mary's sister had had a hand in orchestrating his visit. Sana Hofer was known to everyone as Sana *Basel,* or "Aunt" Sana, and her congenial nature was legendary. No one would think it out of the ordinary to find some new lodger sleeping on a cot in her living room or safely tucked beneath the kitchen table, out of the way of perpetual foot traffic.

Fate had introduced Sana Basel and Ronald in the summer of 1949 at the Rockport Hutterite Colony in Alberta. Her clout as head cook had earned her a once-in-a-lifetime trip to pay a social call to some of the Lehrerleut colonies in the province, including Rockport. Ronald, on the other hand, had spent his youth at the

Rockport Colony and had just returned for the first time in seven years to discuss his family's future with the colony minister.

When Ronald confided to Sana that in a few days he would be taking the train back east to an uncertain future, she didn't waste any time rearranging his schedule. "Come for a visit to New Rosedale Colony in Manitoba," she insisted in her charming way. "Give us a call from the train station in Portage la Prairie, and we'll come to get you." *Gostfrei* Sana Basel was beguiling and had a heart for those whose lives were troubled with ambiguities and indecision. Ronald found himself drawn to the open face and loving manner of this forty-year-old woman who embodied the warmth and caring of a mother and comfort of an old friend. She made him feel cherished, and he hadn't felt that way in a long time. Her compelling invitation was hard to resist.

Once home in New Rosedale, Sana Basel soon received word that her visitor had arrived at the station and quickly dispatched her husband, Paul "*Vetter*," or "Uncle" Paul, and son Paul Jr. to fetch him. They returned in time for *Lunschen*, three o'clock lunch, the only time families ate together in their own homes. When Ronald entered the house, Sana Basel's face lit up and she greeted him enthusiastically, pulling out a chair for him and taking his hat from his hand.

"*Reinhold, sog wos!* Ronald, say something!" Sana said eagerly as she handed the hat to one of her daughters. He was suspected of having heard or seen particular things of interest since he had just traveled across several provinces, and she expected to be entertained. Sana Basel's raised eyebrows were poised for a juicy tidbit of almost any sort, but her visitor proved a disappointment in the gossip department. Ronald preferred to listen rather than be heard and didn't seem to appreciate the fine Hutterite tradition of *Tschelli draufschmieren*, "adding jam" to an unexceptional story. Some would have called him *Maulvoll* or "mouth lazy"—too sparing with his words to be considered entertaining—but in the secluded Hutterite world, his mere presence invited curiosity.

The Hofer boys drifted in from their farm chores, and a handful of regulars stopped by to fraternize and to inspect the strange man in the "English" leather jacket and the black lamb's-wool hat. Mary piled gingersnaps and oatmeal cookies on two Dura-Ware plates and placed them in front of the visitor with the steel-blue eyes and thick, auburn hair, neatly parted down the middle. Back behind the safety of the steaming kettle, she noted that he could use a new pair of pants. She watched Ronald dip the tip of his tablespoon into the jar of honey, tasting it before stirring the rest into his hot cup of chamomile tea. She observed the methodical way he tidied the cookie crumbs on the heavily varnished wooden table, cupping them into his left hand and placing them on his plate. Mary secretly wished she could have served him something better. The fresh lemon pies piled high with meringue and Queen Elizabeth cakes portioned out on Thursday, the colony's baking day, hadn't lasted the weekend at the Hofer house. With seven beautiful daughters who attracted their fair share of interest from eligible *Buben* (young men), Sana Basel's house was always a gathering place, filled with young people who would convene every evening to socialize and sing.

Ronald came for a week and stayed for good. Sana Basel's crowded quarters became his retreat and she a surrogate mother who sympathized with his inner struggles. He lived in a room upstairs with the Hofer boys while Mary lived across the hall, in the girls' room with her nieces. Mary cleaned his room and made his bed every day, but there was never a hint of romance. The only evidence to suggest any concern for his welfare was that she had repaired his tattered pants and left them neatly folded on his bed.

Ronald was consumed with the plight of his father and siblings back in Ontario. His Russian-immigrant parents had joined the

Rockport Hutterite Colony in Alberta when he was nine years old, and the family lived there for almost a decade. But when Ronald was seventeen, Christian Dornn had cut his ties with the Hutterite Church, gathered his eight children, and joined a Hutterite-wannabe community in eastern Canada. The mission and the move were disastrous, as the leader turned out to be a dictator who treated the people in his commune abusively and harshly. When Ronald met Sana Basel, he was on a mission to bring his beleaguered family back to the Rockport Colony, but his hopes were dashed when the colony minister bluntly informed him that he and his siblings were welcome, but their father was not.

At his new home in the New Rosedale Colony in Manitoba, Ronald found relief in toil and in the sanctuary of nature. Strong and fit, he cleared the one thousand acres of land that New Rosedale had recently purchased for four dollars an acre. He removed the oak and poplar trees with a TD-14 Caterpillar tractor and broke up the virgin soil with a Rome plow in preparation for the colony to seed barley and wheat. In the evenings he spent most of his time in his room, reading his Bible.

Two years after his arrival, Ronald came up to Mary's room, unannounced, and asked if she would consider being his girlfriend. She had noticed a shift in the way he was looking at her lately, and once, when she was alone in the house, he had returned from the field early and they'd shared a cup of instant coffee. Caught off guard by his question, she wasn't prepared to give him an answer. "I'll have to think about it," she stammered, lowering her head to avert his piercing blue eyes.

When this was leaked to members of the community, it stirred up a storm of controversy. Ronald was promptly moved out of Sana Basel's residence into a tiny two-room house of his own, and Mary's job of cleaning his room was assigned to someone else. Mary's brother, Jake Maendel, the assistant minister at New Rosedale, wasted no time enlisting Elie Wipf to pursue his sister. Elie was the son of the senior minister at Fairmont Colony, and Jake had gone out of his way to introduce the pair when Mary was barely a teenager. It had been six years since she had seen Elie, but within days of Ronald's proposal, Mary was summoned to her other brother Peter's house, where Elie was waiting. He still possessed the same dark good looks, easy manner, and mischievous smile.

When Mary had met Elie six years ago in Fairmont, she had felt awkward. Elie's sister had invited Mary to join her for tea and cake, and while they ate, Elie had come home from the carpentry shop to catch a glimpse of the young visitor. She remembered feeling intimidated by his imposing frame as he stood in the doorway and teased her that he could run faster than she could.

Mary was no longer a teenager, but she was uneasy sitting on the chesterfield next to him, making small talk about what he was building in the carpentry shop and whether Fairmont had a big garden this year. Elie hadn't come all this way to talk about the colony's cucumbers, but he waited patiently for her to finish. Just as he reached for her hand to tell her she came highly recommended, Peter's wife, Sara, entered the room to offer them a plate of purple grapes. The grapes were a special treat purchased only a few times a year by the colony manager, and Mary would have loved to sample a handful, but she knew eating from the same dish as Elie would imply they were a couple. When Elie said he wouldn't eat the fruit without her, Mary reluctantly broke off a stem, fueling the rumor that they were indeed an item.

Elie returned two Sundays later for a second visit. He arrived in time for the noon meal and had no sooner taken his place with the other men in the adult dining room when tongues began to wag. "She ate from his plate, and now she says she doesn't want him!" said one woman as she took a long reach to pull a drumstick off the roast duck. "*Jung und dumm.* Young and dumb," clucked the neighbor. "She doesn't know what she wants." Newspapers, radios, and television were strictly forbidden on the colony, but people's private lives provided more than enough entertainment with plots as intriguing and unpredictable as a Hollywood soap opera.

Mary wished she was invisible when bits of the conversation drifted to her table a few feet away. She knew many colony members believed she was throwing her luck away if she rejected the carpenter from Fairmont, but for reasons she could not explain and logic she could not defend, she was drawn to the reserved newcomer. She thought about the time they both lived at Sana Basel's house and how she would lie in bed at night and listen to the drone of Ronald's tractor as he worked long hours in the field. At midnight she heard its steady lament as it came closer and closer to home and finally pulled into New Rosedale's machine shop. She heard Ronald open the door and waited for his heavy footsteps on the stairs. She heard the splash of water in the small bathroom sink, the thud of soap against the porcelain as he washed the day's dust from his hands and face, and finally, the click of the bathroom light before he entered the room next to hers and fell into bed, exhausted. She desperately wanted to wait up for him, but with so many people in the house, a private conversation would be impossible. Mary had thought about sneaking out to the field some afternoon to take him a piece of apple pie, but she knew someone would see her, and fresh rumors would fly. It had been almost eight months since Ronald had made his overture, but she had no way of knowing if he still cared for her or if he had become disheartened by Elie's advances.

She dreaded the next encounter with Elie. Mary knew he was the man her brothers wanted her to marry, and she desperately wanted their approval, but she also knew she could not accept his inevitable proposal. She was preparing to go to *Gebet*, the evening church service, when she got word of his return. Grabbing her *Wannick* (jacket), she slipped out of the house, head downcast, and followed the well-worn path toward the church. She was almost at the church door when Ronald and Elie, both hurrying from different directions, unintentionally collided with her—and each other. The confrontation was more than she could handle, and she raced home to hide in the closet upstairs in the boys' room. There in the solitude, with the ironed shirts and polished, black Sunday shoes, Mary wondered what advice her father would have given her. She had heard about his thoughtful counsel to her sister Katrina after she turned down a proposal of marriage from Dafit Wurtz of Deerboine Colony. It was shortly after their mother's death, and Katrina felt duty bound to look after the family.

"Do you love him?" Joseph Maendel had asked her directly.

"Yes," Katrina replied, "but I am needed here at home."

"If you love him, then you must marry him," insisted her father. "We'll get by."

Weeks passed and Mary kept busy with women's work on the colony. One Friday she was in the bakery, measuring out the flour, eggs, and lard for twenty-five dozen buns and fifteen loaves of bread. When the large pillow of dough had swollen to twice its size, she rang the kitchen bell to call the women to roll the buns and shape the loaves. Left to watch them rise and bake in the large industrial stainless steel ovens, Mary's mind drifted back to Elie and the way things had ended between them. She felt bad when she learned he had cried when no one could find her the evening they'd all crossed paths. Ronald, it appeared, had given up on her that night too.

Mary washed the last of the pans and looked forward to her afternoon coffee break. Hot and tired, she began to untie her baking apron when her brother Samuel burst into the bakery, waving a letter in front of her. "Ronald sent me here," he announced to the buns and the bread and an astonished Mary as he tossed the letter on the counter and left. A week earlier, Samuel had given Ronald a new felt hat as an incentive to marry his wife's sister, so the matchmaker secretly hoped the letter's message would put an end to Ronald's prospects for his natural sibling.

Mary stared at the unaddressed white envelope. She trembled as she carefully opened one end and removed a single sheet of precisely folded paper. "*Du Maria*," it began. She was wounded by the harsh "you." "I am not pleased with the stories going around," it continued. "I am writing to you this once, and if you keep this letter to yourself, then there is some hope for us. If not, it's over." It was signed in large, bold script, "Ronald." The letter was as cold as a reprimand from the German schoolteacher, not the kind of note you'd expect from a potential husband. Worse, it implied she was a source for some of the gossip about her and Elie.

Mary stumbled outside the community kitchen into the arms of a beautiful summer day. In the distance she could hear the laughter of children playing tag near the henhouse and the steady hum of the colony's two lawn mowers. Becki Hofer and Martha Baer emerged from a hidden path that led to the river, their stained hands clinging to tin honey pails brimming with saskatoon berries. The predictable patterns of community life remained unaltered, but Mary's world was crumbling around her like the walls of Jericho.

Sana Basel was serving her family chocolate bars and coffee for afternoon *Lunschen* just as her young sister pushed past her, ran up the stairs, and threw herself on her bed, unable to contain her sobbing. "*Wos geht enn für?* What is going on?" a baffled Sana Basel asked Paul Vetter, then followed her sister up the stairs. Standing in the doorway of the bedroom, with a half-eaten Oh Henry! candy bar in one hand, Sana demanded to know what was wrong. Mary had no intention of showing the devastating letter to anyone, but her sister commanded the status and authority of a mother; to refuse her would be a sign of disrespect.

A small red ant scurried across the folds of her bedspread. Mary envied the insect its freedom as she slowly pulled the letter from her apron pocket and handed it to her sister.

Sana Basel adjusted her horn-rimmed glasses and read the confidential correspondence. "*Geht's rüft's in* Jake Vetter!" she instructed her daughters when she read the note, and they ran off to find their uncle. "He'll know what to do."

By the time Jake Maendel arrived, everyone was crowded into the kitchenette downstairs, including Mary, her eyes red from crying. Sana Basel produced the letter and insisted Mary read it out loud. Mary stumbled over Ronald's warning to not share its contents with anyone. When she was finished, the colony's assistant minister didn't say a word. He didn't have to. The controversial relationship between his sister and the Russian-born outsider was over.

Over the next two weeks, Ronald didn't take any of his meals in the community dining room because of a bad chest infection. He was at home in bed when Samuel Maendel dropped in to break the news that the bake house letter had received a public reading. Ronald was crushed.

A few days later, when Sana Basel brought him a pail of chicken noodle soup to nurse his cold, she discovered a man with a broken heart. "*Ich bitt Dich, verzeich's Mir.* I beg you to forgive me," she said when she saw the pain in his eyes. Ronald looked up at the woman whose warmth and kindness had convinced him to join New Rosedale Colony and give community life another chance. "What good is your apology? I don't have her anyway," he replied.

Mother and Father,
two years after their wedding.

> "'*Moch's gut.* Make it good,' whistled Ankela through her troublesome false teeth."

TWO

Die Hochzeit

The Wedding

ALONE IN HER upstairs bedroom, Mary reached for her wedding dress and stroked its soft, rich fabric. It had been meticulously constructed from six yards of beautiful brocade delivered to her door three weeks earlier. The material had come from a reserve of fabrics held on hand by the head seamstress following one of her twice-yearly buying trips to the Winnipeg wholesaler, Gilfix and Roy. Along with the bolts of modest cotton prints for dresses, black rayon for pants, and checkered cotton for shirts, the seamstress kept a judicious eye out for finer fabrics in the event of a wedding announcement.

17

It would not have occurred to Mary to wish for an elaborate, white bridal gown with a matching veil so prized by women in the outside English world. Blue was the traditional color for Hutterite brides, and her simple ensemble was comprised of the same five pieces as a standard Hutterite dress: the *Pfaht*, a *Mieder*, a *Kittel*, a *Fittig*, and a jacket, or *Wannick*. It was as practical and fluid as her everyday dresses, but its texture and color ensured that for the next twelve hours, she would be the center of attention.

Today, for the first time, Mary's *Fittig*, or apron, was the identical deep cornflower blue of her dress. Women's aprons were always a distinctly different color from the rest of the outfit, but friends had pressured her into setting a new trend and cutting her apron from the same fabric as her dress. Mary wistfully thought that perhaps a nice emerald green apron would have given her outfit that extra sparkle.

She slipped on her *Pfaht* and *Mieder* and fixed her *Kittel* with a safety pin. Holding her breath, she centered her matching *Fittig* over her *Kittel* and *Mieder* and wrapped the extra-long apron ties twice around her twenty-four-inch waist, firmly positioning them into a neat bow on her left side. Sometimes a mother or older sister with advanced sewing skills would tailor something as important as a wedding dress, but Mary was an experienced seamstress and had sewn the outfit herself. She tried to catch a full-length glimpse of herself in the small dime-store mirror Paul Vetter had nailed to the opposite wall, but all she could see was her trendy blue apron and its precise bow.

She combed out her waist-length, dark brown hair and carefully parted it down the middle. With practiced hands she began to *drah* it, twisting each side tightly into her hairline and securing the coils with hairpins in the same manner that her mother, her grandmother, and her great-grandmother had done before her. The hairstyle had been fashionable in Austria in the early 1500s and was adopted by Hutterite women ever since for its modesty and simplicity.

Mary lifted her *Tiechel* from the bed and looked fondly at the initials J. M. embroidered into the left corner. Six months before she had turned fifteen, she had sewn the kerchief and added the initials J. M., for Joseph's Mary, as a symbol of whom she belonged to and a reminder of her father's care and protection. She felt a surge of warmth as she thought of him watching her now. The black kerchief with white polka dots had distinguished Hutterite women in North America for more than a century. As a young girl, Mary had tried on her sisters' kerchiefs, or *Tiechlen*, and imagined her own ascension to womanhood. She would take the pointed ends of the kerchief and practice folding the fabric, twice clockwise against her cheeks, before twisting the ends in a knot under her chin. She loved the dark of the fabric next to her clear, pale complexion and the stiffness of the starched cotton against her face. Mary had earned the privilege of wearing one on her fifteenth birthday, the twenty-sixth of May, when she exchanged her childhood *Mütz* (bonnet) for it.

She had risen after the meal in the children's dining room and announced her birthday to the supervising German schoolteacher. "*John Vetter, ich bin funfzehn Johr olt.* Uncle John, I am fifteen years old." She shifted her weight from one foot to the other as John Maendel stroked his graying beard and cautioned her that she was now entering a deeper level of commitment to the Hutterite faith, and this important passage into adulthood must be reflected in her conduct. It was a brief and simple ceremony, but for Mary the honor lay in her unconditional acceptance into the adult world. The next day she put on her *Tiechel* and took her place alongside the other women in the adult dining room.

Today, the simple triangle of fabric would serve as her veil, as much a symbol of her identity as a crown to a queen. She had taken extra care to starch and press it, using the weight of a hot iron to crease a sharp *V* through the middle. She centered it on her head and tightly knotted it under her chin, pleased with the stylish crest it formed at the top. She wore neither makeup nor jewelry; both were forbidden. In a culture that stressed an inner adornment of the heart, her smile would be enough.

As she prepared, Mary couldn't help thinking about what a miracle it was that she was getting married after all. She thought she'd never live down the humiliation of having her letter from Ronald exposed in such a public manner. After that incident she had retreated by throwing herself into the endless cycle of women's work in the community. Months passed; then one afternoon, her sister-in-law Sara approached her at the clothesline. Though it was in her house that Mary and Elie had shared the grapes, Sara matter-of-factly raised the subject of marriage. "I don't want to get married to anyone!" Mary blurted. "The price is too high!"

A week later Mary was hanging out towels when Sara came to her again. "Have you given any thought to our last conversation?" she asked.

"I haven't changed my mind, if that's what you're asking," Mary snapped.

Sara watched as Mary picked up a wet towel from the wicker basket and pinned it to the line. "Look at it this way," she said. "You're living under Sana Basel's roof. She has a husband, three siblings, and thirteen children to take care of. It's time for you to decide your future."

Mary's brother Peter approached Ronald to see where he stood. "I asked Mary to go with me more than a year ago," a bewildered Ronald replied, "but she still hasn't given me an answer."

Peter sent his wife, Sara, to see Mary for a third time and invite her to the same upstairs room where she had braved the ill-fated visits with the carpenter from Fairmont. In Elie's place stood a terse Ronald Dornn.

"Why haven't you answered me?" he demanded.

"How could I?" she replied.

Mary shared her private feelings about Elie's advances and the pressure she felt from her brothers. Ronald was disarmed by her gentleness. His face softened when she went on to explain that she felt as isolated and alone as he did. When Sara offered them a plate of plums, they shared the fruit and agreed to meet secretly every Sunday at Ronald's house.

A few weeks later, when Mary was sorting potatoes in the basement of the community kitchen, she unexpectedly found herself alone with her older brother, the assistant minister, and knew that God had given her an opportunity to plead her case. "Jake, you're the only father I have to go to," she said, "so I'm asking for your permission to marry Ronald." The dark cellar was an unlikely spot for a serious conversation, but if her brother was taken by surprise, he didn't let it show as he continued throwing spoiled potatoes on a growing pile. "I really don't know anything bad about him," he finally admitted, pushing his hair from his forehead with the cuff of his shirt. "I'm not for him, and I'm not against him." The compromise was all Mary needed.

At exactly 9:25 in the morning, Ronald Dornn left his modest lodgings in the northeast corner of the colony and briskly walked the sixty yards to Sana Basel's house to collect his bride. All eyes in the community were glued to their windows to monitor his progress and wait for their signal to follow the bridal couple to church. "*Do kummt der Bräutigam!*" cried one of the cook's helpers from the doorway of the community kitchen, announcing Ronald's approach even as the breakfast dishwater dripped from her forearms. She took in his earnest disposition and the way he wore the perfectly fitted black wedding suit that Mary's sister Katrina had sewn. His washtub hat had been replaced by the traditional black *Schmiedeleut* hat, purchased at Eaton's in Winnipeg. At twenty-nine, Ronald was older than the average Hutterite groom and eight years older than his bride. When the couple emerged hand in hand from Sana Basel's house, the rest of the colony fell in line behind them and followed them into church.

Inside, the church was sparsely furnished but functional. At the front, a low oak table served as a pulpit, with seats on each side for the local and visiting ministers. Ronald and Mary took their places across the aisle from each other while the congregation quickly filled the remaining seats. The loud clack of well-worn shoes echoed against the polished linoleum floor as women moved to the right and men to the left. Visitors from the Old Rosedale, Sturgeon Creek, and Deerboine Colonies were the objects of stolen glances by the New Rosedalers, anxious to see who the minister had invited.

Sam Kleinsasser, Mary's uncle-in-law, was the senior minister at Sturgeon Creek Colony and had been given the honor of officiating at his niece's marriage. *Prediger*, or "preacher," Kleinsasser wiped his spectacles on a fire-red handkerchief—then with one, loud honk, his nose—as he prepared to lead the service. "*Lieben Brüder und lieben Schwestern. Wir haben uns wieder versammelt in dem Namen unseres Herrn und Heiland Jesus Christus*," he began in High German, the formal language reserved for prayers, songs, and sermons.

He looked out at the congregation over his wire-rimmed glasses, and his eyes fell on Sorah Kleinsasser, his dear wife of forty years, sitting with the women in a sea of prints and polka dots. She was the sister of Mary's deceased mother and had arrived in New Rosedale a week earlier to do general mending and patching for Sana Basel and to make a feather quilt and pillows, the customary wedding gift from a mother to her daughter.

Before Sorah's arrival, Sana Basel had directed her daughters to get a big homemade rug and cover the *Kellerlein*, an underground crawl space in each of the homes, where store-bought treats like candies or cookies were stowed. The *Kellerlein* was hidden by a trapdoor at the foot of Sana and Paul Hofer's bed. Sorah was incurably curious, and it took her less than a day to find the treasure chest. Gravity assisted her descent below the floorboards, but her expansive girth made the return impossible. When a rankled Paul Hofer found her, wedged into the square opening, with a package of Fig Newtons in one hand and a box of Paulin's Puffs in the other, she was as flushed as a young lover caught in a compromising position. Today, fully recovered, she sat perched like a duchess between Mary's sisters from the Deerboine Colony, Anna and Katrina.

Across the aisle, behind Ronald, Mary's twelve brothers were as somber as a jury, faces intent, hands folded on their laps. Just a week ago some had been in judgment of their sister's choice at her *Hulba*, the engagement party. The *Hulba* was typically held one or two weeks before the wedding and was the first time an engaged couple was seen together publicly. While it was mostly an occasion for celebration, the *Hulba* also included a special meeting, where the men tested the worthiness of the bridegroom. The suitor was required to rally supporters to speak in his favor while others raised doubts about his virtues. The tradition was rooted in eighteenth-century Russia, when the son of a basket weaver was prevented from marrying a young Hutterite girl because he hadn't learned a trade. For the most part, this ancient Hutterite practice was merely a formality, and the man would be sent on his way in record time to celebrate with his intended. It was rare for a woman to change her mind about a prospective husband or bow to pressure from apprehensive family members and call off the wedding. If that did happen, though, he would be presented with a *Korb*, an empty basket to symbolize the woman's refusal. Followers of the custom reasoned that a dose of embarrassment now was better than a life of misery.

If Ronald was feeling any doubts about the meeting, he didn't let it show as he and Mary went door to door the night of their *Hulba* to formally introduce themselves as a couple. Earlier in the day, Andreas Hofer, the senior minister at New Rosedale, had sent a bottle of rye whiskey and two miniature glass steins on a matching tray to the groom's house. Andreas was one of the first to know of Ronald's intentions to marry Mary Maendel, as Ronald was required to receive his formal permission. The head minister was bound by tradition to set the wedding date and determine which colonies to invite.

That evening, as they made the rounds to receive *Schenken*, Ronald poured out exact measures of Black Velvet for the toasts, and Mary offered the small tumblers to every adult. "To a dozen children and good, strong nerves," offered one resigned father, swarmed by his large clan. "Liff for Jesus," admonished Ankela, a grandmotherly soul who'd already taken out her bottom teeth for the night. Most people gave the couple some practical advice, but some delivered a dose of reality. "You poor snake, you'll find out!" cried one woman to an unsuspecting Mary while gulping back her drink and looking like she could use another.

Everyone was eager to see how the couple presented themselves on their first outing, and children, not content with just a brief glimpse of the betrothed, followed them on their rounds and into the houses. If crowd control became unmanageable, the children were unceremoniously shooed back outside.

When Ronald and Mary finally returned to Sana Basel's house, the girls' upstairs bedroom was packed with young people in high spirits, playing mouth organs, singing, and enjoying rounds of beer and schnapps. The beds and a few pieces of furniture had been pushed against the walls and a circle of wooden chairs set up in the center for Ronald and Mary and their closest friends and family. Some guests leaned against the walls and filled the doorways while others stood behind the wedding party singing sanitized love songs, such as "Are You Mine?" and "You Are My Sunshine." Bottles of beer and chokecherry wine in old whiskey bottles sat on the single dresser next to a tray of glasses and cups that had been brought over from the community kitchen. Most of the guests helped themselves, but some of the young men with eyes for the pretty girls were glad to offer themselves as waiters.

Dating on a Hutterite colony was generally frowned upon. Young people had to rely on work exchanges between colonies, berry picking, Sunday visits, or weddings to size up the opposite sex. The prevailing wisdom among the elders was that if a couple really wanted to get acquainted, they should get married. Ronald had been reduced to discreetly flashing his house lights to signal Mary to come over for their weekly visit, but it hadn't taken long for the whole colony to wonder what was wrong with Ronald's electricity.

Some colonies were known for their beautiful women, but a true trophy wife was considered *fein*, known for her virtue, loyalty, and duty. That night, seated next to Ronald, her eyes shining, Mary was both.

The party upstairs was an occasion for the young people, but the *lustig* (irresistible) atmosphere drifted downstairs, tempting senior colony members to push their way into the upstairs crowd to satisfy their curiosity and enjoy the music. The boys from Deerboine, always eager for romantic songs recounting memories of love letters, stolen kisses, and girls with big, blue eyes, coaxed Sana Basel's daughters into singing the enchanting German ballad "*Es War Einmal ein Mägdelein*" ("There Once Was a Beautiful Maiden"). Someone called for a Hank Williams tune—it was none other than Elie Wipf from Fairmont Colony.

Sana Basel's son, Paul Jr., who listened to CKY radio on his con-traband crystal set, launched into "May You Never Be Alone," his favorite hit from the great country legend.

Paul winked at his friend George Wollman, who had hoped today would be his *Hulba* too. George had had his eye on a pretty girl from Surprise Creek Colony and his mind on a double wed-ding with Ronald and Mary, but when he went to see his love interest unannounced, to spring a proposal on her, she refused to see him because she had just had all her teeth pulled. "Dat just killed da romance," he confided to Paul upon his deflated return home.

"Sing the kissing song!" shouted a flirtatious girl who had loosened the knot in her *Tiechel*. The German love song was the equivalent of tinkling glasses to invite a wedding couple to kiss. "*Mir wöllns auch sehen!*" protested four women in unison, strain-ing to see through the wall of black jackets and pleated skirts that had gathered around Ronald and Mary to give them some pri-vacy for this rare public show of affection. Everyone sang, "*Unser Bruder der soll leben, ja leben, ja leben, und soll seiner Schönsten ein Bussela geben . . .* Our brother he should live, live, live, and should give his beautiful one a kiss . . ."

A few teenagers looking for their own wall of privacy took their drinks outside, where their alcohol consumption wouldn't be monitored. Bolstered by the home brew, they argued with their visiting peers that New Rosedale's seven John Deere 80 tractors outperformed the Allis Chalmers and International models that other colonies had purchased. Sylvester Baer would have liked to join the debate, but he lumbered past the revelers and made his way upstairs to the *Hulba*. His hair and beard were the color of rust, and his pockmarked face was tense. He was nervous about the impending meeting downstairs, where he had promised to defend the character of his friend Ronald.

The upstairs room was cramped with too many bodies, and the air heavy with Lily of the Valley perfume. Sylvester roped his way through a row of harmonica players toward a small window at the back, and with big, fleshy hands, pried it open and propped it up with a ruler. The cold November air brought relief from the flash-back to his *Hulba* less than a year ago, when he had had his own character scrutinized. It had been a considerable challenge for the widower with six children to find a woman to marry him. The girl's alarmed parents tried to talk her out of the marriage, argu-ing she didn't know what she was getting herself into. It took two days of wrangling before the family relented and he was finally able to claim his bride. Sylvester hoped his friend wouldn't have to endure the near-*Korb* experience he had gone through.

"*Reinhold, kummt's gehen!* Ronald, let's go!" called Paul Vetter through the *Hulba* noises as he beckoned him to the meeting downstairs. Ronald stepped through the overflow crowd seated on the narrow staircase with Sylvester on his heels. All twenty of the married men in the colony were squeezed into Sana Basel's small living room.

"Brothers, let's get started," Jake Maendel began. Ronald locked eyes with the aging senior minister Andreas Hofer, who was sit-ting at the front. Andreas had once hoped Ronald would choose his daughter, Emma, for his bride and had gone as far as inviting the *Waiselein*, "orphan," into his own family. When the potential match fizzled, Andreas had been disappointed but tried hard not to let it show. The Maendel brothers sat next to Andreas, and Ronald wondered what each of them might have to say. Mary's brother Samuel, poker-faced and rigid, was still smarting from his failure to broker a deal for his wife's sister. The bake house letter hadn't ended Ronald and Mary's relationship as he'd hoped, and when he'd heard that they would be married, Samuel marched over to his future brother-in-law's place and demanded his hat back.

Jake Maendel cleared his throat and began by commending Mary for being a good Christian woman, born and raised in a good Hutterite family. The others took turns extolling her virtues and praising her for being dutiful, hospitable, and a hard worker. When Mary's other brothers noted that Ronald was an outsider, born in Russia to non-Hutterite parents, Ronald nodded to Sylvester Baer to come to his defense. It took a series of nods and nudges before Sylvester, eyes wide as saucers, propelled himself to his feet. "I can't find any words!" he exclaimed as the room dissolved into fits of laughter.

Upstairs the celebrations were in full swing without the future bridegroom. Ronald had been absent for more than two hours when one of the John Deere boys reappeared for another beer and teased Mary that the men had turned Ronald down and the marriage was off. When Elie Wipf heard this, he came and sat on Ronald's vacant chair. Elie's peers were amused by his pluck, but Mary, unnerved by Ronald's long delay, slipped out of her chair and left the room.

Downstairs, Jake Maendel composed himself and cobbled together a few positive things to say about his future brother-in-law on Sylvester's behalf, pointing out that he didn't drink to excess and was a reliable worker.

Later at the community kitchen, over ham sandwiches and coffee, Ronald tried to make light of the irregular *Hulba* meeting that had lasted until midnight. "No one would speak in your favor," he teased Mary. "They finally told me, 'Have her already!'"

As their wedding ceremony neared an end, Sam Kleinsasser closed his black prayer book and asked the groom, then the bride, to come to the front. Mary extended her left hand toward the *Prediger*, and Ronald placed his right hand on top of hers as they promised to live faithfully together until death. The congregation was feeling restless after ninety minutes of sitting still, and by now most of them were daydreaming about dinner, but when Ronald was asked to make the final vow required of all Hutterite men, everyone leaned forward to hear him promise: "Should I suffer shipwreck of faith, I, Ronald, will not ask my wife or my children to follow me off the colony." There was no kiss to seal the vows; neither did the couple exchange rings. To signify that he was a married man, Ronald would now have to grow a beard.

Over at the community kitchen, Sana Basel moved between the large soup vat at one end and the restaurant-sized grill on the other. She loved being the head cook, one of the few managerial positions held by women on the colony. Today she was filled with the added joy of preparing the wedding feast for her youngest sister. She dipped a large, metal ladle into the steaming soup vat and tasted the simmering beef broth. Sumptuous soups were a Hutterite staple, and noodle soup was the premier soup for Sundays, religious holidays, funerals, and weddings. Earlier in the week, the colony women had made the noodles from scratch with fresh eggs and flour and dried them on long, white sheets in the bakery.

Sana Basel fished out the cooked cubes of beef and meaty bones and put them into a large, stainless-steel bowl, covering the meat with a cotton cloth to keep it warm until serving time. "Here come the big eaters from Sturgeon Creek!" teased Sana Basel as three women from Sturgeon Creek Colony arrived to help prepare the meal for all the extra visitors. Sana Basel was as pleased with their company as she was with their offer to help. Three fifty-pound burlap sacks of potatoes had been brought up from the basement and were waiting to be scrubbed and boiled. The visitors joined several of Sana Basel's helpers, who had already begun to prepare the vegetables in large sinks of water.

In another corner, the younger women were cutting up heads of green cabbage that had been grown that summer in the community garden. The *Dienen* wielded sharp butcher knives with uncanny precision, but when one of them accidentally nicked herself, her coworkers ribbed her that she was having *Heiratsgedanken*, marriage thoughts of her own.

"Did I see right? Is her apron the same color as her dress?" Ankela asked everyone in general as she entered the kitchen. She had just returned from the church service and didn't know whether to trust her failing eyesight. "*Su'e narrischa neue Styles!*" she sputtered. "I can't even tell she has her apron on!" She stopped to rinse her ill-fitting false teeth in the potato water before shuffling off to the dining room. The bride's apron was already a hot topic of conversation among the kitchen help. In a community that generally followed a homogenous dress code, aprons had long been a means to express individuality, and young women would sometimes barter with friends on other colonies for a choice piece of fabric. Mary's apron received unanimous approval from the potato caucus, who considered themselves on the cutting edge of Hutterite fashion.

At eleven thirty the meal was ready. "*Geh glöckel die Glucken!*" announced Sana Basel, pointing to one of the women who proceeded to pull the thick rope attached to an old church bell on the roof of the kitchen. It rang out just as the sun broke through a blanket of gray cloud, spilling golden light onto the cow and hog barns, the machine shop, the *Henna Hüttel* (henhouse), the honey house, the church, the kitchen, Ronald's small dwelling, and the rows of semidetached residences that formed the backdrop of New Rosedale Colony. Ronald felt its warmth as the bridal party stepped outside of Sana Basel's house on their way to the reception. He hoped its light was an omen for a better future.

The couple entered the *Essenstuben*, the dining room, where the head table had been set up against the south wall. Eight-foot wooden tables, placed end to end, ran the length of the east and west walls, and two extra rows of tables were squeezed between them to accommodate all of the guests. Each of the tables was covered with a white cotton tablecloth and set with *Hochzeit G'schirr*, special white dishes with green bands, used only for weddings.

As guests poured into the *Essenstuben*, they were met with the promising aroma of a special meal. A row of hooks just inside the door filled with men's black hats. Wooden benches were soon lined with women looking forward to a day of catching up with sisters and childhood friends who had married into other colonies, and newcomers with fresh chatter about births, deaths, and forthcoming marriages.

Ronald and Mary took the two center seats at the head table, where a single place setting symbolized their union. It would be the only time in their married life they would be permitted to sit together in the *Essenstuben*. Two of Mary's sisters, Anna and Katrina, sat next to her. The third sister, Sana Basel, was needed in the kitchen. Her head and hands were tending to the thousand fine points of preparing a feast for two hundred people, but her heart would be at the head table with them. Sorah Basel filled in for her, happy for her niece but in tears because her own marriageable daughter was *e Tegela ohnes e Deckela*, a jar who hadn't yet found a lid.

Prediger Kleinsasser—finished with his formal duties at the church and as eager as the rest for a good dinner and a glass of wine—took up the position of honor beside Ronald. Traditionally a groom's father and brothers would occupy head table positions, but no one from Ronald's family had been able to attend. When Ronald had contacted his father in Ontario and told him about his upcoming marriage, Christian Dornn told his son, "You are marrying the enemy." Christian had never heard of Mary Maendel, but he had succumbed to the teachings of Julius Kubassek, who was angry that his commune had been rejected by the Hutterite Church.

Mary's brother Jake and her brother-in-law Dafit Wurtz, the

man Mary's father had urged Katrina to marry for love, took up the last two chairs at the head table. Jake trained his eyes on Elie Wipf standing with two *Buben*, "young men," from New Rosedale in the far corner of the dining room. One of them gave Elie a good-natured slap on the shoulder, and they both laughed. Elie appeared to be taking his recent setback in stride, but seeing their glib behavior annoyed Jake, who was left to shoulder his disappointment over his sister's choice.

"Let's pray," announced Dafit Wurtz, who had become the new junior minister at Deerboine Colony. He rose to his feet, and everyone clasped their hands and bowed their heads for the prayer. As soon as the wedding guests said "Amen," a dozen young men burst through the swinging doors of the main dining room, carrying mahogany trays filled with bowls of steaming noodle soup. Wedding meals were always served by the *Buben*, and they hurried in and out of the dining room, squeezing their way through the narrow spaces between the tables, setting out tender chunks of beef, boiled potatoes, cabbage in cream sauce, and crisp dill pickles. The young men took every opportunity to flirt with eligible girls from other colonies as they delivered the food and offered up glasses of beer, wine, Orange Crush, and 7Up.

On the opposite side of the *Essenstuben*, separated by the main kitchen, the children's eating school, called the *Essenschul*, was filled to capacity with fifty colony children and their young visitors. The *Essenschul Ankela* (eating school grandmother) was as busy as a short-order cook during the noon rush, ladling out soup, refilling the bun baskets, and wiping up ketchup spills. She was glad the *Hochzeit G'schirr*, special wedding dishes, hadn't been wasted on this unruly bunch.

Mary was hungry and wished she didn't have to share her bowl of soup with her new husband but insisted he go first and handed him the spoon as she reached for one of the fresh buns.

Trays of food kept pouring into both dining rooms until the adults had had their fill and the tables were sagging from the weight of plates and empty serving bowls.

Mary's brother Darius had just finished his second helping of beef when he broke away from his table to say hello to their step-mother, who had arrived from Old Rosedale. When the colony split, Rachel Gross Maendel had chosen to stay behind because her daughters had married men from the community, but she had urged Darius to move to New Rosedale to be with his older brothers. He was her pet, and the decision had been a difficult one for both of them. Even though Mary had been only thirteen when she had moved to New Rosedale, Rachel was here to wit-ness the marriage of a stepdaughter with whom she maintained a distant, but respectful, relationship.

"*Mer sein recht für cake!*" shouted one of the young men as he entered the kitchen with an empty tray. Fifty round pans of white wedding cake lined the tables of the bakery, ready for serving. The glistening cakes looked like small, snow-covered lakes scattered with stars. They had been baked the day before and decorated with white icing and silverettes. Three of the young women were carving the nine-inch rounds into even slices, stopping occasion-ally to lick the whipped-cream icing from their fingers. Every family would also take a share of cake home. Those pans sat on a separate table, ready for pickup in the afternoon.

"*Gott Lob und Dank für Speis und Trank.* God be praised and thanked for his blessings and provisions." The closing prayer sig-naled the end of the noon meal and the beginning of a short break to allow the *Dienen* to clear the dining room and for the cook and her helpers, the *Nochesser*, "after eaters," to enjoy their dinner.

Pockets of people, some with visitors in tow, returned home to put children down for their naps and take a short rest them-selves. The bridal couple and their entourage were in a celebratory mood and returned to Sana Basel's house to drink home brew and serenade each other with music.

Darius, aided by a glass or two of whiskey, entertained the throng gathered around the Booker coal stove with hilarious renditions of "Froggy Went a Courtin'" and "Big Rock Candy Mountain." One pimple-faced boy, buoyed by the schnapps, demanded the girls sing "Red River Valley," but they didn't want to waste a good song on a substandard suitor. One of his friends took pity on him and played his request on the harmonica.

At one thirty the bell rang, and members of the colony retraced the snowless paths to the kitchen and filled the dining room once more. Fresh from his afternoon nap, Andreas Hofer adjusted his black hat with one hand and clung to his Hutterite songbook with the other, as he followed his daughter Emma to the reception. As senior minister, it was his job to open the celebration with "*Am dritten Tag ein Hochzeit war*," a song depicting the biblical story where Jesus attends a wedding with his disciples and turns water into wine. The song was followed by other traditional wedding hymns, "*O Mein Jesu Du Bist's Wert*" and "*Lass die Herzen immer fröhlich*," the Hutterite version of "Don't Worry, Be Happy." A table of women as uniform as a girls' choir—in polka dot *Tiechlen* and bold, plaid aprons—cut in with an English favorite, "Come and Dine."

All the while, a steady flow of potato chips, peanuts, oranges, ice cream, and cake poured in from the kitchen. The servers launched the loaded trays over singing heads, mindful to not spill too much wine on the oblivious songsters.

By three o'clock most of the children had poked their noses into the dining hall for a peek at the festivities and a glance at the relaxed adults who, flushed with wine, were regaling each other with stories from their own courtships. The children knew that special bags filled with candy, gum, and peanuts were about to be handed out and did not want to miss the customary wedding treats. All the adults received a candy bag, too, but the sweets were the best part of a wedding for the younger ones. By five o'clock the traditional closing song, "*Nun ist die Mahlzeit ja vollbracht,*" had been sung with gusto and the wedding formally ended. Fathers hurried over to the colony machine shop for a quick look at the latest John Deere equipment, while mothers rounded up children for the journey home.

A small group of family and well-wishers stopped to say good-bye to the newlyweds, pressing them with timely pronouncements. "Now you're nicely on the shelf," sighed Rachel Maendel to her stepdaughter as she fastened the snaps on her *Wannick* for warmth on the ride home. "*Moch's gut.* Make it good," whistled Ankela through her troublesome false teeth, squeezing Ronald's hand on the way out. Behind her, a visibly pregnant woman with a shiny round face that bobbed like a bird beneath a tightly knotted *Tiechel* had a warning for the startled bride. "You poor witch; de're telling you lies when dey sing 'Every day da sun will shine.'" She was Bara Baer, the wife of Sylvester Baer—the man Ronald had asked to defend him during his *Hulba*.

Some of the visitors lingered for the supper meal, and young people conscripted into staying the week for the annual turkey slaughter joined Mary and Ronald at Sana Basel's to continue the celebrations late into the evening.

The colony was cloaked in darkness when the couple walked hand in hand toward Ronald's house. Mary's small wooden hope chest, a gift from the colony when she had turned fifteen, had already been delivered. It contained all her possessions: six dresses, her underclothes, hankies, and a small cross-stitch sampler embroidered with the German alphabet and the name Katrina Maendel. It was the only tangible vestige from her mother that she had inherited.

Ronald's home had been furnished with the customary gifts

from the community: a double bed, a table, and six chairs. A large wooden *Schronk* (a fabric storage cupboard) and a Singer sewing machine would be delivered to the couple in a few weeks.

The day had been bittersweet, but Mary was relieved that it had gone so well. She was glad to see Elie Wipf flirt with Emma, the daughter of the senior minister, Andreas Hofer, by stealing her candy bag and daring her to retrieve it. Mary remembered the letter of refusal she had sent Elie after they had shared the grapes, telling him, "You are a very nice man, but God must have someone else picked out for you." She hoped it was Emma.

Ronald gave the doorknob a sharp twist and reached for the string dangling from the ceiling light. The newlyweds looked at each other in astonishment. Someone had unwrapped all their gifts and spread them across the kitchen table. Next to a broom and pail, towels, some cups and plates, and a few pieces of cutlery, an opened card read, "May your joys be many and all your troubles be little ones." Curious Sorah Kleinsasser had treated herself to a little gift-opening for her week of hard work.

On his deathbed, Joseph Maendel had made eerily accurate predictions about each of his children. Of Mary he said, "You will receive much discipline but little love." Mary was glad that part of her life was over. Each night when she returned to the little two-room house after a long and tiring day of community work, she found what she had yearned for, for so long . . . the love of a husband and a home of her own.

The Christian Dornn Family.
Back Row, L to R: Rosa Dornn, eight months
pregnant; Christian Jr.; Christian Dornn.
Front Row, L to R: Ronald, Elsa, and Rosie.

> "Ronald grimaced at the poorly dressed shadow in his doorway, clasping a string of binder twine from which dangled a row of burnt toast."

THREE

"Du Sei Der Gute"
"You Be the Good One"

A FEW MONTHS after her wedding, Mary was at home painting her Booker stove when she was startled by a knock at the door. Local community members just walked into each other's homes unannounced, so she knew the visitor was out of the ordinary. Hastily adjusting her *Tiechel*, she opened her door to a stranger whose posture was as erect as a soldier and whose eyes were anxious and strained. "*Bist du dem Reinhold seine Frau?* Are you Ronald's wife?" he asked her in impeccable High German. "*Ja*," she replied, wiping her paint-stained hands on her long apron. "What do you want?"

37

"I can't tell you," he said. He stepped into the house and asked after Ronald's whereabouts. *"Wo ist der Reinhold?"*

Mary studied the man's large, crooked nose and deeply lined face, looking for clues to his identity. She told him her husband was delivering eggs to Winnipeg and wouldn't be back until suppertime. *"Ich wer warten,"* the stranger informed her and began to pace the length of the small living room as he waited.

Mary ran to fetch Sana Basel to see if she could press some answers out of the mysterious visitor, but he was just as vague with her.

When Ronald returned home, the man's pensive face dissolved into a smile. The last time Ronald had seen his uncle, Alexander Georg, was three years ago in Ontario. Alexander had come to Ronald's father, Christian Dornn, looking for sponsorship to emigrate from Europe, but Christian was trapped in a living situation that limited his ability to support Alexander and his wife, Eugenie. Christian was distressed that he could not provide a better environment for the couple, who had endured unimaginable hardships in the Russian Revolution before they fled from Russia to Poland, and then to Germany, to escape the war. Four of their eight children, including their only daughter, had died of starvation; two sons had been taken by the German army and had never returned.

Alexander Georg now had only one hope for his son Alex Georg Jr. and his family, and he wasted no time appealing to Ronald to sponsor them to come to Canada. Eugenie Georg was the favorite sister of Ronald's mother, and he would have done anything to help her. Ronald immediately retrieved his hat from the hook in the doorway and went over to Jake Maendel's house to plead for consideration. Ronald knew the sponsorship would require the community's approval, but he also knew that his politically astute brother-in-law controlled the votes. Jake agreed to call the men together for a *Stübel* but spoke against the plan on the basis that the colony was already overcrowded and that worldly outsiders would have a bad influence on others in the community.

Through the small open window in her bathroom, Mary could see Ronald coming out of church amid the black suits and hats scattering in every direction. His eyes were downcast, and the knot in her stomach tightened as she went to plug in the kettle.

A short time later, both uncle and nephew sat together in the kitchenette. "I'm so sorry, Opa," Ronald said apologetically. The two men were drinking coffee when the door burst open and a fiery Sana Basel stepped inside. She had confronted her husband, Paul, before he could step over the threshold at home and was incredulous when she heard the colony men had rejected the family's request. "Here's our chance to do our Christian duty and help dese poor people who've been trew so much, and we're saying we don't want dem!" she shouted. The whirlwind ascended in a cloud of indignation and headed toward the opposite end of the colony. "I'm going to pluck his feathers!" the crusader vowed as the door slammed behind her.

Through their picture windows, community members could see an animated silhouette, hands raised, fingers piercing the air, giving the junior minister a piece of her mind. If there was anything that would provoke the wrath of Sana Basel, it was a lack of compassion for people in need. "Well, I can try once more to get the brethren together and see what's going to happen," Jake offered.

At the second *Stübel*, Jake spoke in favor of sponsoring the family, sympathizing with their plight and encouraging the men to vote with a God-fearing conscience. The earlier decision was promptly overturned.

A few weeks later, Adele and Alex Georg and their two sons, Willie and Edwin, arrived at the Winnipeg train station for a nine-month stay at New Rosedale Colony. They moved in with Mary and Ronald but found their new surroundings so peculiar that when Mary returned with food from the community kitchen, the entire Georg family was sitting at her table, crying.

The Georgs were soon dressed in Hutterite clothing and assimilated into the workforce. Adele Georg was beautiful and vivacious, and she enlivened the women's work stations with infectious laughter. "*Was ist, was ist*, why so somber?" she would ask of the women when she reported to the kitchen or the garden or the bake house. She told jokes and startled them with her matter-of-factness. Upon her return from a checkup, she told the women the doctor "*hat in jedes Loch hinein geguckt*, had looked into all her peepholes." Mary cringed at Adele's forwardness, but the irrepressible German wouldn't be stifled.

The new family proved to be charming and dutiful. A year later, when their sponsorship was over, the colony hoped they would join New Rosedale, but the Georgs quietly prepared to move west. Before leaving, they requested that their parents, Alexander and Eugenie Georg, and their mentally challenged brother, Johan, be permitted to come and live at New Rosedale. Once again, Ronald brought his case to the elders, and the senior Georgs with their son Johan arrived from Ontario just as their other son and his family departed for a new life in Edmonton, Alberta.

Ronald barely had time to say good-bye to one set of family members when another group arrived. A month earlier, Ronald's two teenage brothers, Pete and Jacob, had found their way from Ontario to New Rosedale Colony and were living under his roof. Then, before his marriage was a year old, the tidal wave from Ontario struck again, and Ronald's father landed on his doorstep, as welcome as an uninvited thunderstorm. "I have come to see where my children are," a disheveled Christian Dornn said, wild blue eyes peering over his smudged spectacles. Ronald grimaced at the poorly dressed shadow in his doorway, clasping a string of binder twine from which dangled a row of burned toast.

The newlywed's small one-bedroom house was bursting with refugees, so the senior Georgs were put up in the colony kindergarten. Christian Dornn and his teenage sons squeezed into Ronald and Mary's bedroom, and Mary put up curtains to create the appearance of privacy. Still, it was an awkward arrangement made worse by Christian's boisterous snoring. Robbed of a decent night's sleep, Ronald was doubly irate when in the mornings his father would loudly announce, "I couldn't sleep again last night!"

That summer, Jake's favorite aunt visited from Elm River Colony. Maria Maendel had heard Jake boast about the missionary work his colony was doing, and she had been duly impressed. Hutterites were often criticized for not doing enough to help the less fortunate, and taking in Ronald's extended family was a feather in his cap. Maria dropped in to see her niece and wondered out loud where the visitors were staying. When Mary told her they were all sleeping in her bedroom, her aunt was shocked. "Dis is worse dan animals!" she exclaimed, and returned to give Jake a scolding.

"Don't brag that you are doing missionary work and bringing new people into da colony when you are treating them dat way," she told him.

"I don't have any other place for them," Jake insisted.

"Well, den find one!" she demanded.

Soon afterward, a rundown two-story farmhouse was brought to New Rosedale and renovated to accommodate the enlarged Dornn family. Mary replaced their tattered clothing with hastily sewn shirts and pants. The boys and their father were just as quickly folded into the community workforce, and Christian Dornn, relieved to be back in the comforting arms of community life, finally felt safe again.

::

Ronald's father, Christian Dornn, had experienced many years of hardship in his lifetime, both in Russia and in Canada. He had been born and raised in the fertile soil along the Black Sea of the Russian Ukraine. His grandparents first arrived with a tide of other German nationals in the late 1700s, enticed by Catherine the Great, the German-born czarina of Russia, who gave them tax breaks and other incentives to move to the area to farm the land. His family settled near Odessa in the village of *Neuheim* (New Home).

The Russian Revolution was already under way in 1919 when thirty-two-year-old Christian married Rosa Hennig, one of seven daughters from an upper-class German family. Gottlieb Hennig would not likely have given his refined daughter's hand in marriage to the uneducated Christian Dornn, but with reports of Russian soldiers raping single women, Gottlieb knew love was a luxury and safety a premium. His one plea for his future son-in-law was, "Please don't ever hit her."

To compensate for his lack of education and status, Christian worked hard to provide his cultivated wife with a suitable standard of living. He was a beekeeper by trade and could perform other tasks well, so he was sought after as a hired hand by prosperous landowners keen to have him on their payroll. His versatility helped him acquire two teams of horses, some cows, and the only camel in the village, and he became a successful farmer. He earned the admiration of his peers and, more importantly, the respect of his wife. But Christian's contentment was short lived.

One night he dreamed he was standing by an old, deep well that rose up from the long grasses blanketing the expansive landscape of the Russian steppes. A piece of cloth hung over the stony lip of the well, and he began tugging at the fabric to see what it might reveal. The more he tugged, the more the cloth seemed to go on forever, an endless ribbon of soft, white linen emerging from the bowels of the earth. The next day he asked his sister Frieda to interpret the dream, and she told him, "Christian, you will go to a far-off land, and things will be well with you."

Eight years after his marriage, the Bolsheviks murdered his wealthy employer's entire family, and the estate was completely looted. Having plundered the very wealthy, the revolutionists were turning their wrath toward the middle class.

Christian knew his sister's words were prophetic; the dream was a warning to leave his homeland. He avoided conscription by rubbing sand in his eyes to impair his vision, and after bribing a customs official with honey, fled with his wife and four young children to Canada.

After their passenger ship entered the Halifax harbor in Nova Scotia, Canada, in the spring of 1928, immigration officials directed Christian to board the train to Cardston, a small town within sight of the beautiful Rocky Mountains in Alberta. The family moved into a caboose on an Indian reserve and Christian, fluent in German and Russian, soon found work as a hired hand for a local German farmer. The hard work didn't bother him, but the poor pay and long hours without anything tangible to show for it was a strain. It was an intensely lonely time for his wife, Rosa, who was in the early stages of another pregnancy. Living in the middle of the prairies with no one to talk to and a husband who was putting in backbreaking hours, the isolation was often unbearable.

Three years later, with a new baby in her arms and another one on the way, Rosa was still a stranger in a strange land. Christian, like many workers facing the challenges of the Great Depression, was away much of the day, cobbling together as many hours as possible to feed his family.

One morning Rosa was sweeping her front step when she heard a great rumbling noise in the distance. She froze at the sight of a man on a prancing horse emerging from a cloud of dust. The image was a terrifying flashback to the bands of Bolsheviks arriving by horseback to plunder and loot villages with no regard for human life.

As David Entz pulled his horse to a stop in front of Rosa, he saw terror in the woman's eyes and three small children wrapped protectively inside the folds of her skirt. "I am wondering if you need anything?" he asked. When she motioned that she couldn't understand English, he repeated himself in German. *"Ich möchte wissen, ob sie was brauchen?"*

Curiosity had brought the head horseman from a nearby Lehrerleut Hutterite colony to the lonely little caboose in the middle of a field. Rosa nearly collapsed with relief when she heard him speak German, grateful to communicate with someone in her own language.

On Sunday afternoon, David Entz returned with a wagon full of food and friendship. Five Hutterite women, arms loaded with clothing, ham, chicken, fresh eggs, and a dozen loaves of bread, disembarked on Rosa's door and fell on her with questions about life in Russia, why they had left, and how they had come to be neighbors. It was a therapeutic afternoon for Rosa and a rare and fascinating outing for the Hutterite women. Before they left, they invited the family to attend church with them the following Sunday and to stay for dinner.

It was over Sunday dinners with their new Hutterite friends that the family's future was secured. Christian Dornn was desperate for a sense of belonging and security for his growing family. In the spring of 1932, he and Rosa, along with their six children, joined the Rockport Colony in Alberta. Rosa had doubts about the move, but her reluctance was no match for her husband's determination.

She had grown to love the Hutterite people, but their lifestyle was uncompromising, and she was concerned for her children, especially her mild-mannered son Ronald. He was an intelligent boy, making good grades at the elementary school in Cardston, but the nine-year-old had his mother's soft heart, and she worried how the transition would affect him.

She worried that the colony was no place for a tenderhearted child whose eyes welled up when subjected to the Hutterites' blunt manner and candid way of communicating. Through the course of their bloody history, Hutterites had developed a tough exterior; crying was reserved for funerals or physical pain and not wasted on hurt feelings. Ronald's sensitive nature was considered a very odd trait in a boy, and the other children teased him for being a *Brüller*, "crybaby."

Ronald had difficulty understanding the harsh corporal punishment used at the colony school. It was supposed to build character, but to Ronald it was a cruel way of learning a lesson, especially when the schoolteacher routinely gave the strap to all the boys, not just those who misbehaved. If anyone complained that they had done nothing wrong, they were told to consider it a "spanking for future misdeeds."

Solitude became Ronald's close friend when he was recruited to hand-copy sermons for the assistant minister. In German school, the Hutterite teacher had been so impressed with his penmanship and command of the German language that he assigned the young boy the precise calligraphy work usually reserved for more capable hands. As Ronald curved his fountain pen into beautiful Gothic letters on the white lined paper, biblical admonitions interpreted by the Hutterite Church became ingrained in his memory.

- Whoever cannot give up his private property as well as his own self-will cannot become a disciple and follower of Christ.
- The ungodly go each their own egotistical way of greed and profit. To such we should not be conformed.

The adjustment to Hutterite life had been profoundly difficult for the entire family. Their appearance was given a complete overhaul, and instead of English, they now had to learn Hutterisch, the ancient Carinthian dialect synonymous with the culture.

In her quiet way, Rosa did her best to adapt to community life. She loved working in the kitchen with the other women, and they enjoyed the contrast the proper German woman brought to their restricted lives. Still, she missed her family, who had lived near her in Russia, and remembered wistfully the beautiful dishes and teapots she would lend to her favorite sister, Eugenie Georg. Once, when she told the Rockport women how she longed for a starched white tablecloth and a china cup from which to drink her tea, they thoughtfully bought the items at a secondhand store in McGrath and presented them to her.

Over the next three years, Rosa gave birth to two more children, delivered by the colony's midwife. For the most part, her eight children were well cared for and had adjusted to the social structure of this uncommon lifestyle, but Rosa regarded her husband with some concern.

He had taken an extreme approach when they joined Rockport. The Hutterites considered photographs graven images, thus violating the second commandment in the Bible, so they discouraged picture taking of any sort. But most Hutterites privately kept a few cherished photographs taken by enchanted outsiders. If members were discreet, bending the rules here and there was generally tolerated. That wasn't Christian enough for Christian Dornn. When they joined the colony, he burned the handful of irreplaceable photographs Rosa had safely carried overseas in the lining of her coat. He even tore the photos from the family's passports and destroyed them too. She was distressed when Christian took things to such an extreme, especially when he tried to transfer his religious fervor onto Ronald.

Not able to influence his rebellious older son, his namesake, Christian Jr., Christian decided to put his efforts into his second son, Ronald, holding the sensitive young boy to a higher standard and praising him for not being like the others. It was against colony rules to earn personal money, but most of the boys Ronald's age, including his older brother, had traplines in the bush so they could catch small animals. The boys secretly sold the fur in town and bought themselves sweets with the spending money. Ronald desperately wanted to join them, as much for the camaraderie as the candy, but Christian begged him to not become involved in such a worldly enterprise. "*Du sei der Gute*," he admonished. "You be the good one."

By his early teens, Ronald had learned to repress his feelings. Rather than disappoint his father, he turned into a loner and found contentment in the responsibilities entrusted to him by the colony's livestock manager. He delivered meals from the community kitchen to the sheepherders, taking dinner and *Lunschen* on a horse hitched to a light buggy.

In time, he became a sheepherder too, tending the jet-black lambs whose curly hides were destined to warm the heads of the colony men. At age fifteen, when Ronald reached adulthood, he was presented with his own "washtub" hat and promoted to head horseman's assistant. Before long, he was a skilled rider and was granted a team of horses to break in and care for.

Looking after the colony's riding horses was a job he relished, and whenever he could, he would take his favorite stallion and ride up and down the rugged foothills, lulled by the steady, graceful movements of his chestnut friend. In those moments with the wind in his face, he felt alive and free, unbridled from his father's heavy-handedness.

::

A lifetime later, after he and Mary had married, they spent their afternoons grading and packing eggs at the New Rosedale Colony. At those times, his life at the Rockport Colony felt like a dream. "Where were you just now?" she would tease when she would catch him lost in thought. "You don't want to know," he would reply, shaking his head.

In those early months of marriage, when they were still alone, their favorite part of the day was afternoon *Lunschen*, when Mary would run to the kitchen to pick up a fresh pie and hurry home to put the kettle on before her husband returned from the chicken barn. It was during those afternoon coffee breaks that they caught their first real glimpse into each other's lives.

They were unnerved to find that both their mothers had died at age forty-five of gallbladder inflammation. Mary was only one year old and had to rely on a letter her father had written for a window into her mother's tormented demise. In it, Joseph Maendel described his wife's final hours.

> In great agony she tossed and turned in bed and kept repeating, "Oh dear God, where should I go with this great pain." It was almost impossible for me to see my wife in such excruciating pain. It is still a fortunate thing that a person doesn't know these things before he can be so blindsided. I could only say to her over and over again, "If I could only help you how gladly I would do so," but there was absolutely nothing I could do.

With Mary's mother, death had come with an awful suddenness, but for Ronald's mother, Rosa, it was an agonizing and protracted ending. For six long months the family looked on helplessly as she suffered and finally died.

Standing over her coffin, shattered but dry-eyed, the *Brüller* had lost his ability to cry. Ronald was just seventeen. His four-year-old brother, Jacob, was so traumatized by watching the colony men bury his mother, he begged his father to dig her up the next day.

Rosa Dornn had been the heart of the family. Without her, life was about to take a sharp turn for the worse, for she was the only force that might have prevented Christian Dornn from the irrational and misguided decision to sell his soul to Julius Kubassek.

Julius was a persuasive Hungarian with a shadowy past. It was said he had been a Communist leader in the Red Army. He carved out a meager existence for his wife and thirteen children in British Columbia and became enamored with community life after reading about the Hutterites in a book from the library. Compelled to travel to Alberta to visit them, he and his large family were taken in by the Raley Hutterite Colony in 1939. From the moment he arrived, Julius began to chastise the colony leadership for not exercising more control over its members. While the community cared for his large family, Julius also criticized them for their lack of involvement in missionary work.

He took his provocative message to neighboring colonies, including Rockport, where he soon had a convert. His views struck a chord with Christian, who was seduced by Julius's revolutionary ideas. The two men began to spend their Sunday afternoons poring over the Scripture, discussing in great detail Julius's vision of community, while Rosa lay dying in the back bedroom.

As soon as Julius entered her home, Rosa could sense a contentious spirit and warned her husband that nothing good could come from this man. Sometimes Julius stayed so late he needed a bed for the night, but she refused to let him sleep in her home.

After nine months, the Hutterites were eager to be rid of their antagonist. They gave Julius enough money to travel east with his family, where he was free to turn his grandiose ideas into reality. Bitter that the Hutterites hadn't embraced his hard-line ideology,

Julius denounced them as ignorant and inferior and declared them "the enemy."

He set up a makeshift commune on a run-down farm in Bright, Ontario; anointed himself leader of what came to be called "Julius Farm"; and collected followers from a hodgepodge of disenfranchised families in the area. Christian desperately wanted to be one of them, but his ailing wife wanted nothing to do with *der Mensch*, "that man."

Julius kept in touch with Christian through letters, which Ronald had to read to his illiterate father. On paper, Julius was convincingly inspired, and no one could have predicted the true nature of this man or the vulnerability of his lonely convert.

Soon after his wife's death, Christian began a campaign to join Julius in Ontario. "*Ich hab eine Bitte an euch, wenn die Männer mich lassen,*" he said. "I have a plea for you, if the men would allow it." Ronald cringed when his father rose and made his plea after the church service in Rockport to request permission to move his family out east. Bringing the matter so openly to the entire community defied protocol, and Ronald felt embarrassed by his father's tactic. Cash-strapped Julius had instructed his disciple to not come empty-handed and personally wrote the colony minister a letter asking for eleven thousand dollars in cash. The people in Rockport were alarmed at the prospect of losing the Dornns. In the ten years since they had joined, they had become more than valued members of the community; they had become family. But Christian would not give in, and with heavy hearts, in August 1943, the people of Rockport granted him his wish.

The elders were generous to the departing family but ignored Julius's financial ultimatums. The Dornns received seven thousand dollars in cash, more than half of the colony's entire income for the year. As well, they took their household goods and furnishings, two teams of horses, two colts, four bags of flour, bolts of fabric, and a case of beer and homemade wine.

These items were all sent in advance by boxcar, accompanied by Christian and his eldest son, Christian Jr., while Ronald was left to escort his younger siblings by passenger train a week later. Everyone on the colony stopped work to see them off. Most of the women were in tears as they pressed fresh buns and baked chicken into their hands for the long train journey.

As the minister drove them to the train station in Cardston, Ronald's eyes fell on the beautiful fields of grain lining the road from the colony. He remembered the Alberta summers working the land with his horses and the winters apprenticing as a stockman. He had struggled to assimilate at Rockport, but the experience had given him a strong work ethic and taught him many useful life skills. He wondered if he would ever see this place again.

When the family arrived at their destination in Ontario, they were faced with a grim reality. Julius was a severe and calculating leader who expected unquestioning loyalty. He qualified all of his demands with biblical references. Those who defied his rules were bound to a bench and whipped. Working conditions were primitive and chaotic, clearly lacking the organizational sensibilities of a Hutterite colony. Incoming and outgoing mail was censored, and letters the Dornn family had promised to write to the people of Rockport never made it to the post office. All of their household furnishings, including their shoes and clothing, had been distributed among strangers in the community, and the rest of their belongings were locked away. Family ties were severed, and males and females were split into separate dormitories. Ronald and his four brothers were not allowed to communicate with their three sisters. Everyone was required to speak Hungarian, and all personal property, right down to calendars and spools of thread, was confiscated.

Christian Dornn had placed his family in the hands of a dictator. Rather than stand up to the man he once idolized, Christian submitted himself and his family to years of mistreatment. His final humiliation came when Julius flew into a rage and banished him from Julius Farm for advising would-be converts that they'd be better off to join the Hutterites in western Canada than to do what he had done. Julius forbade Christian's children from visiting or bringing their father sustenance, leaving his youngest sons, fifteen-year-old Pete and eleven-year-old Jacob, lost, afraid, and not understanding why their father had been sent away.

For weeks, Christian lived in an abandoned shack in the woods. When Julius found this out, he put a lock on the hut while Christian was out hunting for food. Cold and hungry, Christian turned to a local farmer and begged for work in exchange for food and board.

Ronald fled west and returned to Rockport Colony to see if the family would be afforded a second chance. He remembered his sense of despair when he was told by the colony minister that he and his siblings were welcome but their father was not. Sana Basel's kind words had given him hope and enticed him to come to the New Rosedale Colony in Manitoba.

In the entryway of Ronald's small house at New Rosedale, the exiled Christian Dornn had finally reached safety. "I have said it, I have always said it, and I will say it again: *Gemeinshaft ist der einzege Weg*. Community life is the only way to heaven," a defiant Christian proclaimed as he fell into Ronald's arms, battered and penniless, twenty-four years after fleeing Russia. Despite the flood of unresolved emotions between father and son, the defeated patriarch knew "the good one" would take care of him.

Oma, Opa, Father, Mother, and baby Edwin in New Rosedale Colony. Far Right: Edwin's Luckela looks on.

> *"'Mein Gott, you've named her after the Indians!'* Eugenie Georg exclaimed."

FOUR

Tea Bags and Sugar Lumps

IT WAS A hot afternoon in July, and the excitement in the air was palpable. It could only have been inspired by the annual arrival of the watermelon truck. The semitrailer had come to the New Rosedale Colony all the way from Texas, and images of the succulent red fruit on such a sweltering day nearly had people in altered states. Gusts of wind blew swirls of dust around barefoot children and weather-weary adults as they advanced from every direction to help unload it. My mother, Mary Dornn, was among them, nine months pregnant and looking for all the world like she'd gotten to the truck first and swallowed a Texas-sized watermelon whole.

At five o'clock the following morning, she was ready to release her burden, but the nurse at the Portage la Prairie hospital crossed her legs and told her the doctor wouldn't be in until seven. She would have to wait. It was a torturous delay, redeemed only by the eventual news that she had given birth to a healthy baby girl. Bearing and raising children is the highest calling in Hutterite culture and a woman's most important role in life. Large families were considered a blessing, but it had taken four years and one miscarriage before Mother had delivered her first child, my brother Edwin, who was two and a half. Edwin and my other brother, Alexander, one and a half, now had a sister.

The lyrics to a hit song playing on the radio in her room, "Marianne" by Terry Gilkyson and the Easy Riders, captured Mother's imagination. The name *Marianne* was sung with two distinct syllables in the catchy tune, which gave me my name. "See you next year, Mrs. Dornn," the nurse called out sarcastically as my parents left the hospital with their new daughter. Colony women were admitted to the maternity ward at the Portage hospital with a certain frequency, but their liberal birthrate was often frowned upon by the outside world. The nurse was hoping Mother would get the hint.

"*Mein Gott*, you've named her after the Indians!" Eugenie Georg exclaimed when Mother arrived home and proudly announced my name. Though she was our great aunt, we called Eugenie *Oma* or "Grandma" because she was a devoted surrogate grandmother to her late sister's growing collection of grandchildren and a constant presence in our home. Oma lived next door with Alexander, or *Opa*, our "Grandpa," and their remaining son, Johan, who despite a mental handicap was a valued member of the community. Opa was a gifted woodworker and assisted the colony carpenter making tables, chairs, dressers, and hope chests for members who were getting married or coming of age.

Oma was convinced my parents had named me after Dad's friends, George and Bob Marion, from the Long Plains Indian Reserve that bordered New Rosedale. The Marion brothers were often hired by the colony for carpentry work or clearing land, and Father frequently invited them to the house for *Lunschen*. In Oma's opinion, Mary-Ann sounded exactly like Marion, and she refused to have anything to do with me until I was given a proper German name. When my parents relented and began calling me by the popular German name Ann-Marie, which sounded a lot like my name in reverse, Oma began to dote on me. I experienced no significant side effects from my impromptu name change, and neither, I'm sure, did the Marion brothers.

As soon as she arrived home from the hospital, Mother entered *die Wuchen*, a six-week period of special treatment extended to women after the birth of each child. This included a nine-week exemption from colony duty. Peterana was the cook for nursing mothers, and she delivered delicacies to our house every day. Rich foods like *Nukkela Suppen* (buttery dumplings), waffles soaked in whiskey, and plump cuts of chicken were carried over from the community kitchen in bowls and stainless-steel pails. While the rest of the colony ate regular fare at the long tables in the community kitchen, Mother had the privilege of inviting family and friends to dine with her at home. Most often, her guest of choice was my father.

Mother also received the customary community gift of one quarter pound of tea, one and a half pounds of coffee, a cup of cream daily, three pounds of sugar, nine boiled eggs weekly, and two bushels of *Rescha Zwieboch* (crisp buns), favored by all those with their natural teeth. Women who miscarried in the second trimester received a half portion.

The local carpenter carved a baby bath from a piece of wood, and eight pounds of feathers were brought to Mother so she could make a down pillow and quilt for her new daughter. Two quarts of whiskey and one quart of wine were also provided for visitors who came to toast the new arrival.

For the first two weeks after a baby's birth, mothers are cared for by their own mothers or an older sister, often brought in from another colony. It was her sister Sana who stepped into the role as Mother's *Abwärterin*, or "one who waits on you."

"Dis is a holiday for me!" Sana Basel said cheerfully as she swept in every evening, having fled her own busy household. She was an old pro and loved nothing better than caring for babies on the late shift. A night owl, she would bring me to Mother to be nursed and then, hoisting me over one shoulder, retreat to the wooden rocking chair in the oversized bedroom closet to indulge in her love of reading. The two sisters slept together in the same bed to accommodate my feedings, while Father was relegated to the couch in the living room so he could get a proper night's sleep.

All of the young girls in New Rosedale between the ages of eleven and fourteen waited anxiously to see which one of them would become Mother's apprentice. In addition to an *Abwärterin*, mothers also chose a *Luckela*, "baby holder," to help care for the infant as well as clean the house and look after the other siblings. A *Luckela*'s role generally lasted one year or until the mother gave birth to a new baby and selected another apprentice.

The position was coveted, and parents often lobbied on behalf of their adolescent daughters to influence a mother's choice. Certain homes were considered more desirable than others in which to work, and Mother, who had gone through the process twice before with my two brothers, had developed a reputation for treating her young helpers with appreciation and kindness. She entrusted the responsibility to her twelve-year-old niece. Hilda came to our house every day during *die Wuchen* to acquaint herself with her new charge and obligations before Mother returned to collective duty.

The birth of a child brought all of the relatives and other community members out to inspect the new member, and a full assessment was made of the personality traits predominant in the baby. Everyone had an opinion and rarely waited to be asked before passing judgment. Those who considered themselves particularly enlightened on such matters could trace character flaws in adulthood to within a few days of birth. "She looks like a boiled potato," complained an *Ankela* to Father as he offered her a generous tumbler of dandelion wine. "And she sure can holler!" added Paul Vetter, stopping in to see where his wife spent her evenings and to enjoy a complimentary shot of rye. Oma quickly turned me over and pointed to my wide back. "She will carry herself beautifully when she grows up," she forecasted over my wailing.

The colony women came to cluck and coo, pointing knowingly to the neat piles of cloth diapers on the dresser. Expectant mothers received thirty yards of white cotton from the colony seamstress for diapers and nightgowns, and Mother had created a generous wardrobe for me. "Dose poor diapers, de're gonna learn someting!" chuckled Annie Stahl, patting them down with her hand.

Annie was a jovial busybody with an entertaining story up each sleeve. When Mother reached into her bra for a safety pin during a diaper change, Annie launched into the latest chatter from Hillside Colony about Esther Wollman. Hutterite dresses didn't have pockets, so most of the women used their bras to store small items such as hairpins, safety pins, and Kleenex. Esther, Annie reported, carried tea bags and sugar lumps that way too. When an outsider had dropped in to see Esther's husband, she sent one of her children for him and offered the stranger a cup of tea, nonchalantly pulling a tea bag and two sugar lumps from her bosom. When she asked whether he took cream, the flab-bergasted businessman jumped out of his chair and cried, "No thanks!" as he fled the scene.

The women listening to Annie's story cupped their hands over their mouths to stifle their laughter. Loud laughter, especially among baptized members, was considered unseemly and inappropriate, but it didn't help matters when Annie took the liberty of adding, "Laughing is healty. It's as important as a good bowel movement!"

::

I was born the day my father was voted cow man and the year Fairholme, a new colony, was established six miles south of New Rosedale. Each Hutterite community is structured to support approximately 125 people to ensure that everyone has meaningful work to do in the community. When New Rosedale's burgeoning population exceeded the customary limit, it was time to buy more land and "branch out."

New Rosedale's elders were led to the site of the new colony by one of their dairy cows that got lost in the woods. Quick to recognize the potential of the rich farmland dense with trees, wildflowers, and tall prairie grasses a stone's throw from New Rosedale, Jake Maendel negotiated the sale of its twenty-three hundred acres for fifty-five thousand dollars in the spring of 1959.

The assistant minister of an old colony automatically becomes the head minister of the new one. Fairholme would belong to Jake Maendel, and he would be its leader for the rest of his life. For months, the sound of hammers could be heard from six miles down the road, where Caterpillar tractors were clearing brush and houses and community buildings were being repaired by the men. When I was just nine months old, lots were drawn to see who would join

Jake and his family in the new colony. Twelve households were selected, including Sana Basel's family and three of Mother's brothers, Peter, Fritz, and Hons Maendel. Fate chose our family, too, which included Mother, Father, my brothers, and me; Oma, Opa, and Johan; Father's dad, Christian Dornn; and Father's brother, Christopher, who had by now also fled the clutches of the Julius Farm. Father's younger brothers, Pete and Jacob Dornn, were still too shaken with their experience in Ontario to commit to staying in New Rosedale. They had "run away" from the colony just before they were due to take the serious step of adult baptism.

Like the more than four hundred Hutterite communities in North America, Fairholme was patterned after the mother colony established in South Dakota in 1874. At the center of the colony was the kindergarten, the church, and the colony school, but the heart of Fairholme was its large kitchen with separate dining rooms for adults and children. The community kitchen was our center of gravity.

In the back, a commercial-sized bakery was filled with long, wooden work tables, cooling racks, mixing bowls, baking utensils, and stacks of pans, tins, cookie sheets, and pie plates. The room felt serene as it was bathed in sunlight year-round, and over time the walls absorbed the creamy smell of thick *Schutten* (cottage cheese) pies, the sweet yeasty aroma of cinnamon buns, and the buttery goodness of poppy seed *Krapflen* (pockets).

A stairwell on the far side of the main kitchen led to a cement basement that smelled like new potatoes just dug from the ground. It housed two large walk-in freezers and several cellars to store root vegetables. Next to the freezers was a generous pantry with a year's supply of canned fruits and vegetables, pickles, jams, and soups. Jars of canned peaches, crab apples, and saskatoon berries lined the shelves, waiting for a cold winter's day when community palates would crave something that reminded them of summer.

The walk-out basement opened from the outside, providing easy access to the communal showers and laundry facilities near the front. Each family had a wash day, and the two washing machines and one ringer were in full use every day except Sunday. In the spring and summer, the basement doubled as a cannery and as a second kitchen to make *Specksaften* and sauerkraut, and to clean fish.

The main kitchen was a bustle of activity, where the women on cook week created three meals a day under the watchful eye of Ona, the head cook. Ona had a round face with a prominent nose, which was a useful tool, considering her vocation. She was an excellent cook, and her ample body supported the notion that she enjoyed her work. The heat in the kitchen often forced her to take off her *Wannick* (jacket), and the loose flesh on her upper arms hung in folds when she lifted the stainless-steel lid and peered into the steaming soup vat. When the taste of the broth pleased her, her cheeks flushed ruby red and her face beamed.

Her menus followed a weekly and seasonal pattern, and all meals were made from scratch with the freshest ingredients. Fruits and vegetables were eaten in season, and the pantry and root cellar ensured an abundant supply of nourishment in the winter months. Many of the recipes, like *Maultoschen* and *Tröplich suppen*, were centuries old, originating with the early Hutterites in Europe.

The community kitchen stood across from five neat rows of homes that reached like outstretched arms toward it. Each row, with units for two or three families, had been modified from old army houses that had been hauled from a military base fifty miles away. Our house was in the last row, farthest away from the kitchen. Three large oak trees shaded our front lawn, and to the west, four long clotheslines perpetually billowed with diapers, underwear, sheets, and shirts.

Four days shy of my first birthday, Mother made good on the

hospital nurse's prediction and brought home another addition to our family, an adorable baby girl. I threw all my dolls in the garbage, certain Rosie was mine. Fortunately, Mother was in *die Wuchen* and could keep a close eye on me, because I insisted on being involved in every aspect of her care, especially the diaper changes.

My earliest memory is waking up from an afternoon nap to the sound of the floor polisher and the smell of fresh wax. Mother loved clean floors, and she washed them several times a week. All the chairs would be upside down on the big, honey-colored pine table in the living room so she could access every square inch of floor space. "Every time da wind blows, dat woman washes her floors," noted Annie Stahl from her back window. "*Die hat kein Huckorsch!*" she said, shaking her head before she returned to threading her needle. "That one doesn't have a sitting-down arse!" Through sleepy eyes, I would watch as Mother's pleated skirt kept time to her movements while she slowly swayed with the polisher across our vinyl flooring.

Our white walls were bare except for a clock, a calendar, and a wooden plaque that read in beautiful calligraphy *Herr, ich traue auf Dich* (God, I Trust in You), a gift from Sana Basel's daughter Becky. Two doors at the back of the living room led to the bedrooms. The room on the left belonged to my parents, and the larger room on the right was for the children. Our beds were fitted with handmade feather quilts and pillows that always had a soft smell, like the outdoors after a summer rain.

Just inside our front door was a coal stove where Mother often stood with a baby in her arms to warm herself. Across the hall from the living room was a small kitchenette. It had a serviceable wooden table with six chairs, a few cups and plates, some cutlery, a white plastic washbasin, and an electric kettle. No family was allowed to own a fridge or stove, but underneath the kitchen window, Mother's black Singer sewing machine stood in a wooden case, with mounds of cloth taking the shape of flowered dresses or checkered shirts growing from it. A heavy door in the back led to another bedroom, where my father's dad, Christian Dornn, slept. We called him *Oltvetter* or "Grandfather," and for better or worse, he was the only natural grandparent we had.

Every colony had an eclectic cast; the taskmasters, storytellers, comedians, and simpletons all brought something of value. We were bound to a society that needed to get along in order to survive and, like it or not, had to find ways to adapt to the failings of others. Because Oltvetter Dornn got along with bees better than with almost anyone else, he carried on the trade he'd learned in Russia by working in the colony's apiary. It was furnished with a small cot so he could rest among his bustling friends when he became tired.

Unlike bees, however, flies he could not abide. He rarely went anywhere without one of his custom-made flyswatters and should have received the Order of Canada for his contribution to reducing the fly population in North America. When he ran out of flies at home, Oltvetter would invite himself over for a few hours of fly patrol at a neighbor's house. In the event he was offered a ride to town, he brought along a flyswatter with a shorter handle and didn't hesitate to give the insect a forceful whack when it landed on the driver. He was a good shot and, as a courtesy to the startled motorist, always killed the fly on the first try. Every night after supper, he sat in his chair outside our front door, swatter in his hand and fedora on his head, until the heavens lowered a blanket of night on the colony and he retired to the house for evening prayers.

Regardless of age or capacity, each member had a station to fill and meaningful work to do. No one received a salary, but everyone's needs were met. Sharing a common faith, most colony members were satisfied with a sustainable lifestyle that nurtured them physically and spiritually from cradle to the grave. Everyone ate, worked, and socialized together for the good of all. Women did the cooking, baking, and gardening while the men carried out the farming, mechanical, and carpentry chores.

My father approached his new position as cow man with his usual thoroughness and dedication. He had inherited an infected herd of dairy cows from his brother-in-law, Samuel Maendel, and spent weeks scrubbing and disinfecting the barn and removing all the sick animals.

Over the next year, he turned the stable of diseased cows into a thriving dairy operation. Fairholme was one of the first colonies in Manitoba to be awarded a milk contract for sixty-two thousand pounds of milk a month. But Father wasn't done yet. Once the milk parlor was up and running, he developed an artificial breeding program and routinely sold his calves for top prices at auction. Other colonies, including Old and New Rosedale, soon became his customers.

::

At two and a half years of age, I started *Kleineschul*, or kindergarten. The *Kleineschul* was a vibrant part of our community, where our formal religious training began. We were taught traditional German prayers, stories, and songs, which our young minds soon committed to memory.

The Hutterites created kindergartens three hundred years before the modern European kindergarten system was established. Early in their history, Hutterites prospered as physicians, farmers, and artisans, and enjoyed universal literacy. Children from royal households often attended Hutterite schools, including their kindergartens.

In the mornings before breakfast, Mother would take me to the kindergarten, and that was where I spent the balance of my day until I was five years old. I remember bowls filled with cream so thick it couldn't be poured, baskets of golden buns, and jars of strawberry jam awaiting us on the low, wooden tables in the *Kleineschul*. *Schmond Wacken* (dipping cream) was my favorite breakfast. Freeing myself from Mother's grip, I hurried to my seat. We eagerly clasped our hands and bowed our heads to repeat our German prayers in unison before diving in, scooping generous dollops of jam onto the linen-colored cream and plunging the soft, fresh buns into the decadent dip until there wasn't a white streak left at the bottom of our bowls.

When our bellies were filled, we were entertained with songs, stories, and games. We also had regular outings to see the geese or visit the colony garden. We developed our fine motor skills opening pods in the pea patch and pulling out baby carrots to see what size they were.

The *Kleineschul* was run by three *Kleineschul Ankelen* (kindergarten grandmothers), a post assigned to senior women on the colony whose own children were grown and whose experience and wisdom were valued by the community. In Fairholme, Sana Basel, Suzanna Basel, and Ravekah Basel shared the position in rotation, each with a distinctly different approach.

Suzanna Basel was Hilda's mother, and when Hilda was my *Luckela*, she often brought me to her house. In fact, I had spent so much time there, I sometimes referred to Suzanna Basel as *Muetter*, or "Mother." She indulged me with candy, but best of all, she let me clean her dentures. Every day I would climb onto a stool next to the bathroom sink, sprinkle her false teeth with Ajax, and scrub them with a toothbrush under running water. Then, without fail, I would try them on. I couldn't wait for the day to be fitted with a pair of my own.

The only drawback to being at Suzanna Basel's house was her teenage sons, who weaned me from my beloved bottle when I was two. They teased me mercilessly. "*Du bist schon bald e Ankela, und trinkst noch von der Boddel!*" they said. "You are nearly a grandmother, and are still drinking from a bottle!" Teasing is a form of entertainment on the colony, especially among teenagers, who in the absence of radios and televisions are left to invent other means. Anyone with a bad habit developed a thick skin or reformed. Fed up with their taunts, I asked Mother to throw my bottle in the garbage, because I couldn't bear to do it myself. She had retrieved my dolls from a similar fate, and I happily accepted them back, but when she offered me my bottle the next day, I bit my lip and determinedly pushed it away.

I loved it when it was Suzanna Basel's turn in the *Kleineschul*. She gave me sweeping privileges, such as helping her with dishes, threatening the children if they misbehaved, or calling them inside for the noon meal. If anyone defied my orders, I didn't hesitate to march over and slap them with my bare hand. Most of the time I was slapped right back, particularly when it involved an older child. I immediately took up such serious incidents of insubordination with Suzanna Basel, who couldn't bear to discipline me when I overstepped my authority, and she would comfort me as only she could.

During our afternoon naps, all the children slept on rows of mattresses in the sleeping area. The boys were on one side of the room and the girls on the other, but I slept with Suzanna Basel on the double bed in the corner. Leaning heavily on the edge of the big bed, she would take off her plain black shoes and place them evenly in the corner. Then, with a heavy sigh, she would remove her glasses and *Tiechel* and put both on a low, wooden table nearby. "*Ann-Marie, schlofst du nonnitt?* Ann-Marie, aren't you sleeping yet?" she would ask with a yawn as the back of her head fell on the pillow next to mine. The plain hair needle that held up her long, dark hair was always the last thing I saw as I, too, drifted off to sleep.

Ravekah Basel was Jake Vetter's wife and a stern antidote to Suzanna Basel. She was strict with all the children, especially those she regarded as spoiled. Raising children on the colony was a cooperative effort, and if you were indulged by someone or not properly disciplined at home, another would be sure to take note and provide the necessary adjustment. Ravekah Basel believed that Suzanna Basel was ruining me. Her corrective measure was washing my hair. Oma was responsible for my hair, and with her meticulous tendencies, I didn't need a touch-up. But such protests were futile with Ravekah Basel. She undid my perfect braids and pressed my head under the sink of water, nearly drowning me as she unspoiled me by scrubbing my head hard with her fingernails. When Oma found out about this, she offered to help Ravekah Basel in the *Kleineschul*, and from then on, I was never without Oma as my guardian angel.

When Sana Basel was in charge, we had a riot. She had an easy command of the children and was an all-round favorite. Upon her arrival, she would blindfold herself with a dish towel and would get down on all fours for a game of *Blinde Kuh*, "blind cow." The children squealed with delight, swarming around her and trying to dodge her clutches as she tried to capture and identify each of us. Eventually, we were all caught, and she would good-naturedly rough us up until our laughter gave away our identity. With her hair out of place, *Tiechel* dangling from around her neck, and glasses askew, she finally called it quits, amid howls of protest. Afterward, her peace offering was a story. The mere mention of storytime had us arranging ourselves in a circle on the floor around the chair on which she sat. "Be quiet, and I will tell you da story of 'Rass, Wa, Tri,'" she began, pushing her disheveled hair back from her face and adjusting her *Tiechel* in a tight knot under her chin.

Storytelling is an art form among Hutterites, and Sana Basel was our version of a hit TV show. Our eyes were glued to hers, and our young bodies involuntarily leaned in as her voice rose and fell at key moments in the story. Subtle hand gestures heightened the drama and had us hanging on every word.

"Dere once was a Russian coat maker. He had a long coat and was walking on da road. All at once he sees a wolf. Well, what shall he do to da wolf? *I will offer him a coat*, he tot. So he said, 'Wolf, don't eat me, I can make fur coats, I will make you one.'

"'Yes? How do you do it?' da wolf asked.

"'Oh,' said da coat maker. 'I hold you by da tail and take a measuring stick and count in Russian.'

"'Oh,' the wolf said. 'Do dat to me; dat's good.'

"So da coat maker took a big stick, and then took a good hold on da tail. And he counted in Russian, 'Rass, Wa, Tri.' Oh, da wolf was so scared, he said, 'You want to kill me.' He ran home. He ran home for more wolves.

"Here dey come, more wolves. What should he do; where should he go? He got scared. So dere was a tree; he climbed up da tree. Here come da wolves; dey all came, but how can dey get up dere? Dey can't get up to da man. So da angry wolf said, 'I will stand here and you climb and climb one on top of dah udder, and den when we're all up dere, we can reach him.' So dey climbed and climbed. Suddenly dah man in dah tree gave a sneeze, 'Achee,' and dah wolf at dah bottom tot he said 'Rass, Wa, Tri' again. He gave a big leap, and down fell all dose wolves, and dey cried and went home and didn't come back."

We had heard the story many times, but she added exciting embellishments each time she told it. Her ability to freshen it up and make it seem new was always very satisfying. If anyone dared to make a noise during the performance, a nearby child would kick his or her leg on everyone's behalf. Disturbances were not tolerated.

When *Kleineschul* was dismissed, we fled through the small gate in the fence that surrounded the building. My best friend was my cousin Sandra, the daughter of Peter Maendel. Sandra was full of energy with a constant smile on her face, and in those early years we shadowed each other, never tiring of the day's routine. Sometimes we would race toward the whitewashed walls of the hatchery and join the constant stream of underage callers who found the smell of warm sawdust and the lure of fluffy, yellow goslings irresistible. We loved the hatchery, which was off-limits to children, but scoldings from Michel, the short, stern man in charge, seldom deterred us. Sometimes, he would meet us at the door with empty feed bags from the back room and send us out to pick grass. An hour later, our bags full and our hands stained green, we were allowed into the hatchery, where hundreds of chirping chicks scrambled toward the intoxicating scent of fresh grass.

We never wore shoes in the summer. Every path was thick with caramel-colored sand, and every field was a carpet of bluebells, asters, and black-eyed susans. The leaves on the trees were so green that they looked like they had been newly painted when they reappeared each spring, and in the fall, the bushes surrounding the colony were heavy with pin cherries, blackberries, and saskatoons. In winter, an embankment at the back of the kitchen was transformed into a toboggan hill. There were never enough toboggans, so we would grab pieces of cardboard from the *Stonter* (trash barrel). Our long dresses were reinforced against the cold by leotards and thick, homemade woolen socks, and our heads were enclosed in long scarves tightly wound around our necks.

We loved our little corner of the universe and were, for the most part, happily confined to it. But my near idyllic childhood was in sharp contrast to the struggles my parents faced. Beneath the peaceful facade of community life, the political landscape offered another reality. Father was still an outsider, and the tension of seeing him continually marginalized by Mother's own brothers took its toll, casting a troubling shadow over our future.

Hanna holding Eugenie and Renie.

> "Our new little 'boiled potato' had my mother's heart-shaped face with ears that stuck out in the most charming manner."

FIVE

Renie

I WAS TWO months shy of my fourth birthday when Mother brought Reynold Henry Dornn home from the hospital in Portage La Prairie. Her hasty departures and subsequent returns with another baby were an annual event, so his arrival was neither remarkable nor unexpected.

The previous year she had presented us with Phillip Mark. Phillip responded to being sidelined by choosing his thumb for a best friend.

Our new little "boiled potato" had my mother's heart-shaped face with ears that stuck out in a most charming manner. From the start we called him Renie. He was *en Schmondengela*, a "creamy angel," with full, apple cheeks and tufts of curly, red hair. I was permitted to hold him after he was fed and changed, a privilege I relished. He smelled wonderful, sprinkled from head to toe with Johnson's baby powder.

The following spring, Mother gave birth to a delicate, blue-eyed baby girl she named Eugenie. Oma was thrilled to have a namesake at last, but Father was beginning to feel like Paul Vetter, who, after Sana Basel had given birth to their twelfth child, loudly complained, "All I do is hang my pants on a hook at night, and da next ting I know, my wife's having anoder baby."

Mother's sister Katrina came from Deerboine Colony to help as *Abwärterin*, and over the course of her weeklong stay, she persuaded Mother to let her take Renie home with her. Assuming temporary custody of a child from a close relative was a common practice on the colonies, easing the burden for those in the prime of their childbearing years. Katrina Basel's four daughters were in their late teens, which reassured Mother that one-year-old Renie would not lack his share of love and attention. Mother's other sister, Anna, also lived in Deerboine with her large family, and Katrina Basel argued that with Mother's extra demands, Renie would be in good hands.

Shortly after Renie left for Deerboine, Eugenie began showing signs of asthma. My parents were baffled by her symptoms, and her illness sent them on a frightening roller coaster ride to have her diagnosed and treated. In the fall, when the air was thick with dust and debris from threshing the nearby fields, Eugenie's *Luckela* took her for a short walk, and my sister suffered her first serious asthma attack.

While she gasped for air, Father rushed to Jake Maendel's house to request a vehicle to take Eugenie to the Portage hospital. Jake accused him of wanting the vehicle for his own pleasure and flatly denied his request. The two men spent the entire afternoon arguing. Father would leave and then return, hoping his renewed pleas would have some effect. Jake, failing to recognize the gravity of the health problem facing this tiny child, remained unsympathetic.

It was a scene that would repeat itself over and over in the coming months whenever Eugenie was besieged by an attack. Unlike most of the other colony men, my father was not afraid to challenge his brother-in-law's authority. This agitated Jake and clouded his judgment when it came to my father. Like the unrighteous judge in the biblical parable, Jake would sometimes relent, but not out of a sense of justice—but because he wanted to be rid of his persistent petitioner.

Jake Vetter was a handsome man, with high cheekbones and dark, deep-set eyes. He had his father's height and solid frame and a neatly trimmed beard that hung from his chin like an inverted triangle. When he was appointed head minister at forty-eight years of age, he had reached the pinnacle of his career. His wife, Ravekah, a petite, comely woman, had borne him two sons and seven lovely daughters who would help promote Fairholme's notoriety as a colony with beautiful women.

In spiritual terms, Jake Maendel was "shepherd of the flock," providing doctrinal guidance, administering discipline, and settling disagreements. He was, in effect, the CEO of a sizable corporation, involved in every aspect of community life. No purchase was made without his knowledge or the approval of the council he headed. Shrewd and convincing, he was a natural orator who would use his persuasive manner to move his agenda forward.

If you were out of favor with him, he had the authority to prevent you from leaving the colony to go to the doctor, to town on business, or for a Sunday visit. He could also obstruct you from obtaining a managerial position. Jake's sweeping powers were enough to keep most of the men in line and agreeable, but his political maneuverings did not impress my father. He often found himself out of step with Jake's agenda and at odds with his tactics.

The tone for his brother-in-law's incumbency had been set at the particular *Stübel* in which the men deliberated the division of common goods when New Rosedale "branched out." The meeting, in accordance with established custom, was to determine which tractors and farm equipment would go to Fairholme and which would stay in New Rosedale. Everything was documented and agreed upon to ensure the money and assets would be divided equitably. The men decided that New Rosedale should get the Taylor *stuck*, "piece," even though it was a prime piece of Fairholme's land. But when the time came for the distribution of property, Jake Maendel claimed he had lost the dividing papers and refused to give up the land that New Rosedale had been promised. The incident caused a huge uproar. None of the men believed Jake's story, but he declared victory, and the land remained with Fairholme, further corroding the respect my father would have for the man under whose leadership he would be governed.

Several months after Katrina Basel had taken Renie into her home, my parents were able to visit him at Deerboine. When they arrived, they found their son in the midst of potty training. Katrina Basel's daughters, Hanna, Katie, Dora, and Judy, were energetic surrogate mothers, who delighted in their cousin. Whenever they opened their arms, he would run to them with laughing eyes and a big, toothy smile. It was clear that Renie was happy and well cared for, while Eugenie's health was still a considerable challenge. After the weekend visit, Mother agreed to extend Renie's stay.

When my parents returned to Fairholme, the political drama continued. The medical community knew little about the causes of asthma at that time, and my parents never knew when or why Eugenie's illness would flare up and out of control. Due to the difficulty of getting her to the doctor on time, Mother and Father were beginning to fear their young daughter would not survive. Sometimes, Father would wait until Jake Vetter had a visitor, knowing the *Prediger* would be forced to appear reasonable with a community member's request, or he would seek him out in the honey house where Jake sometimes worked. Once, when a large barrel of honey had slipped from the wooden shelving, my father opened the door to find his adversary covered head to toe in sticky liquid. Seizing the moment, Father boldly asked for use of the Econoline van. "Take it and get out," an embarrassed Jake Vetter barked.

A few months later, my parents returned to Deerboine, only to find that my aunt's family had grown even more attached to their *fest* (compact), rosy-cheeked son. Mother decided to extend his stay over the winter months while she continued to focus on treatment for her ailing daughter.

By the following March, Renie was almost two years old and had been away from our family for almost a year. Mother went to Deerboine with the younger ones, including Eugenie, for her annual weeklong sewing visit. The cooler weather had eased Eugenie's symptoms, and Mother felt reassured because Rivers Hospital was nearby, in case of an emergency. Edwin and Alex, who were in school, stayed behind in Fairholme, as did I, in Oma's care.

Armed with the latest ration of approved fabrics, Mother was thrilled that the head seamstress had chosen some daring, bright colors for the young girls. Some of the Fairholme women grumbled that the fabrics were getting too worldly and would lead to *stolz sie*, but Mother felt a bit of pride could do a person some good. She piled her yards of black rayon, printed cotton, and checkered flannel over Katrina Basel's sewing machine, and the two sisters spent the week catching up with each other's lives and shaping the material into a season's worth of clothing—black pants, jackets, and flannel shirts for my father and brothers, and flowing flowered dresses and underwear for my sister and me. Mother enjoyed tapping into her creative energy and welcomed spending time away from the tensions back in Fairholme.

At the end of the sewing week, after wrangling a vehicle from Jake Vetter, Father set out for Deerboine to bring his family home. I could accompany him, he offered, on the condition that I sing for him all the way there. Deerboine was a three-hour drive, and it was rare for us to spend so much time together and even more unusual to have my dad all to myself. That alone made the occasion memorable, but nothing equaled our unspoken anticipation of having Renie back by his second birthday.

The only time I ever saw my father truly relax was when he sang. Our extensive repertoire contained exclusively religious songs except for one popular children's tune titled "I Wonder Why Folks Act So Queer Whenever I'm About." Father had me sing it solo for his amusement, but the rest of the time I took requests in German and in English, and he joined me for most of them. I managed to last for two hours, delivering song after song in a loud and enthusiastic voice, just the way Father liked it. Beneath his black hat, strands of rich auburn hair glinted in the bright sunlight. His strong, freckled hands steered the wheel, and I sat beside him in the front seat, eating dust and inhaling diesel fumes as we rumbled down the road to Deerboine. My concert came to an abrupt end when, without warning, I collapsed on the front seat, fast asleep from the exertion. For the rest of the trip, Father had only a bag of sunflower seeds to keep him company.

When we arrived at Deerboine, he nudged me awake and together we walked into Katrina Basel's house. I carefully tucked myself behind Father as we entered, because I needed a line of defense from Katrina Basel's husband, Dafit Wurtz, who loved to say outrageous things to people, especially children. "Who on earth let you in? *Geht's Heim!* You're ugly! We don't want you!" he shouted, a wicked grin on his face. He looked like a portly friar in his creaky rocking chair, loudly snapping his suspenders with his giant thumbs. He knew he scared me, and he loved it. "Hurry up! Someone bring me a knife. I want to cut her arm off," he said, lunging toward me.

Renie darted around the corner to see who was at the door, saving me from sure death at the hand of a madman. Renie was a miniature version of Father, with intense blue eyes and tousled reddish hair, wearing a gray, checkered shirt and thick woolen stockings. "*Wer issen dos?* Who is that?" he asked Mother, pointing to Father. Father was taken aback by the question, and Mother raised her brows and cupped a hand over her mouth.

"*Kommt's einhin!*" said Katrina Basel from her small kitchen in the back, where she was cutting up a fresh banana cream pie. "*Sei vernünftig*," she said to her husband, warning him to behave as she waved us in. My *Basel*, Deerboine's head gardener, had a round, sun-kissed face and bronzed hands from the hundreds of hours she devoted to planting and hoeing the community garden. A shy woman, Katrina Basel would often lower her head and clasp her hands when she laughed or smiled, a habit that gave her an endearing quality. I quickly finished my pie and asked Mother if I could give Renie a ride in the wooden sleigh that stood outside my aunt's house. Mother bundled him up against the cool spring air, and I took him by the hand and led him outside. Waiting for me on the porch was Ida, a girl I had played dolls with on my last visit. She had on a new dress and a matching *Mütz* (bonnet) that gave me a pang of jealousy.

"They say Renie doesn't belong to you anymore; he belongs to Deerboine," she said, crossing her arms in front of her and trying to look official.

"*Wer sog enn so?* Who said so?" I demanded.

"Everybody is saying that," she taunted in that singsongy way that Deerboiners talked.

I turned red with rage. All my anger surged into my right hand, and I slapped her across the face with all my might. "*Du lügst!*" I said, branding her a liar as she sped home, howling.

Most of the winter's snow had melted, except for dirty skiffs under the trees and in the ditches, and I had a hard time pulling the sled. I was completely enchanted by Renie, who was just like one of my dolls, his face swaddled in a tight green scarf. I kept turning around to stare at him instead of watching the road, and when we turned a sharp corner, the sled landed in the ditch, propelling Renie face-first into a patch of dead branches. One of the twigs became lodged in his nose, and little drops of blood trickled from one nostril onto his upper lip. He began to cry as I grabbed him under his arms and half dragged, half carried him back to Katrina Basel's house. Renie ran to Mother, and she comforted him and wiped his bloodied nose.

When he calmed down, I insisted on having him back to clean his fingernails. Tidy children were my specialty, and those with dirty extremities and runny noses were subject to lessons in personal hygiene whenever in my care. I hunted for toothpicks in the bathroom medicine cabinet but found none, so I pulled off a stiff piece of treated straw from the handmade broom at the door's entrance. I had watched some of the men in Fairholme use a sprig of it to clean their teeth and reasoned that it would do the job. Little Renie trustingly held out his hand, and I went right to work with the sharp strand, digging away at the dirt. My intent was admirable, but my technique was lacking, and blood came gushing out as I invaded the sensitive area beneath his nail. Immediately, Renie's mouth fell open, his eyes squeezed shut, and he was crying again. Mother had to intervene and come to his rescue once more.

After a time on Mother's lap and in the comfort of her arms, I won my brother over one last time and we played together on the floor with his small John Deere toys until suppertime. I was careful to stay away from any efforts that would draw blood or cause bodily injuries, worried that Renie might insist on staying at Katrina Basel's house and prove that awful Ida right.

After supper I found that Mother had agreed to a request by Katrina Basel to briefly extend Renie's stay. Katrina, her husband, and her eldest daughters had just been offered the rare privilege of visiting some Lehrerleut, the most traditional sect of Hutterites, in Alberta. Hutterites rarely take a holiday, but when they do, the trip is limited to traveling to colonies in other provinces. This opportunity came with little advance notice. Due to a shortage of room in the vehicle, Hanna would be staying behind in Deerboine, so Katrina Basel appealed to have Renie stay with her to ease her daughter's disappointment. It was agreed that Renie would be returned immediately after the trip. Mother was satisfied with the new arrangement, but Father was not, troubled that his young son didn't even recognize him. But a Hutterite mother's wish prevails when it comes to decisions about the children. I sided with Father and pouted the whole way home.

During her stay in Deerboine, the only thing that concerned my mother was that, intermittently, Renie appeared to favor his right side when he walked. She probed him a number of times, but he insisted that nothing was hurting. Mother raised it with her sister and her girls, and they agreed to watch for any changes. Renie was in such high spirits that no one felt a pressing need to have the matter immediately investigated.

Within a day of my parents' return to Fairholme, and on the heels of the Wurtz family's departure, Renie began running a fever and vomiting. Hanna mentioned this to the women in the community kitchen when she went to get him some *Milch Gerstel*, "milk soup," often served to people who are sick or have weak stomachs. The women told her it was flu season and that other community members were sick in bed with similar symptoms. Hanna assumed Renie had the flu, too, but was uneasy about the fact that he refused to eat anything.

Peering out the back window, Hanna noticed a grain truck from Fairholme parked at a relative's house. The worried nineteen-year-old quickly wrote a letter outlining Renie's condition, addressed it to my mother, and left it on the front seat of the vehicle. She expected Mother would contact her and give her some guidance, alleviating some of the responsibility resting on her shoulders. Renie's high temperature and listlessness continued for the next two days, but the fevered child didn't complain of any pain, so Hanna held out hope that the symptoms would soon abate. To allay her fears, she frequented a small closet in her room in which she knelt and prayed.

Early the next morning, Hanna knew she could no longer ignore the warning signs. Something was gravely wrong with Renie. With no response from my mother, and no improvement in Renie's health, she walked to the minister's house to ask for help. John Wurtz drove them to Rivers Hospital, where the doctor promptly admitted the ailing boy and requested that his parents be called immediately. No one on the colony had a home phone except the minister, so John Wurtz placed a call to Jake's house in Fairholme. He left word of an emergency and stressed that my parents must come to Rivers Hospital without delay. Jake dispatched one of his daughters to give the ominous message to my parents, who were caught completely off guard with the news of a crisis in their young son's health; they had not received the letter Hanna had written.

Jake was expecting Father when he arrived at his doorstep, breathlessly appealing for a pickup or van to make the trip. Jake flatly denied Father's request, calling the trip unnecessary and claiming no vehicles were available. Dad pleaded that his young son's life was at stake and the hospital needed signed consent forms in order to proceed with the crucial surgery. It was the same argument he had used over and over with Eugenie, and Jake's heart seemed as hardened as Pharaoh's. "Well, phone New Rosedale Colony and see if you can get a vehicle from them," he suggested. Father knew full well that Jake would call ahead to ensure no transportation would be available from that source either.

Mother, beside herself with worry, rushed around at home aimlessly. "What's wrong?" I asked her.

"Renie is sick in the hospital, and Dad and I must try to go and see him," she said, trying unsuccessfully to appear calm.

"I want to go with you," I said.

"No, no, not today," said Mother, shaking her head. "We'll bring Renie home with us when we come back," she promised.

Critical hours went by. Dad still didn't have a vehicle, so he hurried to the colony's machine shop and spotted one of the big cattle trucks used to transport livestock. The keys to the truck dangled inside. If he took the truck, he knew he would have to answer to Jake Maendel and the *Stübel* council, as well as bear the reproach of the community. He also knew that if he didn't get to the hospital on time, his son might die. There was no time to debate the moral dilemma. Frantic, he gathered up Mother, and they stole away in the bulky vehicle.

Half a day had gone by with no word from my parents, and the surgeons at Rivers Hospital had become increasingly concerned with the delay. John Wurtz, who had been relegated to the waiting room with Hanna, was asked to sign the papers so the doctors could operate. As the colony's minister, he had the moral right to authorize the procedure. When the paperwork was complete, he and Hanna were told there was nothing more they could do, so they returned to Deerboine.

When Mother and Dad finally arrived at the hospital, it was late evening. Sickened by an unspoken fear that they might be too late, they made their way down the long hospital corridor to Renie's room, where they found their small child out of surgery, unconscious, and hooked to numerous tubes and intravenous drips. Renie was moaning and fitful, and my parents could clearly see that he was critically ill. A nurse came in and curtly told them the delays had created complications. "By the time the doctors performed the surgery, his appendix had ruptured," she said. Unwilling and unable to consider the obvious, my parents held a vigil at his bedside all night long, hoping and praying he would rally. At 3:00 a.m. one of the doctors padded into the room, checked the wound on Renie's abdomen, and left without a word. If there was any hope, it would not come from the doctor.

There was no change in Renie's labored breathing throughout the night, and by the next morning my distressed parents were overcome with exhaustion. A nurse directed them to a kitchenette down the hall for something to eat and drink. They both badly needed the break, and the smell of the coffee and toast was the only thing in the last twenty-four hours that seemed familiar. Everything else had been incomprehensible.

Father had just taken his first sip of coffee when a sudden fear rose up like bile in his throat, and he was compelled to return to his son's side. He urged Mother to stay and close her eyes for a few minutes of rest while he returned to check on Renie. The small hospital room that had been stifling with heat just an hour ago felt suddenly cold and hollow. The nurse had disappeared, and the only sound breaking the silence was the tick, tick, ticking from the metal clock on the stark white hospital wall—8:00 a.m. He approached his son's bed and gently bent over the little body. Renie was dead.

Mother knew in an instant what had happened when the

nurse entered the doorway of the coffee room. She rushed down the hall, where she found her husband overcome with grief and racked with guilt, sobbing at his son's bedside. Mother threw her arms around Renie and pressed him against her bosom with an anguished cry. She took his small hand, still attached to tubes and syringes, and held it tightly in her own, trying somehow to bring life to the limp child underneath the stark hospital linens.

An hour later, Father quietly asked the nurse to have Renie released to his custody, as it was the Hutterite tradition to prepare and bury their own. The necessary papers were signed, and Renie's lifeless body, covered by a white sheet, was handed to my father. In shock, my parents stumbled down the long hospital corridor and out to the hospital parking lot. They didn't have much trouble finding the big cattle truck in which they had arrived. Mother seated herself, and Father placed Renie in her arms. But the burden of holding her dead son was too much. She slumped over and wept uncontrollably.

Father realized he couldn't leave the body with Mother, but neither could he bring himself to lay his little boy on the cold, corrugated floor in the back of the truck. He returned to the hospital to ask for some cardboard on which to lay the body, and then slowly drove to Katrina Basel's house at Deerboine Colony, four miles away.

My parents never imagined that the year they spent without their son would end in such tragedy. When Hanna was told Renie was dead, she went into hysterics. One of the women who had come to offer support gave her a cup of water heaped with sugar to help stabilize her. Other women arrived to wash Renie's body, while Father looked for a box in which to place his son. Needing to salvage a little piece of the boy she had loved so much, Hanna removed the identity tag that the coroner had placed on his toe and held it against her chest as she cried. A sturdy banana box was located, and Father placed Renie into it and carried the container to the back of the truck. Together, my parents began the long and desolate journey to finally bring Renie home.

Back in Fairholme, I was getting worried. My parents had been away overnight, and by suppertime the following day, we still had no sign or word from them. Oma didn't appear to know anything and was growing tired of my questions, so I decided to bide my time outside on the porch steps. I heard the cattle truck before I saw it, inching its way around the corner and into view. I started running toward the truck as it came to a halt, but I stopped short when I saw Father's face. I had never seen him cry before, and I would not have thought he even knew how. "*Wos fahlt enn?* What's the matter?" I asked, peering through the open window.

Dad slowly pushed the truck door open and slipped out, unable to look at me or to put his sorrow into words. Perplexed, I jumped in beside my weeping mother. "Mother, didn't you bring Renie home with you?" I asked. I had visions of showing off my new little playmate to friends and relatives, especially to Suzanna Basel. "*Jo,*" she replied, blowing her nose on a handkerchief, her face flushed from crying, "but he is dead." Her words took my breath away.

I saw Dad remove the closed banana box from the back of the truck and carry it into our living room. Mother and I followed, she shaken and unsure, and I in disbelief, unable to make sense of her awful words. I entered the house just in time to see my father lift a white bundle from the box and hand it to my mother. Some of the senior women on the colony, led by Sana Basel, arrived almost immediately, ushering Mother into the back room and shutting the door. Preparing the dead was their privileged domain, and the proceedings were carried out quietly and in secret. They sponged Renie's body with soapy water and rubbed him with a rose-scented deodorant cream they found among Mother's things on her dresser. Quart jars of ice were applied to the small corpse to cool and preserve it.

The young women came with large pails of steaming water to wash Mother's floors and to strip the bedding and take the sheets to the communal laundry to be washed. Preparing the house for mourners was a practical way of serving those touched by tragedy. The hours dragged on, and I, desperate to be with my mother, tried to force my way in to see her. I was decisively ushered out by one of the women; and overcome by this inexplicable turn of events, I began to cry. "Don't cry, dear child," said Oma, who had arrived from next door. She pressed my head against her bosom before she, too, vanished into the secret society of the back room.

The carpenter delivered a small wooden coffin, and the women finally carried Renie out and positioned him into it. He was dressed in a little white shirt and black pants that someone had supplied from their own child's wardrobe. His head rested on a feather pillow, and his small hands were folded across his chest. A small drop of blood seeped out from under his nose, and I worried it might be from his fall off the sleigh.

The coffin was placed on a bench in the middle of our living room with Mother and Dad, Sana Basel, Oma, and an inconsolable Hanna crowding around it. Dafit Vetter and Katrina Basel arrived a short time later, physically depleted from the long drive back from Alberta. Katrina stroked Renie's body from head to toe, as if this could stall his passage from this world to the next and somehow ease her profound heartache. The room filled with relatives and friends, and the overflow crowd peered through the living room window. They sang German mourning songs until late into the night, and Katrina Basel and her daughters told stories about Renie, about what a tease he was and how he loved to play practical jokes and laugh. Others in the room offered words of comfort or assurances that Renie was now a beautiful angel with God in paradise.

While the wake was taking place in our living room, Ona, the head cook, was in the community kitchen, estimating how many people had arrived from other colonies and how much food she would need for the night lunch. A handful of young women were buttering piles of fresh bread and filling them with slices of ham for sandwiches. They chattered as they worked, disclosing details they had seen or heard about the tragedy. Katrina Basel, one said, had rushed back from Alberta and was totally devastated. Another speculated on who was coming and who had already arrived for the funeral. A third had caught a glimpse of Renie in his coffin and could not get over his beautiful red hair. Finally, two of the girls took a tray of sandwiches and a carafe of coffee to my parents' house for immediate family and friends.

To those milling around outside, one of the girls announced, "*Lunsch iss recht*," signaling it was time to attend the community kitchen for refreshments. After the customary sandwiches in the main dining room, everyone retired for the night, some with visitors who would remain for the funeral the next day. Renie's body was taken to the community kitchen and placed in the walk-in fridge, where he lay all night with the leftovers.

Early the next morning, the coffin was returned to our living room, where people came to view his body and offer condolences. In the afternoon the open coffin was placed on a bench in the center of the community dining room for the funeral service. Dafit Vetter, who had come to love Renie as one of his own, had been asked to officiate. His brusque and rough exterior that frightened me most of the time gave way to a gentleness that was oddly authentic. Standing in front of the gathered crowd, he chanted the ancient mourning songs, one line at a time, while the people echoed his lament in loud, plaintive voices, as melancholy as the early Hutterite prisoners who sang in their cells to console each other during times of imprisonment. To the Hutterite community, suffering is an inevitable part of the Christian experience, and songs of bereavement written centuries earlier were sung to comfort my parents. There were no musical instruments to embellish the voices; haunting and emphatic, they rang out for those whose own words were silenced by sorrow.

> *Parents do not weep my passing.*
> *Wipe the tears from your sweet cheeks.*
> *I know you are crying because I was so young,*
> *But grieve not because I died,*
> *For I am free from all pain and suffering.*

After the last prayer, the young men on the colony surrounded our family and waited for the senior women to cover Renie's body. Sana Basel stood directly in front of my parents, hands raised and arms open like Moses on the mountain, speaking words of comfort and blocking their view while the lid was secured on the simple wooden coffin. The men lifted it to their shoulders, and we followed behind for the quarter-mile walk to the colony graveyard. Katrina Basel and Sana Basel, arm and arm with my parents, led the procession; and behind them, a column of men in black and women in fluttering *Tiechlen* moved like shadows against a lonely prairie sky.

At the cemetery two men lowered themselves into the grave to receive the coffin, and Katrina Basel and Mother both cried out as Renie was positioned into his final resting place. The steady thump of shovels pierced a mound of earth nearby, and the hollow thud of soil against wood was the only other sound disturbing the silence. People slowly started filing out of the cemetery toward their homes, leaving in their wake those who loved Renie best, two families with broken hearts.

A week after the funeral, Father accidentally stumbled across the letter Hanna had written. He found the envelope under a clump of dirt near the machine shop, half buried in the same sandy soil in which Renie's body now lay. How it got there and why it had been dropped was a mystery, but its disturbing discovery contributed to my father's mounting doubt about community life. In the weeks and months to come, the events that led to Renie's death settled around his heart like a shroud, cloaking his thoughts with uncertainty and forcing him to contemplate a decision that would forever change our lives.

> "Although Jake Maendel
> wasn't everyone's uncle,
> he was mine."

*Jake Maendel, a gifted
and persuasive orator.*

SIX

Die Teacherin

The Teacher

THE COLONY CHILDREN all called him Jake Vetter, and although Jake Maendel wasn't everyone's uncle, he was mine. At two o'clock on summer afternoons, when we saw him walking from his house to the church with a bag of licorice in one hand and the leather strap in the other, we grabbed our pillows and blankets and followed. From every corner of the community we tumbled after him like goslings pursuing their mother.

Stern and aloof, Jake Maendel was in charge of afternoon naps for school-aged children in the summertimes. Naps were designed to keep us out of trouble and to continue to provide structure to our school-free days. While other cultures discouraged sleeping in church, ours, in its way, embraced it.

I would find my cousin Sandra, and she and I would claim a spot on the cool, hardwood floor beneath the rows of pews and inhale the velvety scent of varnish that permeated the darkened church. The spicy smell and dignified atmosphere transported us to a sacred place. If we lay very still, we could almost hear the echo of our parents singing and the vibrations of Jake Vetter preaching the sermon in his captivating, monotone voice.

Huddled together, nose to nose under our blankets, we were as inseparable by day as if someone had tied us together. Sometimes our sleepy eyes surrendered freely, but generally I would whisper something foolish and Sandra would giggle. Jake Vetter, who patrolled the aisle in his soundless bedroom slippers, suppressed any noise or chatter with a whack from his fearless strap. His aim was singular and fierce, and when he wasn't sure which bump was the guilty one, he just guessed. As long as the end result was silence, he didn't care. More often than not, the strap landed on me. I found it terribly unfair that Sandra didn't declare her guilt and take her punishment, but she was just too happy to have gotten away with it. Unable to defend myself, I would turn over and sniffle our lump to sleep, two pairs of bare feet sticking out of one end of the blanket and two *Mützen* (bonnets) peeking out of the other.

An hour later, flushed and rested, we would stir but didn't rise until a snoring Jake Vetter, his hand still clutching the strap, awoke on the front bench. "*Kommts her!*" he would command, telling us to "come here" as his hands wrestled with the bag of licorice. We would stream to the front, and he would playfully hit us over the head with a long rope of red licorice before handing it to us.

In the summer of 1965, Sandra's and my kindergarten days were over, and our routines shifted significantly. We both turned six in July and without ceremony graduated from childhood to the status of young girls. We were now required to eat with the other children in the *Essenschul* (children's eating school) and to attend *Gebet* (evening church services) seven days a week. With the exception of our summer afternoon naps, church had been off-limits. At first, daily attendance seemed overwhelming, but the sure knowledge that we would get the strap at the *Essenschul* if we dared miss did wonders for our attendance record. On weekday evenings, church began at five o'clock, just prior to supper. Mother would starch and iron her *Tiechel* while peering out of the front window, and when people began spilling out of their homes and heading for church, she knew Jake Vetter had been spotted leaving his house, clutching his sermons and songbooks.

"*Reinhold, Gebet!*" she would shout to Father, scrubbing up in our small bathroom. Father seized his black hat with one hand and the front door with the other, and Mother fell in line behind him, hastily fastening her *Tiechel* under her chin.

"*Ann-Marie, Leg dein Mütz on!*" she reminded me as the door closed behind her, and I quickly fastened my bonnet. My brothers, Edwin and Alex, and I knew enough to follow our parents out the door to the white stucco building with the gray roof across from Sana Basel's house.

Mother was slender and fashion conscious and a woman deeply devoted to her children. She had promised herself on those awful nights so long ago when she ached with loneliness for her own mother that when she had children of her own, they would never feel like a burden. From morning to night, when it came to her family, her energy was boundless. From a young age I was very attached to her. I clung to her skirt when we went to town and were subjected to the often cold and suspicious glances of English people in stores.

During those years, I had a recurring dream that Mother and I had accompanied the colony seamstress to a fabric store in

Winnipeg. It was a large warehouse, and there were shelves and tables of fabric as far as the eye could see. A rack of buttons in every color imaginable down one aisle caught my eye. After a time I realized Mother was gone, and I was alone in a store filled with English women. Panicked, I ran around trying to find her, but the tables were so laden with fabric, I couldn't see over them. I ducked down low, and in the distance I saw her unmistakable pleated skirt. The way she dressed was my shield, and when she spoke to me in our language, her voice was my sanctuary.

In church we were seated according to age, with males and females on opposite sides of the aisle. The youngest sat in the first row so the minister, not our parents, could keep an eye on us. I squeezed into my spot next to Sandra, and we exchanged a quick smile, proud and nervous to officially be among the grown-ups. Weekday evenings, church was relatively brief, but on Sunday mornings, the *Lehr* (morning service) stretched from half an hour to ninety minutes. Sandra and I would pass the time by discreetly drawing on each other's arms with hairpins, all the while staring straight ahead, our eyes fixed on the *Prediger*, who, with a fleeting look our way, commanded our best behavior.

The 350 sermons used by the Hutterite Church were composed nearly 500 years earlier and had been passed from generation to generation. They were as ancient as the method of singing that began the service. The minister would chant a line of a song, and the congregation would respond in a forceful, shrill manner. Annie Stahl, who considered herself gifted in the singing department, sang the loudest, and her voice was so piercing she could make the dogs howl. But to hear her tell it, if God gives you a talent, by golly, you should make good use of it. Sandra and I emulated the skilled sounds of our mothers coming from the middle rows behind us, for this sacred screech was applied only at solemn occasions, such as church and funerals, and would take some time to master. The elderly, like Ankela and my Oma, had earned their place on the cushioned back rows with others of their vintage, where the pressure to perform was not as great.

Even though my Oma, Eugenie Georg, had joined our Hutterite colony, she held on to her German heritage. She made no attempt to *drah*, or twist, her hair; wear a polka-dotted *Tiechel*; or speak the Carinthian dialect like everyone else. Instead, she combed her long, white hair straight back under a solid black kerchief and adhered strictly to High German. Perhaps it was the persistent sadness in her pale, oval face and eyes that never smiled that made Jake Maendel and other members of the community turn a blind eye to those things. They knew Oma had endured the loss of children and her homeland, which was enough sorrow for several lifetimes. But she had also lost Opa two years after we moved to Fairholme. He had died a torturous death from lung cancer.

My memories of him are vague, but the awful ordeal was etched in Oma's face. Once a heavy smoker, Opa was forced to kick the habit after joining the colony, but it was too late. As the disease destroyed his body and rendered him helpless, my mother's presence seemed to be the only thing that could soothe him.

Oma couldn't bear to watch her husband's terrible demise. "*Ach Gott!*" she cried every time he soiled the bedsheets.

"Looking after you is not trouble at all," my very pregnant mother, who exhausted herself looking after him, constantly assured him. Day and night, she faithfully changed his bedsheets and gently washed his feeble body.

Opa was a man of few words, but when he spoke, what he said was memorable. His cool head and diplomatic skills fascinated colony people, whose direct manner of speaking was primarily designed to promote humility. Others often tried to involve him in their skirmishes just to see what he would say. Once, two colony men passionately argued their opposing points of view in front of him, after which, he calmly concluded, "*So viel Wahrheit gibt's uberhaupt nicht.* That much truth doesn't exist."

Such stickhandling endeared him to the entire community, and in the days before he died, Opa requested to say good-bye to every colony member. One by one, they came to bid farewell to the gentleman among them. On the afternoon he died, tears streaming down his pain-racked face, he clasped Mother's hand in his and said to her, "Good-bye, Mary. *Gott wird's dir belohnen.* God will repay you for what you've done for me."

::

In the fall, Sandra and I began German and English school. German school was taught by a Hutterite teacher and was held one hour before and one hour after English classes. I was already fluent in High German, thanks to Oma, who held fast to her German heritage even though her family had immigrated to Russia under Catherine the Great's persuasive incentives. Thus, it was from our new English teacher that I would get a real education.

Mrs. Phillipot was Catholic, or so we were told. She was from the nearby French community of St. Claude and had been hired by the colony to teach grades one to five. Hutterite schools abided by the Department of Education's curriculum but were allowed to retain their distance from the outside world by having the school on colony property. At the beginning of the year, Mrs. Phillipot would rely on the older girls as interpreters, since our English language skills were poor. But there was nothing wrong with our eyesight.

On the first day she swept onto the colony in a white Buick and into the school wearing a fitted, crimson dress with a double strand of pearls around her neck, smelling of cigarettes and English clothing stores. Her lipstick and nail polish matched the color of her dress exactly. Her high cheekbones were dusted with a soft sweep of rouge, and her dark brown hair was done in the same precise manner as Queen Elizabeth, whose picture hung immediately above her desk. Her feet were squeezed into jet-black, pointy high heels, and a matching purse glistened like polished ebony as she placed it on her desk with a thump. She was the most groomed and glamorous creature we had ever seen in our lives, and we nearly went cross-eyed looking her over.

After the roll call, during which we had to spring to our feet and reply, "Present, Mrs. Phillipot," she arranged for basins of water and large bars of soap to be brought to the back of the class, and we were lined up and ordered to wash our hands and then have them inspected—palms up, palms down.

Mrs. Phillipot felt obliged to impose her standards in cleanliness, not that some—like young Roland, who loved skunks and mice and frogs better than anything—couldn't use a proper scrubbing. Roland hung out at the machine shop with his older brothers, and his hands were ingrained with grease and dirt, and that's the way he liked it. Mrs. Phillipot tried valiantly to separate the boy from the grime, but then he would pass gas, and she would flee for her economy-sized can of lilac air freshener. "Phee-yew, phee-yew," she lamented, streaming the poison up and down the aisles while the rest of us coughed and rubbed our watering eyes until we nearly lost consciousness. When it was particularly foul, she would shout, "Roland, go to the washroom and don't come back!" With a gleeful smile, Roland happily spent much of the school year in the bathroom, looking out the window at the squirrels.

After the hand inspection, the girls had to line up and remove their *Mützen* for a hair assessment. Some of the girls had quickly stuffed their long hair into their bonnets, more concerned with getting to the *Essenschul* in time for the 7:30 breakfast than having a good hair day, and it came tumbling out in a disheveled mess. With Oma as my hairdresser, I never had to endure a scolding from Mrs. Phillipot about my lack of neatness.

When we were clean to Mrs. Phillipot's satisfaction, the basins were put away, and we finally got down to the business of schooling, which began with singing "O Canada" and saying the Lord's Prayer. During "O Canada," Mrs. Phillipot stood at strict attention at the front of the class and led the singing, but as soon as we started saying the Lord's Prayer, she would grab a yardstick and march around the room, pounding it on the floor as she went. "Our Father . . ." *thump, thump, thump,* "which art in heaven . . ." *thump, thump, thump.* If we dared to turn our heads and look at her, she'd bop us over the head with the yardstick, leaving us with the impression that Catholics did not approve of the Lord's Prayer.

The school year took shape with reading, writing, and arithmetic assignments, none of which interested me as much as what our teacher was wearing. I learned my colors from her outfits, the days of the week from when she wore what, and my numbers from how often she changed high heels. Day after day she wowed us with her perfectly tailored clothing and exquisitely matching necklaces, earrings, and bracelets.

Every day when the bell announced the noon meal, classes were dismissed, and hungry students ran to the *Essenschul.* Mrs. Phillipot would briefly escape to her special room in the back of the classroom, close the door, and apply a fresh coat of lipstick. The room was off-limits to the rest of us and held a particular mystique, because along with school supplies, a couch, a small table, and two chairs, we knew it was where Mrs. Phillipot kept her extra pairs of high heels. When she opened the door, the draft would smell of new books and perfume.

Mrs. Phillipot ate at the community kitchen with the rest of the women, but she never walked there by herself. She was escorted. It didn't seem right that someone so beautifully dressed should be alone, so a bevy of girls would wait for her outside the school and fight over who would attend her right side and who her left. No matter how cross or frustrated she had been with us in the morning, when she pushed open the door, we all jockeyed for position. The older girls usually won out, leaving the rest of us to follow, but even that was a thrill. Watching the sleek, tapered heels of Mrs. Phillipot's shoes disappear into Fairholme's sand, making small, square holes all the way to the *Essenstuben*, we wondered how such thin heels could support her entire body weight and whether her next meal would be the breaking point.

We released Mrs. Phillipot on the adult side of the communal kitchen to eat with the women and proceeded to the *Essenschul*, where I was now taking three meals a day with the rest of the children between the ages of six and fifteen. A latched opening in the far wall gave us access to the main kitchen, through which the cook's helpers passed bowls of *Alla Kartoffel*, "egg fries," and *Focken Klops*, "pork burgers," that the teenage girls would set on the tables. We were again seated according to age, with the boys on one side and girls on the other. Andrew Gross, the assistant minister, supervised and kept *Ordnung*, "order." Under his watchful eye, we closed our eyes and lifted our folded hands to say our prayers before and after each meal. At breakfast and supper meals, we would kneel for extended versions of our table prayers, addressing God in the most reverent tones, "*O Du Allmächtiger, Ewiger, Gnädiger und Barmherziger Gott* . . . Oh, almighty, everlasting, gracious, and merciful God . . ."

During *Mittog*, the noon meal, we kept our *Essenschul Ankela* Rahel on the run. If we ran out of something, we simply shouted for more: *Brot*—bread! *Milch*—milk! Hands were engaged more often than the cutlery, and reaching was more popular than passing.

After *Mittog*, we waited outside the adult dining room until Mrs. Phillipot emerged, and we accompanied her back to school for afternoon classes, where we inevitably practiced our spelling. She was obsessed with dictation, and we had a test almost every day. Standing at the front of the class in her finery, she called out words for each grade. "Grade ones, 'cat.' Grade twos, 'never.' Grade threes, 'corral.'" Mrs. Phillipot had a habit of running her fingers up and down her pearls, which made a soft, purring sound that was intoxicating and did nothing to improve my spelling. We were lined up at the front of the class according to test results, and I was always dead last with Roland, the wildlife specialist.

Roland was an accepted part of the décor in Fairholme, and Mrs. Phillipot was no threat to his self-esteem. And regardless of what she might think, he had his talents. Sandra and I were indebted to him for helping us adjust to the new responsibilities that came with our age—in particular, feather picking.

Winter was pillow- and quilt-making time on the colony, and twice a week, all through the summer and early fall, our mothers harnessed us with a *Federsock* (feather sack), and hoisted us over the fence into the path of a thousand honking geese to collect feathers. It took forever to fill our sacks, and the tiresome job cut into our playtime. At first we included leaves and twigs and goose droppings, but Oma warned me that even if my gentle mother let me get away with it, she would not. Sandra's mother took Oma's side.

We were always on the lookout for dead geese, easy targets for a sack full of feathers, but Fairholme had the heartiest flock in the country. None of them were going to croak on our account. Roland's frequent offers to kill one for us were becoming harder to resist, and once, in a weak moment, Sandra and I gave in to temptation and said yes. We covered our eyes and turned away to purge ourselves of sin by association. Behind us came an awful thrashing and flapping and grunting and quacking as Roland attacked a large gander. It was hard to tell which utterances came from the boy and which from the goose. "*Sie iss tut!*" he shouted as he sped off, bloodied and triumphant that the goose was dead.

The soft down feathers on the belly were just what our mothers wanted, and we stuffed our *Federsöck* until they bulged. The fear of being caught and getting the strap in front of all the children in the *Essenschul* was too much for us to ever consider a second offense, although nothing excited us more than finding a goose that had died of natural or near-natural causes.

As children, we found contentment in the bosom of colony life and in the routines that directed every new season. The honey-colored paths that led us to school and play and occasionally into mischief remained a sea of softness, and Jake Vetter rewarded us for keeping them that way. He instructed us to gather all harmful debris, in particular broken glass, wherever we could find it, and when we had a little tin can's worth, to bring it to his house in exchange for candy and bubblegum. We scoured the paths and lawns and ditches like human vacuum cleaners, for Jake Vetter always had some new American candy on hand from his frequent visits to Hutterite colonies in the United States.

Once, Sandra and I decided to make a determined effort to learn how to blow bubbles. But we didn't have any gum, so we spent an entire afternoon combing Fairholme's trails. All we had to show for it by the end of the day was two rusty nails, not enough to earn our reward. Dusty and disappointed, we lay down on a patch of grass under the shade of a tree and watched the clouds go by. When Roland spotted us with our tin cans, he caught on right away. "Would you like to know where Jake Vetter puts the pieces of glass we bring to him?" he asked, his eyes twinkling. "*Jo!*" Sandra and I said in unison.

Down in a dark corner in the kitchen basement, Roland pointed us to a large basin crammed with pieces of glass. We quickly filled our tins and ran to reap our reward.

::

We had everything you could wish for in Fairholme—beautiful friendships, a strong sense of belonging, enough excitement to keep us looking forward to each new day, and in our hour of need, there was always Roland.

Of course, I knew it was a sin to take so much pleasure in Mrs. Phillipot's worldly wardrobe. I knew that from Sana Basel, who sometimes came by the house in the evenings to help with our bedtime routines and to tuck us in.

Bedtime fell at the same time for everyone on the colony, and because children were always barefoot, we had to wash our feet in a pail of water on the front porch. Our neighbors were doing the same thing, and calls for a race or queries about a missing child's whereabouts were often exchanged across the lawns. My younger sister, Rosie, who was a five-year-old hurricane, and I lifted our long skirts and vigorously stomped our feet in the water until most of the dirt was gone, then wiped them on a towel before following our equally diligent brothers into the house. Sometimes, Mother had to expel the whole lot of us back outside for a second wash. Inside, we knelt to pray, sang our evening songs, and then Father read us a German Bible story while Mother burped her babies.

After Renie died, Sana Basel had begun to pay special attention to our family. She had many grandchildren and was welcome in any number of homes, so it was always a privilege to have her with us. Her version of the biblical story of David, a mere *Tüpfel* (dot) on the horizon who dared to take on Goliath, held us spellbound. We sat on the floor in front of her chair, and she'd lean forward and ask, "How could that little boy, with a pathetic slingshot dangling from his wrist and five small stones rattling in his pocket, take on an enormous giant in a suit of armor?" Her eyebrows shot above the rim of her glasses as she pronounced how Goliath fell to his death *"G'rod so wie Pienets!* Just like a peanut!"

As a baptized member of the Hutterite church, Sana Basel felt it was her duty to *vermohn,* "warn," the younger generation of the pitfalls of life, and nobody could make hell as hot as Sana Basel could. After Goliath's spectacular demise, she cautioned us about *Jüngste Tog,* Judgment Day, the unexpected moment when the heavens would open and God, along with a host of angels, would burst upon the earth to judge every person and determine who was going to heaven and who would go to hell. As if *Jüngste Tog* weren't terrifying enough, Sana Basel told us the story of a young girl who was so disobedient to her mother that one day God had had enough. The floorboards gave way beneath her, and hell swallowed her whole. That sorry story popped into my mind every time I didn't want to do what Mother said.

Nobody knew, Sana Basel told us with conviction, when *Jüngste Tog* would come, but we should always be prepared, because God could read our thoughts, and they would also be judged. That was very unfortunate, because I spent most of my days dreaming about Mrs. Phillipot's wardrobe and perfume, and I knew that kind of thinking was *Irdisch* (carnal).

Even Mother's brother Fritz, the colony turkey man, was jeopardizing my chances in the hereafter. Fritz Vetter loved nothing better than a little escape to the Portage dump in his smelly old truck to forage through other people's garbage. While some, like his wife, Suzanna, did not appreciate his scavenging ways, I shared his enthusiasm. Every broken piece of furniture had potential to him; I was just as determined to find discarded bottles of perfume identical to the kind Mrs. Phillipot wore. Uncle tried to help me by suggesting which bottles he thought belonged to *reiche Leut* (rich people), but he was so covered in turkey dust and feathers I preferred to rely on my own judgment.

Fritz Vetter was a small, stooped figure with a long, scraggly beard, who spoke with his hands. It didn't bother him at all that his right thumb faced the wrong direction. Poor Fritz Vetter. He'd just lost his daughter Lena to the evils of the outside world, and he was so lost in the pain of it all that here I was, dabbling in temptation right under his nose, and he couldn't see it.

Just before school had started, my dad's youngest brother, Jacob Dornn, had stolen my uncle's beautiful, nineteen-year-old daughter Lena Maendel in the middle of the night. At least that was Fritz Vetter's version of the facts. The commotion woke the whole colony, and lights flew on in all the homes as people strained to see the taillights of Jacob's car and Fritz Vetter running over to our house. Shouting from our hallway, he angrily demanded that Father have Jacob bring his daughter back. Father, roused from a deep sleep, tried to get to the facts.

"Did she take a suitcase?" he asked, running his hand through his hair that had taken the shape of a stack of hay.

"Why?" Father's brother-in-law shot back.

"If she packed her suitcase, then she went willingly," Father said quietly. The door slammed, and Fritz Vetter went home only to find Lena's suitcase missing from under her bed and her clothes gone from her closet. She was perfectly prepared to be "stolen." Young people "running away" from the colony before they were baptized for a taste of outside life was fairly common, but so was having them apologize and return because they couldn't make the adjustment. By morning, the story was percolating in the nearby colonies, and people were saying that's what you get when you try to do good and bring in outsiders.

At least Father's other brother, Pete, wasn't coming to steal the women. He just came to sell them . . . beauty supplies. After leaving New Rosedale, he'd found work as a door-to-door salesman for the Rawleigh Company, selling household cleaners, spices, and hair products out of the back of his car. He would arrive on Sunday afternoons, his trunk loaded down with jars, cans, and bottles of products from chicken soup base to hair gel to toilet cleaner.

The sight of half a dozen women bent over the trunk of a runaway's car was more than the elders of the community could tolerate, for they were quite certain nothing good could come out of that particular scenario. But Uncle Pete worked fast. He was a born salesman, and he successfully convinced the women, including Mother, that they absolutely couldn't do their hair without Dippity-Do when for five hundred years they had. It was a pink hair gel with an irresistible fragrance and became a best seller among the colonies.

Pete's trunk was as close to a hairdressing shop the women would ever come to, and the Dippity-Do for $1.50 made them feel that they could give those English women some competition. Even Ankela fell for it, but she never used hers. Every day she just visited her plastic jar of Dippity-Do and inhaled its flowery fragrance for a pick-me-up after her noon nap.

Dippity-Do Pete's intrusion into our sheltered way of life didn't seem to have much of an effect on anybody's conscience, including my siblings, who all appeared undaunted by *Jüngste Tog*. We slept in the same room on two full-sized beds. Three-year-old Phillip slept between Rosie and me in one bed, and Edwin and Alex slept in the other. I could tell by how quickly they all fell into a sound sleep that Sana Basel's warning went in one ear and out the other.

Oltvetter, whose loud snoring rattled the house, seemed to think his salvation was secure too. Maybe he supposed he'd been to hell already with his harrowing experiences at Julius Farm and during the war. On Wednesday evenings, after our prayers, my brothers and I would go to his room, kneel on a chair, and sort through a burlap sack of pinto beans for the Saturday noon meal of beans, bacon, and fresh buns. As we separated the good beans from the bad, he regaled us with stories about his life in Russia and how the revolution had ruined so many lives. Our mouths gaped open when he explained how he had hidden his wealthy employer's jewelry and valuables in a manure pile and was nearly caught when the soldiers poked at it with pitchforks. His stories gave us nightmares, but we always came back for more.

Hell wasn't hot enough to stop me from thinking about Mrs. Phillipot's outfits. After much agonizing, it occurred to me that Sana Basel's warning included an escape route. "Nobody knows when *Jüngste Tog* will come," she had said, emphasizing that God could read our thoughts. Thus, I began a nightly ritual. "God, I know tonight is *Jüngste Tog*," I would whisper during evening prayers, "and you are coming for sure." It was a ridiculous routine that provided me tremendous comfort. I had God in a corner, and the Almighty would have to postpone Judgment Day indefinitely because Ann-Marie Dornn at Fairholme Hutterite colony knew all about it.

After our baths on Saturday nights, we would congregate in the living room in our pajamas and Father would conduct wrestling matches. "Ready, set, go," he would call out, and Edwin and Alex would run from opposite ends of the room and spar and brawl until they were exhausted. My brothers took the matches very seriously, and Father couldn't contain his amusement. Pint-sized Rosie should have been no contest for me, but when our turn came, her fast, slick moves brought both me and the house down. Father threw his head back and laughed until his sides hurt. He had a wonderful laugh. It was a rare, carefree moment for a man who craved order in work, in life, and in relationships.

Order brought my father peace. Sometimes at dusk, Edwin, Alex, Rosie, and I would follow him to the pasture to watch him feed the milk cows. Father would put on his leather working gloves, cut the binder twine, and pull apart bales of hay, spreading them evenly in a long row. The Holstein cows sauntered toward the fence as Father iced the hay with molasses to stimulate their appetites and increase milk production.

Father was well suited to the structure and routine of community life and embraced the words written in the Hutterite Chronicles of 1525:

> To have all things in common means to love our neighbor, to have with him, to want with him, to suffer with him and to endure the ups and downs with him.
>
> In Heaven (as it should be on earth) there is no ownership and hence there is found contentment, true peace, and blessedness.

But like the unease a man feels when a room is too hot or his suit is a size too small, my father was always strained, torn between the tenets of the Hutterite faith and his experience in Fairholme.

Months after Lena had eloped with Jacob, a new crisis erupted. The women leaving the community kitchen with warm rhubarb pies for *Lunschen* saw their husbands exiting the church after the yearly *Stübel* and quickened their pace home. Mother caught sight of Sana Basel blazing a trail to our house, her square heels hitting the ground with a steady thud. You could feel the tension in the air. Mother knew without being told that Father was in the thick of it. So did Sana Basel. Paul Vetter had told her there had been fireworks and retreated to his office in the back of the house to revive himself.

Women made it their business to find out what their men were up to behind closed doors, and if their own husbands were vague on the details, they'd get them from someone else. Oma, sitting on our front porch with her knitting, was shouting at Oltvetter for being so evasive. The two were like oil and water and didn't get along at the best of times. "You've cackled and cackled and you still didn't lay an egg!" she scoffed as she grabbed the yarn in her lap and followed Sana Basel into the house.

"*Reinhold, wos' iss enn fürgongen?*" Sana Basel demanded, pumping my father for information as Mother entered the kitchenette with the pies.

Father did not mince words. Anger rose in his voice as he spoke and told her how Jake had given the men the yearly *Rechnung* (account) of Fairholme's income while her other brother Hons, the colony manager, who handled all the money and paid all the bills, had nodded his approval from the front bench. "*Recht oder unrecht, mir bleiben z'somm.* Right or wrong, we stick together" is how the two brothers described their relationship.

"I listened as Jake gave us the figures from the cows, hogs, chickens, geese, turkeys, and bees, and then I stood up and said, 'Now, Jake, you're a good artist and you've drawn a very nice picture here, but it's wrong. The income you have reported for the cows is much lower than it should be, and I can prove it to you! I have copies of all my receipts for sales and supplies, and so does Feed-Rite. Another thing,' I said, 'you have us making a good dollar with the apiary, and we didn't even have bees this year!'" Father had made a mockery out of the figures.

"You've sure got nerve, to take on Jake in front of all da men like dat! He must feel humiliated," Sana Basel proclaimed, diving into her piece of pie.

"We should be doing really well financially here in Fairholme," Father continued, "but we're not, because of the way Jake and Hons are managing the affairs! I just find that so offensive."

"Dose Maendels, dey shure can cackle," called Ankela from the hallway, noting the Maendels' penchant for exaggerating. "For every two dollars dey make, dey spend tree," she continued. "Dey're real treshing machines with da money."

"*Koom einhin! Wegen stehst enn in Gangel?*" Mother said, motioning her into the room, but Ankela refused, preferring to listen in from the hallway.

"*Ich will nitt, Ich will kolla einhin losen,*" Ankela insisted.

Oma put down her knitting and looked Father straight in the eye. "You better be careful or you'll end up in *der Strof,*" she cautioned, warning that he might be disciplined.

"Oma," Father replied, "I chose community life because I wanted to obey the will of God and live an honest and sincere life. I expect the same from our leaders." He reached for his hat and left to milk the cows, slamming the door behind him.

"If Ronald didn't speak up, who would?" clucked Sana Basel to Mother. "Da men all have big mouths at home, but when they go to *da Stübel*, dey turn into *Tag Mandlen* [dough boys]." Swallowing her last bit of coffee, she took her leave.

In June, one year after Renie's death, Mother was back from the hospital with our annual gift. "*Doh iss dein Brüdela. Er heist* Carl Jacob," she said, introducing him as she offered me the squirming bundle. My six-year-old arms nearly gave way to the weight of the nine pounder.

"We won't give you away," I whispered to him as I squeezed him tight.

"I longed for an older sister and found her in Sana Basel's cherished granddaughter."

Catherine Hofer, Sana Basel's cherished granddaughter.

SEVEN

Secret Flowerpot

THE WINTER AFTER Carl Jacob arrived, my tormented fears about *Jüngste Tog* returned; it had occurred to me that if I could outwit God, he would surely find a way to outmaneuver me. Sana Basel had warned us that if our last deed on earth was noble, then we would go to heaven, but if we were caught behaving badly or merely thinking unworthy thoughts, then we would burn in hell for eternity. I was haunted by her words. Adding to the pressure was our German teacher Katya, Jake Maendel's daughter. She had full, red lips and eyes so big and round that they could instill the fear of God in you with their earnestness. The beautiful nineteen-year-old shared her father's ruddy complexion and persuasive oratory skills. She echoed everything Sana Basel had said about *Jüngste Tog*, and I came to the decision that the surest way for me to get to heaven was to commit suicide. I would do something really nice for Mother and then end my life.

On Sundays, we were treated to a bottle of pop with the noon meal. I loved Orange Crush until I heard Strankel, "String Bean," tell one of his friends that if you put two aspirins into a bottle of 7Up and drank it while it was fizzing, it would kill you. Strankel was a fountain of useless information and always up to some foolish scheme. The previous week, he had been selling suckers to the *Essenschul* children for one and a half cents each, so of course we all had to come up with two pennies. Everyone considered him a simpleton, but his pockets were constantly jingling with our nickels and dimes. Now, I was counting on his formula to help me kill myself.

Mother was besieged by cranky, crying babies when I arrived home, so I offered to wash the dishes and clean up the kitchenette while she put the little ones down for a nap. I hurried through my chores and found two aspirins in the bathroom medicine cabinet and a bottle opener with the cutlery.

Then I remembered my Japanese orange collection and the effort it took to accumulate it. Weeks earlier, the colony had distributed *Weihnachtsgeschenken*, "Christmas goods." By tradition, the bell would ring on the afternoon of Christmas Eve, and every household would rush to the community kitchen with sleds and toboggans and wagons for their share. Beneath a cardboard sign with the initials R. M. D. (Ronald Mary Dornn) stood boxes and boxes of store-bought cookies, candy, fruit, and nuts. Halvah, ribbon candy, shiny chocolate coins, licorice, toffee, Dubble Bubble, broken chunks of Sweet Marie bars, Sultana cookies . . . on and on it went. A child's dream: it was like being let loose in a candy store with a year's worth of treats right in front of our eyes.

The excitement had started to mount on the last day of school, when the Eatons' truck arrived and two delivery men brought dozens and dozens of wrapped parcels into the classroom with our names on them. Our gift from the colony had arrived! Visions of tea sets and dolls and toy guns and yo-yos danced through our brains. We could hardly suppress our exhilaration, even though we knew what they contained; in November, we had given the teacher our order from the Eatons' catalog, with a price limit of $2.99.

No one had a Christmas tree in their homes, and we did not receive gifts from our parents; but on Christmas Eve, we laid one of our wool socks on the table, and Mother and Dad would fill them with peanuts and a single Japanese orange from our bursting *Kellerlein*. The orange was exquisite but so small it went down before you could properly taste it. That year I had started collecting them, and I made the rounds to all my favorite homes to ask for another. Then I bartered with the other children for more so I could have a real feast.

Like precious little eggs, I had amassed thirteen oranges in the back of my underwear drawer, and I wasn't about to deny myself one last moment of pleasure. Then and there I consumed them all, leaving an arc of peels across my bed. By the time I added the aspirins to the 7Up, my stomach was pitching, and I felt as if I already had one foot in the grave. As I watched the aspirins dissolve, I remembered how much my parents cried when Renie died, and how awful it felt in my heart for so long, and my resolve began to evaporate.

Dying was turning out to be a very inconvenient undertaking, and I realized I was going to have to get used to the threat of *Jüngste Tog* for the rest of my life, just like everyone else. Besides, in my

young girl's way of thinking, there was always something exciting around the corner to look forward to. Any day now I would
be receiving a special invitation not to be missed! Whenever the
mood struck him, often over the Christmas holidays, Jake Vetter
would invite a handful of children to his house for the evening.
We were always summoned at the last minute and in the same
manner. One of the young *Dienen* would open our front door
and yell, *"Ann-Marie, der Jake Vetter werd G'schichtlen verzählen,"*
announcing the exclusive invitation. And while she was off to
the homes of other invitees, I would dash off at full speed to my
uncle's house at the opposite end of the colony. Only about five of
his nieces ever made the list, so we felt very special. We descended
on the rickety ladder into his *Kellerlein*, surrounded by shelves
stacked with fruits and nuts and box after box of chocolate bars.
At six-by-six feet, the *Kellerlein* was bigger than anyone else's on
the colony. It even had its own lightbulb.

We found our places on the hard ground around him, and he
offered us each a handful of toffee. Jake Vetter preferred girls as
an audience because we were less troublesome—not as likely to
fart or fidget. He looked like a character straight out of the Bible,
perched on a wooden stool, with his full beard and his thinning
hair combed neatly back. Dark suspenders crisscrossed his checkered shirt, and his feet were wrapped in thick, burgundy slippers
that had been crocheted by his wife. He always left the *Kellerlein*
opening ajar so his daughters could pass him fresh cups of tea and
so his wife, who must have been as captivated as we were, could
listen in while she did her knitting upstairs. For two hours, with
the toffee melting in our mouths, we were transported to Egypt
and suffered with the children of Israel as they endured plague
after plague before Pharaoh finally relented and let them go.

After the story, Jake Vetter would go on at length about the
meaning of all that, the hardening of Pharaoh's heart and the

years of anguish the children of Israel endured. I had no way of comprehending the similarities between this story and his troubled relationship with my father. In my view, Jake Vetter was simply a masterful storyteller who left us spellbound, just like his sister, Sana.

::

The long, lazy days of fall were magical in Fairholme. The trees in the colony apple orchard hung low with a bumper crop of fruit, while up above, the velvet skies were dotted by hundreds of Canadian geese flying south in V-shaped formations. As the sun retreated, we were warmed by steaming vats and crackling fires.

The kitchen was a giant ventilator, circulating aromas of *Strankel Worsch,* bacon, and fresh bread. Meaty tomatoes were transformed into jars of soup, joining the hundreds already lining the burgeoning shelves in the basement pantry. Deep-red beets, boiled whole and eaten with the skins left on, and thick cobs of corn slathered in butter and salt tasted *mächtig gut,* "incredible." I admired Sana Basel's cherished granddaughter, Catherine Hofer, and she and I would grab one of those beets on our way out of the *Essenschul.* We would take it home and hide in our bedroom closets, where we applied the vegetable to our cheeks and lips and pretended to be Mrs. Phillipot.

Though Sandra and I remained inseparable, I longed for an older sister like Sandra had, and Catherine filled that role for me. She was a year older, but more mature and sophisticated, just like an older sister should be. Tall and slender, with jet-black hair, she carried herself with grace and had a reputation for being dutiful. Mrs. Phillipot liked her because she was diligent in school, and I liked her because she could satisfy my curiosity about almost everything.

We formed a club, just the two of us, which convened Sunday afternoons when all the adults and children took a nap. Catherine gave it the exotic name Secret Flowerpot. We would fish a large dill pickle from a gallon jar in the walk-in fridge and choose the softest buns in the kitchen for inspiration. Then we would sit on the wooden tables in the bakery, our legs dangling down and the warm sun on our backs, as we discussed a week's worth of Mrs. Phillipot.

Catherine told me that Mrs. Phillipot dressed according to her moods: when she wore red she was mean, in blue she was pleasant, and on pastel days she was nice to everybody. I liked Mrs. Phillipot so much in red that I hadn't noticed, but I promised to pay more attention.

Mrs. Phillipot was our closest specimen from the English world, and nothing she said or did escaped our scrutiny. One thing that had us scratching our heads was why Mrs. Phillipot wore nylons. In our practical world, they made no sense whatsoever. They didn't keep her warm in the winter, and they didn't cool her off in the summer. It was the oddest thing the way they matched the color of her skin and were next to impossible to distinguish with the naked eye, except for the slight crinkling at the knees when she stood up from a sitting position.

The topic had come up among the children at school, and we tried to penetrate the English person's mind with wild guesses and ridiculous theories. Someone said Mrs. Phillipot wore nylons for health benefits, such as the prevention of *Reisen*, "arthritis," but then another claimed it was to keep hair from growing on her legs. She certainly had the baldest legs we ever saw. Even Roland weighed in on the debate, speculating that she wore them to shield herself from our germs. Anything was possible. One of the older girls finally worked up the nerve to ask her, and at first she seemed taken aback by the question, but then insisted they really did keep her warm.

We giggled, thinking she took us for fools. Catherine considered all their theories, took a bite of her pickle, and said thoughtfully, "It has to be for style, because that's what Mrs. Phillipot cares about the most." Catherine always had the right answers!

I grew to rely on Catherine for answers to an abundance of questions. Our imaginations were fueled by the poetry Mrs. Phillipot read to the older students. We were smitten with a poem by Canadian poet Pauline Johnson, called "The Song My Paddle Sings." We quickly memorized it, reciting it over and over again as we imagined ourselves floating down the Assiniboine River in Pauline's canoe. The way she strung words together made us feel there was hope for the English language.

West wind, blow from your prairie nest
Blow from the mountains, blow from the west.
The sail is idle, the sailor too;
O! wind of the west, we wait for you.
Blow, blow!
I have wooed you so,
But never a favour you bestow.
You rock your cradle the hills between,
But scorn to notice my white lateen.

I stow the sail, unship the mast:
I wooed you long but my wooing's past;
My paddle will lull you into rest.
O! drowsy wind of the drowsy west,
Sleep, sleep,
By your mountain steep,
Or down where the prairie grasses sweep!
Now fold in slumber your laggard wings,
For soft is the song my paddle sings.

August is laughing across the sky,
Laughing while paddle, canoe and I,
Drift, drift,
Where the hills uplift
On either side of the current swift.

The river rolls in its rocky bed;
My paddle is plying its way ahead;
Dip, dip,
While the waters flip
In foam as over their breast we slip.

And oh, the river runs swifter now;
The eddies circle about my bow.
Swirl, swirl!
How the ripples curl
In many a dangerous pool awhirl!

And forward far the rapids roar
Fretting their margin for evermore.
Dash, dash,
With a mighty crash,
They seethe, and boil, and bound and splash.

Be strong, O paddle! Be brave, canoe!
The reckless waves you must plunge into
Reel, reel.
On your trembling keel,
But never a fear my craft will feel.

We've raced the rapid, we're far ahead!
The river slips through its silent bed.

Sway, sway,
As the bubbles spray
And fall in tinkling tunes away.

And up on the hills against the sky
A fir tree rocking its lullaby,

Swings, swings,
Its emerald wings,
Swelling the song that my paddle sings.

Pauline Johnson's father was a Mohawk chief. In pictures, she looked so beautiful in a fringed buckskin dress and bear claw necklace; we could feel the wind blowing its bitter chill over the prairie as we glided through the pristine waters of some mighty river, our voices swelling and falling with every slip and dip of her pen.

Hutterites in Canada generally felt a kinship toward the neighboring aboriginal communities because neither was well accepted by the mainstream. The women from the nearby reserve often appeared after supper, and our cook would pack up the leftovers for them. (We were so spoiled we didn't eat leftovers.) The women brought with them hand-painted, birch-bark brush holders and beaded broaches and necklaces in exchange. Although jewelry was prohibited on the colony, Indian beadwork worn discreetly was tolerated. Sometimes the women would make a stop at Sana Basel's house. She knew them by name and offered up treats from her *Kellerlein*, but her generous nature irked Paul Vetter, who complained loudly as she carried box after box out to the car.

"Your husband, he talk too much," one Indian woman observed when they were out of earshot.

"He sure do!" agreed Sana Basel. "He sure do!"

Loaded down with leftovers, the back ends of their dilapidated vehicles dragged on the ground as they pulled away in a cloud of dust. Some summer nights, the haunting sound of drums from the powwow at the Long Plains Reserve would seep through our open windows and lull us to sleep. Every year, a group of curious teenagers stole a colony vehicle in the night and returned with fascinating stories of feathers, regalia, and wild dances. The natives weren't tempted by our lifestyle any more than we were by theirs, yet a quiet understanding remained between us, fortified by our shared status as second-class citizens.

Saturdays were all-out cleaning days on the colony. Every person and their floors were washed and polished, including the community kitchen, the kindergarten, and the school. When the older girls washed the floors at the school, there was always an audience, because they were given the key to Mrs. Phillipot's little back room, where she kept her beautiful shoes. Lined up in a neat little row were black, blue, white, and brown high heels, each more stylish than the other. It was impossible to resist the urge to try them on, and soon all the girls were clippety-clopping up and down the aisles. I was desperate to experience the sensation of heels sinking into the sand the way they did when Mrs. Phillipot was walking to the *Essenstuben*, so when Sandra and I were given a turn, I chose the sleek, black patent pair, stuffing them with toilet paper until they fit.

Our feet felt like they had been poured into a vase, and they ached as we marched all over the school yard, wondering how Mrs. Phillipot made it look so easy. The older girls made us wash each pair inside and out until every speck of evidence was gone before returning the shoes to the exact spot from which they had been taken. Mrs. Phillipot never knew what a thrill her shoes gave her students at Fairholme Colony on her weekends off.

Sometimes, when we had a little pocket change, we would sneak off to Bambi Gardens. It was a seasonal resort area a quarter mile from the colony. A large, round Coca-Cola sign beckoned us on as we started down the long, winding road to our desired destination. As we drew closer, we could hear the owner's yappy Maltese barking feverishly. Approaching the canteen, we could see the wading pool, the swings, and the Assiniboine River slowly rolling past like a picture book. Off to the right were the campers.

Mrs. Bamberack always seemed so strained in contrast to the tranquil surroundings. We could hear the familiar clatter of the wooden stick as she propped open the canteen window through which she shouted nervously, "What do you want, girls?" If we dared dip our feet in the pool or sit on the swings, she would say, "The wading pool and the swings are off-limits and for the use of my customers only. Now, come along, get what you want, and off you go." We'd make our way to the window and longingly eye all the wonderful treats. The smell of cigarettes would rush at us while our eyes searched the shelves behind her for ripple chips, McIntosh toffee, ice cream, Coca-Cola, and 7Up. If we took too long, Mrs. Bamberack would prod us. "Come on now. I don't have all day. Make up your minds and off you go."

Beyond candy and Mrs. Phillipot's fashions, we did not envy English people their stressed lives. For Catherine and me, it was enough to walk in the woods in the summertime and play miniskirt, fastening the bottom of our skirts to our waistlines and feeling the cool wind on our legs.

In the glistening days of autumn, when Fairholme was blanketed with leaves from one end of the colony to the other, the women would rake the lawns, and the teenage boys would come with wheelbarrows to collect the individual piles and deposit them in one huge mound in an open space near our house. The larger it grew, the more irresistible it became, until we hurled ourselves into the golden bed of foliage. Our sides would hurt from laughter, and our clothes and hair would be matted with bits of twigs and debris. The older boys would eventually set the pile on fire, and we would run down to the *Kartoffel Kammela*, "potato cubicle," in the community kitchen and retrieve a potato from a heap as high as the leaves we had been playing on. Then we would hurry back to toss it into the blazing bonfire, deeply inhaling the sweet, tobacco smell of burning leaves and inching as close as we dared to warm our shivering bodies from the chill of fall, though each year the bottom of Rosie's dress was charred from getting too near to the fire, and Mother would throw it away.

When the fire subsided, the boys would start pulling out the blackened potatoes with long rakes. Nobody got their original potato back, but we all claimed to identify the first one out of the fire as our own. Our hands and faces would be smeared with soot when our mothers would come to collect us for a scrubbing and bedtime routines. Sleep was never sweeter than in the fall when, drunk with fresh air and exercise, we ducked under thick feather comforters and dreamed contentedly of the days ahead.

Late fall was the most romantic time of year at Fairholme. The Manitoba Hutterite colonies were responsible for 95 percent of the province's geese production, and every year Fairholme produced twenty thousand birds for market. The *Buben* (young men) from the Riverbend and Oakbluff colonies were always invited to provide the extra manpower needed for the two-week slaughter. They were industrious, courteous, and most importantly, flirtatious. When the bell rang after breakfast, lines of men and women fitted with aprons and rubber gloves made their way to the *Gonsstoll* (goose barn) behind the hatchery.

Out in the back, the young boys rounded up the geese while two *Buben*, armed with an ax and a block of wood, chopped off the birds' heads and hung the carcasses neck down on a circle of hooks to let the blood drain. The geese were handed off to my cousin, John Maendel, through an opening in the wall covered by a rubber flap. John had an artful way of swinging the door of the boiler while keeping his eye on his stopwatch. It took exactly one minute to steam the feathers off six geese, and he had the timing down to a science. Inside the steamy *Gonsstoll*, women were stationed along the sides of large, rectangular plywood boxes built to collect the feathers that would be sold to markets in Minneapolis and Chicago for two dollars a pound.

While the geese were suspended from the ceiling by hooks, rows of women, two to a goose, plucked the feathers while the *Buben* ran to supply their favorite *Diene* with a fresh bird. The Fairholme girls used the opportunity to tease them about how *longsäm*, "slow," they were, while married women shared advice about sensible things, like how to stop children from sucking their thumbs or wetting the bed.

As the community worked amid the blood and the goose heads and the feathers, the young women would start to sing. Their clear, beautiful voices surged in a unison so powerful you could almost feel your feet lifting off the ground. "In that beautiful land where it's always springtime and the flowers bloom on and on." At three o'clock, the colony boss brought special store-bought treats for *Lunschen*, and the children received handfuls of candy or bubble gum. Benches of straw bales bordered the length of the room where the adults rested and enjoyed soft drinks, ice cream, and coconut cookies.

Late in the afternoon, as the piano-sized boxes filled with feathers, the *Buben* couldn't resist the invitation for some sport. One after another, a *Boa* (young man) would grab his favorite *Diene* from behind and throw her into the box of feathers. She would resurface covered in feathers and soft down, feigning astonishment, while onlookers laughed at their antics. The older women criticized the single women for being *bubisch*, "boy crazy," and wild, but everyone knew the annual goose slaughter was a way for young people to share time together and playfully acknowledge their interest in a potential husband or wife.

In the evening, after the older crowd had retired to their beds, the young people gathered at my friend Catherine's house. Guitars were forbidden, but her dad, Paul Jr., had one hidden in a closet, and the romantically inclined would pile into a back room to socialize and sing. At midnight, Paul Jr.'s thoughtful wife, Katie, who enjoyed the young people, would serve tea, chocolate bars, and fruit before everyone went home for a good night's rest in preparation for another big day of work.

Wing feathers were not salable, but they were collected in gunnysacks for the women to make quilts and pillows out of them. After the goose slaughter, Sana Basel always took a big sack of wing feathers, and in the cold winter evenings, the call would go out to come and *Federschleiss* (feather strip) at her house. The women sat in a semicircle in her living room, each with a pile of feathers in her lap. The feathers were stripped down on each side, and the stems were thrown on the floor to be made into whistles for children. *Federschleissen* was our invitation to the theater, filled with good food, lots of laughter, and the latest gossip about who got married, who was in *die Wuchen*, who died, who rose from the dead, and who found Jesus.

The only thing more engaging than *Federschleissen* was when my mother's sister Anna came from Deerboine for her yearly visit. She always stayed at Sana Basel's house, and whenever those two Maendel sisters got together, it was worth dropping everything to pay them a call. Sana Basel's husband, Paul Vetter, nearly had heart failure when those two teamed up. He was neat and orderly, and that's the last thing you'd ever accuse them of. Within hours of Anna Basel's arrival, she and Sana Basel turned the house upside down. Side by side they sat on the brown sofa in the living room, sacks of feathers sprouting between their knees.

They clutched the delicate down in their well-worn hands and discussed its quality and potential while wisps of feathers floated around the room and dotted the furniture. Nothing held their attention for long, and by the end of the day, the house was a jumble of fabric and feathers. Garbage bags filled with rags for making rugs were brought down from the attic, and the colorful fabric was scattered about in careless heaps. Sana Basel took out her spinning wheel and started to spin some sheep's wool while Anna Basel unfolded the sewing machine and began construction of a durable pair of underwear.

Paul Vetter couldn't stomach chaos. He either evacuated himself early or remained barricaded in his bedroom. At *Lunschen*, the two sisters went in pursuit of his chocolate bars, which he kept under lock and key in a desk drawer.

"*Voter, bring uns Bars!* Father, bring us some bars!" Sana Basel demanded.

He wasn't in the mood to break bread with the two mess makers, but he was due for a coffee, and the only way to get it was to dodge the mayhem in the living room and make his way to the kitchenette in large strides, complaining as he went.

"Good God, this house is a pig barn! How on earth can you two create such an awful mess?"

"*Och stilla, Voter,*" replied Sana Basel in a soothing voice. "Don't scold, Father. You know that we'll clean everything up. Hush, hush—here's some good coffee."

Sana Basel was fairly used to his discontent, and he understood that his objections fell on deaf ears. Still, they tried resolutely to change each other's habits. And in their spare time, they had raised thirteen children together.

Eyeing the coffee, Paul Vetter plunked down on a chair, his thumbs in both suspenders, glaring at his sister-in-law with unmistakable indictment. "Anna, *dos bist du Schuld!*" he declared, laying the blame on her. "It's a downright sin to be capable of making such a sorrowful mess!"

Anna Basel nodded her polka dots in Paul Vetter's direction, wordlessly confessing her collusion as her face disappeared into her coffee cup. Then she and Sana Basel would try to distract my uncle with interesting gossip.

"I don't care!" he shouted midsentence as they tempted him with a delightful tale, but then he'd press them for details, and they knew they had him.

They cooed and massaged and waited on him, but if he caught sight of Catherine and me passing by the window, pushing baby carriages outside, he would open it and bellow, his cheeks expanding and retreating like a goldfish. "*Dindlen kommts her!*" he'd beckon. "Something outrageous is going on in here. I beg you to come and clean up this piggery." And then he'd dash back beyond the living room to the safety of his office.

Fairholme had a reputation as a free-spirited colony and was criticized by other colonies for being too worldly. The young women dared to wear their skirts an inch shorter than in other colonies, but Jake Maendel did not concern himself with such matters. In the winters, when all the young men on the colony disappeared after supper, everyone knew they were huddled on bales upstairs in the pig barn, watching the Stanley Cup finals on a small black-and-white television.

Despite Jake Vetter's willingness to look the other way in some areas, his management style continued to clash with my father's when it came to a moral code for community life. Father's current position as cow man in Fairholme did nothing to improve his status with Jake either.

Back at New Rosedale, Father had been the appointed chicken man, assuming the position from Sylvester Baer, who stayed on as his assistant even after their unforgettable *Hulba* incident. The two had remained friends and worked well together in the colony's new, large-capacity chicken barn. My father, who had never worked with chickens before, read everything he could on the subject before immersing himself in his new job. He constructed wooden water and feed troughs for six thousand birds, paying special attention to details, such as spacing to avoid overcrowding. Diligent and methodical, he was driven by the motto he adopted in his youth: "Things that you do, do with your might; things done by halves are never done right."

While Sylvester had been satisfied to deliver a dozen cases of eggs to a handful of faithful weekly customers, Father set his sights on a bigger market and drove to Winnipeg to approach Safeway to buy his eggs. The large grocery chain offered him forty-three cents a dozen, but when the competition, Burn's and Co., promised him half a cent more per dozen, he signed a deal with them. Egg production soared to over a hundred cases of graded eggs per week, and over the course of three years, Father had helped to establish New Rosedale as the largest egg producer in Manitoba.

My father always took pride in a job well done, but sometimes, when alone with the chickens, he wondered whether he had made the right decision by giving community life another chance. At New Rosedale, he had a kind and gentle wife who took good care of him, but the absence of brotherly love in the colony, at least the kind the Bible spoke of, left him questioning his judgment. He was troubled that his strained relationship with the senior Maendel brothers had not improved after his controversial marriage to their sister. Instead, they continued to downplay their brother-in-law's achievements, praising the chicken men from other colonies as superior, even though the profit margins year after year proved otherwise.

My father applied that same exhaustive work ethic to his role as the cow man at Fairholme, and as a result, he helped to establish a dairy and breeding program that was booming. As had happened at New Rosedale, though, he didn't get the credit. His profit was applied to other enterprises.

::

The summer I turned nine, Father's commitment to community life was challenged once again, and Jake Maendel did what he swore he would never do: summon ministers from surrounding communities to help him deal with the mess. "That will be the day, when I need other ministers to help me run my own colony," he had once bragged.

The crises began in the usual manner. Father asked for something, and Jake said no. At first, the two were at loggerheads, because Jake wouldn't repair the barn's water pumps. It was hot outside, and the cows' water supply and milk were in danger of drying up. Father was so annoyed that Jake would jeopardize the colony's milk contract that he retaliated by refusing to milk the cows. Then in August, as Father was struggling to keep up with the demands of his thriving livestock operation, he repeatedly asked to buy a wagon so he could cut grass and use it for cattle feed. Again and again Jake denied his request.

It galled Father that he was breaking his back to make a success of the dairy without any support or acknowledgment. He went to Winnipeg and bought a new wagon for five thousand dollars and charged it to Fairholme's account. To buy something without permission was unheard of; not even ministers were allowed to do that. When he arrived home with his new purchase, the whole colony erupted, and Jake immediately called a *Stübel*, where he rebuked Father and told him he would be disciplined for flagrant insubordination.

"Jake," Father responded, "before you punish me, you must first be punished." Father's anger made him fearless. "You and Hons are buying trucks without asking, and you know as well as I do that all big items are to be approved by the community."

There was an audible gasp in the room as Father appealed to the rest of the men sitting stiffly on the wooden pews. "I asked and asked Jake for a wagon to feed my cattle, and he refused to even bring the matter to council. So I did what the minister and the boss do. I went out and bought it without permission. I acknowledge that it is against the rules, and I am willing to subject myself to the same punishment as they get."

Mother's other brothers were also in attendance, and during the discussion, Hons Maendel shifted uneasily on the front bench while Peter Maendel tried to mediate. "What," he asked Jake, "was your reason for saying no?" The question hung in the air like a bad smell.

The *Stübel* was dismissed, and a diminished Jake went home and called twenty-five ministers from other Manitoba colonies to deal with the matter. Their decision was compromised by Jake's own disregard for colony rules. Father was forced to apologize, but he made the apology on the condition that he would be allowed a wagon. It was agreed that he could have a wagon, but not that wagon. His hasty purchase was to be returned immediately, and the colony would buy a new one.

Mother's brother Peter accompanied him to Winnipeg to make the return. They spent the better part of a day going from one implement dealer to another to find a similar wagon, but there was none to be found. At the end of the day, they quietly returned to Fairholme with the same wagon and said nothing.

"What are we living in the colony for?" Father asked Mother late that night as they both lay in bed, unable to sleep. "Why are we living our lives in a constant state of conflict?"

The answer came with the morning light, and Father's frustrations were replaced by a steely calm. He knew what he must do.

Ann-Marie Dornn, age 9.

"'Ann-Marie,
your mother and
father are running
away!'"

EIGHT

Weglaufen

Running Away

ACROSS THE WESTERN sky, the rich red, orange, and gold tones of a spectacular Manitoba sunset were bringing the soft summer day to a close. We felt spoiled by its beauty in Fairholme, for over and over again, even in the harshest of winters, we were treated to its splendor. Against this magic expanse of space, I was playing dodgeball with the children from the *Essenschul*. We all had the giggles, and our laughter infected a group of adults who had come to watch. The women on cook week, having put in a full day in the kitchen, folded their arms across their chests, ready for a little fun. They chortled with amusement as I, as wide as I was tall, kept eluding the ball. The older boys were on a campaign to take me out, and the laughter escalated as the bare misses whizzed by.

Above the merriment, a voice pierced the warm air. "Ann-Marie, your mother and father are running away!" I froze and turned toward home. To a Hutterite, nothing is more shameful than the word *Weglaufen*, "running away." *Weglaufen* was for rebellious young people who needed to get it out of their systems, not for mothers and fathers with a bushel of children. Entire families simply didn't leave colonies. It was unheard of.

I remembered in previous years how, one by one, Sana Basel and Paul Vetter's daughters had started leaving Fairholme for that big, sinful world. Who wouldn't want to wear a short skirt or cut her hair like Mrs. Phillipot just once in her life? There just seemed to be no end to this exodus, but through the tears and protests, their parents had the hope that they would soon be back to get married and settle down in the comfort and security of colony life. They always came back to visit on Christmas Eve.

I would watch from our kitchen window for car lights at Sana Basel's when her daughters would sneak home. In the pitch dark, the driver would quickly turn off the lights, and dark figures would rush into her house. In less than a minute I was there. Her daughters were still in the hallway, their hair cut short and the change in their appearance dramatic. Their knee-length coats hung open, revealing long legs and miniskirts. Paul Vetter was frantically shouting for them to cover up. "*Legt's ench on! Ich bitt ench Diene n legt's ench on!* Get some clothes on! I beg you, girls, get some clothes on!" he said. "How can you come home like this?"

Sana Basel was getting food and coffee ready in the kitchenette. "*Kommt's einhin,*" she invited, trying to be heard above the commotion. "Father, be quiet and let dem come in."

Paul Vetter disappeared into the bathroom as the girls slipped out of their coats and into the living room to greet a large contingent of siblings, nieces, and nephews who had come to welcome them home. Chairs were placed against the wall all around the room, and the children sat in the center of the floor. "I see London, I see France, I see someone's underpants," one of the children piped up. Paul Vetter emerged from the bathroom, red faced and balancing a pile of towels in his hand. "Cover yourselves up, girls. It's a terrible sin to dress like this," he insisted.

"You never know what's under dose skirts until you git married. Den you find out, and I can tell you, dos women are full of surprises," said James, their newly married neighbor who had popped in for a look-see. "*Du geh Heim!*" a flustered Paul Vetter exclaimed, pointing him in the direction of the door while placing towels over his daughters' exposed knees and thighs. I wondered if Sana Basel had warned her daughters about *Jüngste Tog* as well as she had me.

The dodgeball hit me hard in the abdomen. The game was over. I rushed toward home, trailed by a probing entourage. Rounding the corner, I saw two strangers lifting our family table onto a truck parked out front. Behind them came my father with the chairs. What was happening was unmistakable.

Out of the corner of my eye, I saw my brothers and sisters dashing home from every direction. Word had gotten around, and we all singly and breathlessly arrived at our front door. Father ushered us into the house and into one of the bedrooms, away from prying eyes. The event that was unfolding had, in that moment, driven a wedge between us and the rest of the community. Watching the spectacle from their lawns and out of their back windows, colony members were in as much disbelief as we were.

Sitting on the edge of the bed, wide-eyed and speechless, we waited for our parents to enter the room. We were all still young enough to have a child's trust in our parents but old enough to recognize the seriousness of what was taking place. My oldest brother, Edwin, was twelve, Alex was eleven, and in a matter of days, I would be ten. Rosie was poised to turn nine, Phillip was seven, Eugenie was five, and Carl, the baby, was four. Together we waited for our parents to help us make sense of this madness.

Days earlier, I had been confronted at the *Essenschul* by one of the older girls when I arrived for the noon meal. "Your dad is running away from the colony, and he's taking your whole family along!" she said. I could feel her hot breath against my face.

"You liar!" I shouted so everyone could hear me.

"Well, then why is he wearing ass pockets?" she wanted to know.

I felt my face grow red and my throat go dry. Pushing past her, I took my seat next to Sandra. My mind reeled and my hunger vanished. It had escaped my observation that Father had acquired store-bought pants. I wanted to run home, but I couldn't. Clasping my hands, I recited the traditional table prayer with the others. After a few bites, I waited for closing prayers and hurried outside. I didn't dare mention the incident to my parents, for fear there might be some truth to the troublesome exchange. I removed it from my mind as only a child can.

Now Mother stood solemnly behind Father as he told us plainly that we were leaving the colony the next morning. We were asked to please cooperate and be good. Alex cried that an adult had told him our parents were leaving the colony and taking us straight to hell. Hutterites are taught that the colony is the ark of God, and like the story of Noah in the Bible, those inside the ark are safe, and those who refuse to enter perish. "*Ich komm nitt mit*," Alex objected. "I'm going to hide tomorrow and stay here." My parents knew their second son had the stubbornness to complicate things and tried their best to calm him, but he was not persuaded. Father resorted to threatening Alex with the strap if he pursued his own course.

Father never told us why we were leaving but had, in fact, spent the last year preparing for this moment. The previous summer, he had taken an unapproved trip to visit his sisters in Ontario. Jake had refused to even consider granting him permission, and when Father requested Jake call a *Stübel* to see what the other colony men would say, that, too, was met with a firm no. "I want you to remember that I came to you and asked for your consent," he told Jake, closing the door behind him. Father then took a load of cows to the livestock market in Winnipeg, borrowed some money from his brother Dippity-Do Pete, and left by train for Ontario.

He stayed away for six weeks, contemplating our future. His daring move was the talk of the community. Some of Mother's brothers told her he had left her for a new life in the outside world, and others told her to lock him out when he came home. Mother held fast to the letters he wrote to her every day and anxiously waited for his return. His sisters, who had long since left the Julius Farm and settled in rural Ontario, cautiously advised him that it would be difficult to find a decent job to support so many children, but deep in his soul their brother's mind was made up.

Jake hadn't seen it coming. With such a large family, and with Oltvetter and Oma living next door, he never expected my father would leave the security of colony life. But after Father defied his orders and went to Ontario, Jake began to grow anxious about what his brother-in-law was capable of.

Upon his return, instead of being disciplined or excommunicated, Father found he had more leverage than ever. Hay and feed supplies for the cows were delivered on time without a hassle, and if he required a vehicle, one was promptly made available. Father was milking the cows one day when Jake unsteadily came to ask him if he felt what he'd done was right.

"If you would have treated my request with respect, or at least tried to appear reasonable, I would not have taken this trip," said

Father. "But Jake, we are like two immature boys arguing all the time. How can you stand there and begin your sermons every day with the words '*Der Frieden des Herren*,' 'The peace of God,' when we have such disrespect toward one another?"

Angered by Father's doggedness, Jake promised "to deal with him" and left, but nothing came of the threat. An uneasy calm prevailed until just before Easter, when Father felt compelled to find out where he stood.

Easter is a time of renewal and the most significant religious holiday for Hutterites. Not only is it the time of year when serious young adults are baptized and become full members of the Hutterite church, but it's also the only time its members take communion. The communion service lasts for three hours. Special loaves of bread are baked by the women in the bakery for this solemn occasion, and everybody's *Luckela* arrives early to care for the children so all the members of the church will be in attendance. All the women and girls, even those too young to attend, got a new dress. Watching the *Dienen* going to church in gorgeous new outfits was not to be missed.

Before the sacred holiday began, my father went over to Jake's house and informed him that he would no longer be attending church. "In the Bible it says if your brother has ought against you, leave your gifts at the altar and go and reconcile," Father said. "We don't even consider straightening our matters out, and I don't want to be a part of this anymore."

The startled minister was moved to take action. He called a *Stübel* to clear the air, but as he stood at the front, defending his past actions, he began to contradict himself. This disturbed the rest of the men, who started to argue about the discrepancies. Finally Jake announced, "Well, we're going to apologize." The room fell silent as Father stood to his feet and said to the *Prediger*, "Jake, you've said up until now you have always done your best and have done nothing wrong. What do you have to apologize to me for?"

Immediately the men were up in arms because Father wouldn't let a minister apologize to him. "I'd like to explain myself," Father said, and he gave them a parable. "Supposing you accuse me of stealing something from you and I repeatedly deny it and argue my innocence all night. Then, all of a sudden, I say to you, 'Okay, I'm sorry,' and you ask me, 'Did you steal it?' and I say no. Would you accept my apology?"

Infuriated, Jake ordered Father to leave the meeting so he could speak privately with the men and determine a course of action. But Father said to him, "Jake, if you send me out now, I will take that to mean that you're through with me, and I won't come back."

From then on, Father's resolve exceeded the fear and doubt any reasonable man might have had about leaving the security of community life with a thirty-eight-year-old wife, seven children, and not a penny to his name. At forty-six, Father had never had a bank account, held a mortgage, or paid a bill. All he had was a grade-eight education and the heart of a laborer who knew the value of honest, hard work. After the *Stübel*, he devoted himself to his dairy cows and waited for his children to finish the school year.

One week before we "ran away," Father took Edwin, Alex, Rosie, Mother, and me on a secret outing. Dad was vague about the trip, except to say that we were going to a place called Dahl's Farm, because Mr. Dahl needed someone to clean his house. We didn't get off the colony very much, so it sounded like a wonderful adventure.

Phillip really wanted to come along, but at his age Mother knew he would be more of a hindrance than a help. She told him he had to stay home. "Then I'm going swimming," he sobbed. This alarmed Mother, who knew that the Assiniboine River was dangerous. Several Hutterite colonies were established on its banks, and its undercurrents had become legendary. Too many Hutterite young people, with no opportunity for formal swimming lessons, had lost their lives in its waters. Swimming was discouraged, and certainly stripping down to a swimsuit not condoned, but on hot summer days with no air-conditioning, rules and propriety gave way to the compelling desire to cool off. Typically, the teenage rule breakers influenced the younger crowd in need of excitement. The older ones often jumped into the river fully clothed, and the moment was not lost on the younger ones, like my brother, who would gleefully follow suit. Mother firmly warned Phillip that if he went near the river while we were gone, he would be disciplined when she returned.

Dippity-Do Pete had given Father an old brown pickup with a used camper in exchange for repair work on his home in Winnipeg. My father hid the truck in the bushes surrounding Fairholme. Mother, Dad, Rosie, and I climbed in the cab, and Edwin and Alex hopped into the camper, which was fitted with a yellow foam pad they could lie down on. Then off we went. After what seemed like a long time, we turned into a lane that went on for half a mile. It was very muddy, and the truck swerved all over the road as Dad fought for control of the steering wheel. Finally, we came to a stop in front of a small, yellow house with green shutters. Only our parents knew that this isolated little farmhouse would soon be our home.

Mother told my sister and me we had to help her clean the house, and she would give us a chocolate bar later. Dad went off to work, and the boys, to their delight, found two rusty old bikes in a nearby shed. They happily spent the day learning to ride them. We were given explicit instructions to not tell anyone where we had been when we got back to the colony.

Inside, the three of us—Mother, Rosie, and I—toured the lifeless, empty house. It was very dirty and smelled musty. The job got bigger by the room. Mother opened some windows to let flies out and others in. She appointed my sister to clean the bathroom, and me the kitchen. I was to wash out the cupboards and then the floors with the rags, pails, and *Specksaften* she had brought with her. Mother vanished to the basement, where she spent the day scrubbing a filthy cistern and removing the dead mice.

I filled the kitchen sink with water. A bottle of Ivory liquid dish-washing detergent had been left behind, and when I squeezed the bottle, a thick, milky solvent flowed into the hot water that released the most amazing scent. On the colony we used the practical and versatile *Specksaften* to clean everything. This was my first experi-ence with dish detergent, and I was amazed English people actually did their dishes with something that smelled this fabulous. As I inhaled deeply, the steam rose and filled my enchanted nostrils. It smelled better than Mother's perfume, and I couldn't resist squeez-ing a small amount into my hand and daubing it on my neck. It was a bit sticky, but I felt unaccountably beautiful.

The Ivory detergent put considerable pleasure in my work, and it took me all day to do the job. Father returned for us in the evening. Mother, Rosie, and I had done as much as we could, and the boys were getting restless. We piled back into the truck, tired but happy to be going back.

On the way home, I rested my head on Mother's shoulder and listened as she began to tell Father about a dream she'd had during her afternoon nap that week. Mother took her dreams seriously, for they often foreshadowed things to come. She was very conscious of their impact, because her own mother had been warned about her death in a dream that Joseph Maendel described in a letter:

A few days before she took sick, Katrina had a dream. She had taken her afternoon nap in the same bed upstairs, and when she came down at 1:30 she said to our daughter and me, "I was awoken by a dream and my sleep vanished from me." We eagerly asked, "What was your dream?" She began, "I dreamt a big storm or a weather system was coming toward me. I screamed and tried to run this way and that, but I couldn't get away. It frightened me and I woke with a start." We couldn't interpret the dream for her, but a few hours before she died, she reminded us of it and said, "This undoubtedly is what my dream was about."

"I dreamt," Mother said, "that a team of horses going very fast drove right through Fairholme and took off a corner of a house. I sat straight up in bed, I was so frightened," she told Father. She was unsure whether the horses had run into our house or the house of the assistant minister, Andrew Gross, which stood directly in front of ours. "Something terrible is about to happen," she predicted.

By the time we reached Portage la Prairie, I had dozed off. Suddenly my mother called out, "Police!" Dad stepped on the brakes, and I was jolted out of my slumber. "It looks as if they're stopping all the cars," Father said with a puzzled look, bringing his vehicle to a halt. He rolled down his window, and a police officer nearly blinded us with his flashlight. "What's your name, and where are you heading?" he asked.

"My name is Ronald Dornn, and I'm on my way home to the Fairholme Hutterite Colony," Father replied.

"Well, apparently somebody drowned there today," the officer stated casually.

"Who was it? Do you have a name?" asked Dad, panic filling his voice.

"Oh, dear God," whispered my stunned mother.

"No, I don't," he responded as he waved us off.

Father breathed new life into the old truck as he took off in earnest. Frantically, and out loud, my parents prayed that Phillip was safe. They alternated between begging God for his life and contemplating whether this was a sign from God that they shouldn't be leaving the colony.

My brothers started banging on the camper window, upset by the way Dad was driving. They couldn't imagine what had gotten into him as they knocked about in the back. Mother motioned for them to sit down and be quiet.

Dust and bits of gravel blew up behind us as we turned onto the sandy road to Fairholme. It was a dark night, and we were full of fear. In the event of such a tragedy, vehicles used to assist in the recovery of a body would traditionally be parked beside the home of the family who had lost a member. "Look, Ronald, they've parked the vehicles beside my sister's house because we weren't home," said my mother, bracing for the worst. "No, that's not your sister's house, Mary," said Dad. "That's the assistant minister's house." We drove up to our house and rushed inside. Oma had put the children to bed and was sitting in the dark, waiting for our return. "They can't find Ewald," she said, referring to Andrew Gross's son. It was a pain she understood only too well. Mother rushed past her into the children's room, where she threw her arms around a warm and sleeping Phillip.

"They say he went swimming after supper," Oma continued, "and now they can't find him." Relief and sadness flooded our rigid bodies. Mother returned and ordered us to bed. My parents were filled with gratitude that Phillip was safe but deeply saddened by the news. Eighteen-year-old Ewald was one of my dad's best helpers in the cow barn, and Father was very fond of him.

Over the next few days, the predictable pattern of community life was turned upside down as the men searched the river. Ewald was handsome and likable and very popular with the girls. The whole colony was stunned by his loss. He had gone swimming after supper, and a strong undercurrent had carried him away while his two friends stood by helplessly and watched. His wary father had warned him not to go into the river, but Ewald was too old to be told what to do. "Then I'm off to build your coffin," his father had said bluntly, trying to shock him into submission. Incredibly, his father's terrible prediction came true.

Catherine and I sat on the riverbank, watching the men search the water with boats and tractors. I found her a great comfort in times like this. She displayed maturity beyond her years as she patiently explained how lucky and happy Ewald was to be with God. "We poor souls," she continued, "must work hard to live good and productive lives."

Many colony members came and went during the course of the day, including Ewald's grieving family. Food and fresh coffee were brought from the community kitchen for the workers and for those holding vigil. Hours turned to days with no trace of the body.

Finally, it was decided that the best way to recover Ewald's body would be to slaughter a pig weighing about the same as Ewald, and release it on the spot where he had disappeared. As soon as Catherine and I heard this news, we rushed to the pig barn. Since her dad was the pig man, we didn't want to miss the slaughter, but by the time we got there, all out of breath, the pig was already on its way to the river. Rushing back to the river, we found we had missed the launch as well.

They eventually found Ewald's body, and the funeral was held a few days later. His bloated remains were sealed in a steel coffin from an English funeral home, but even with this precaution, the putrid odor seeped through, making the circumstances surrounding the tragedy that much sadder. Because the coffin was closed, Ewald's body could not be seen or touched, which suppressed the traditional good-byes.

Ewald was gone forever, and now, a few weeks later, we were leaving Fairholme too. Left in our wake was a community still reeling from its earlier loss. Like Ewald, we would no longer be a part of colony life, but unlike him, we would have to build a new life for ourselves elsewhere.

My parents went back to packing while their children wandered about the house in a daze. I went to look for Oma and found her in Mother's small kitchenette. Her face was buried in her apron, and she was weeping so hard her whole body shook. As I entered, I heard her crying to God under her breath, "*Du lieber Gott.* Oh, dear God."

I came undone. The sight of my cherished Oma in such a state was devastating. I threw my arms around her thick waist and started sobbing. She was my beloved grandmother who had taught me how to knit, fold clothes, and make tea. I was her favorite, and she mine. We ate and slept together on weekends and spent hours in her chamomile patch, picking the miniature, daisylike flowers that filled her house with fragrance as they dried. Every Saturday, when she could have chosen any one of the most capable colony girls to wash her floors, she chose me, patiently sitting in her rocking chair and pointing with her cane to the spots I'd missed. I couldn't bear the thought of life without her.

"Don't cry," she whispered, composing herself as she quickly wiped her tears with her apron and smoothed her hair away from her face. Choosing her words carefully, she took a deep breath before she spoke.

"Ann-Marie, you must listen to your father and mother. They will need your help now more than ever. You have to be strong and set a good example for the younger ones. Your father is doing a very courageous thing, but you are too young to understand that right now. Someday you will understand and be grateful."

I promised her I would do as I was told. I would have promised Oma anything.

When night fell, our house was nearly empty. The big truck was gone, and a sense of apprehension hung in the air. Little was said. Mother pointed my sister and me to a mattress on the living room floor, where we were to spend our last night as happy, carefree Hutterite girls.

I had worn my favorite dress that day. It was covered in small bursts of color and looked as if someone had taken a paintbrush and daubed red, yellow, and green blotches all over it. I loved the way it fit and wore it more than any other of my dresses. My fashionable mother had tried unsuccessfully to replace my well-worn, faded dress with new ones. That night, I couldn't bring myself to take it off, an unspoken good-bye to a good friend. I slipped under my feather comforter and lowered my head on the soft, feather pillow. It took a long time before all the unanswered questions tumbling around in my head were overtaken by fatigue, and I fell asleep beside my equally subdued sister.

The next morning I awoke to the sounds of sobbing. Sana Basel and Mother were holding each other, weeping as if their hearts would break. Sana Basel knew my parents' struggle intimately, but her arms did not want to let her sister, with whom she shared so much history, go.

Father had been up since 5:00 a.m. to milk the cows and do his chores for the final time. Then he went to see Jake Maendel. "Jake, I'm leaving the colony," Father informed his brother-in-law. "Here are the records for the cows. Everything is in order. You've got milk for a whole year and then some. There're a lot of little heifers coming in, and whoever takes over from me, the barn is ship shape. Now Jake," Father said, looking him straight in the eye, "you and I have been at odds since the beginning, but I think you would have to agree that I gave my best years to the colony. I have been a hard worker and have done a good job of everything I've been assigned to. I'm starting over with nothing.

Your sister and our seven children are relying on me. I am asking you to give me one milk cow for my family."

"Absolutely not!" came the swift reply.

It was the last time the two men would ever see each other.

I wanted to run over to Sandra's or Catherine's house and tell them it was all a big misunderstanding, that we weren't really leaving after all, and that this was just a bad dream, but I couldn't. It really was happening.

"I'm going to da kitchen," Sana Basel said, her voice cracking. "It's not right dat you're leaving empty-handed!"

We went next door to Oma's and had hot oatmeal with brown sugar and cream for breakfast. It had no taste. Father was eager to go. He went out to put the mattress on which we had slept into the camper on the back of the pickup. Edwin, Phillip, and a reluctant Alex climbed in while Rosie, Eugenie, Carl, and I followed our parents into the front, a band of Hutterites on a risky venture. Sana Basel returned and pressed a chicken and a bag of noodles into Mother's hand. It had started to rain.

No one said a word as we pulled away. I felt a lump in my throat, and tears well up in my eyes, but I didn't dare cry. I looked straight ahead and tried to remember Oma's words. "In God's name we go," Mother said softly.

The rain started coming down harder as we drove, and Mother and Dad sang a few German songs to lift their spirits and soothe their nagging fears about the future. Before long, Rosie started complaining of a stomachache and then began throwing up. In between spells of vomiting, she would curl up in a ball with her head on Mom's lap and cry. We turned onto a long lane, and I recognized the isolated farmhouse in the distance. The rain had turned the road to gumbo, and the truck created deep ruts in the mud.

By now, Rosie was doubled over, and my parents realized they would have to take her to the hospital. Leaving the rest of us behind and me in charge of the younger ones, they drove to the children's hospital in Winnipeg, thirty miles away. I stood outside and watched as Dad once again navigated the long lane. Mud flew up behind the wheels of the truck until he reached the adjoining road that led to the city.

Once inside, seeing our table, chairs, and beds around the house, I was left with the indelible impression that this was now home. My stomach started to hurt, but not in the same way as my sister's. It was with the kind of aching loneliness that would last for a long time.

My parents returned late that night without Rosie. She had been admitted and stayed in the hospital for a week, during which time she turned nine. One of the nurses surprised her with a cake. On the colony, birthdays were acknowledged but not celebrated, and none of us had ever had the pleasure of a birthday cake. Thrilled with her good fortune, Rosie decided to take the plate of cake around the hospital ward and in her best English offered it to delighted fellow patients. "Want some, take some," she would chirp. When I heard this, I wished with all my heart I could be hospitalized for my tenth birthday a few days later. In reality, the only thing I suffered from was homesickness. I wanted to go home, back to Fairholme Colony, where I belonged.

In our German family Bible, below the recorded births of all her children, Mother wrote in her plain hand, "Friday, July 16 we left the colony, 1969."

Christian Dornn had exchanged his freedom for security, and now his son was giving it all up for the chance to be free.

The Dornn children at Dahl's Farm. Back Row, L to R: Phillip, Edwin, Alex. Front Row, L to R: Carl, Ann-Marie, Rosie, Genie.

NINE

Our Year at Dahl's Farm

THE SUMMER OF 1969 was the loneliest summer of our lives. We lived in the middle of nowhere and knew no one. It rained all the time, and the flies and mosquitoes were intolerable. If we went outside to play, we were up to our elbows in muck. If we stayed in, with no television or toys to amuse us, the boys would wrestle or play tag, tearing the house apart. On the colony, we would have been to the *Essenschul* for breakfast, then off playing with our friends by 8:00 a.m., but the social and physical structure that had given order and purpose to our lives had been ripped out from under us.

In Fairholme, we had spent relatively little time with our siblings except for evening prayers and bedtime routines; our new circumstances brought us in much closer contact with each other, and that led to a lot of arguing as we worked to redefine our relationships. Mother found herself with a houseful of lively children who didn't know what to do with themselves.

The shift in family dynamics placed a greater sense of responsibility on my shoulders and Rosie's to help with the younger ones, do the dishes, and clean up after our brothers' muddy outdoor exploits, for it did not occur to our Hutterite-minded mother that boys could wash their own boots.

Every morning, seven forlorn sets of eyes followed Father as he twisted and zigzagged his way down our soggy lane to go to work. He had found employment through the Holdeman, a conservative faction of Mennonites who had sometimes come to Fairholme for an evening of gospel singing as part of their outreach program. One of the Holdemen had told my dad about Pete Siemens, a wealthy grain farmer who owned a feed mill and a substantial land base in the Domain area, a small village thirty kilometers west of Winnipeg. Mr. Siemens had employed Hutterites before and found them hardworking and reliable. He hired Father for $1.50 an hour to assemble and service his farm machinery and to seed, thresh, and combine large fields of oats, barley, and wheat. Mr. Siemens was exacting, and Father put in long days doing field work. He missed his cattle, but he put that out of his mind as he toiled in the hot sun.

Mother, too, struggled in the heat—of our kitchen. There was no more running to the community kitchen for fresh, home-cooked meals or buns, pies, and cakes just out of the oven. In Fairholme the bell would ring at fifteen minutes past seven and eleven in the mornings, and fifteen minutes past five in the afternoon for what was known as "first call." Those with very young children sped toward the kitchen, for it signaled that the meal was ready and they should come to fill their pails and dishes with a delicious variety of fresh food to take home. Older people had the option of having their food delivered to their homes instead of going to the *Essenstuben*. On the half hour, the bell would ring again and the rest of the community would stop what they were doing and head to the kitchen to eat.

Since the age of seventeen, Mother had followed the traditional pattern of work rotation on Hutterite colonies. That was the age when women stepped into their adult roles and were paired with other women between the ages of seventeen and forty-five to spend alternating weeks baking, washing dishes, or cooking. With up to one hundred community members to feed, good organization was important. The menu was set out in advance by the head cook, and the supplies were always on hand in the kitchen. If Mother had stayed at the colony, she would, at age forty-five, have been eased into retirement as the younger women took over, but now her retirement had been put off indefinitely.

She was an excellent cook and with the proper ingredients could replicate all the mouthwatering Hutterite meals our spoiled palates were used to, but we couldn't afford the ducks for Sunday dinner or the thick cream for *Schmond wacken* dipping or the fresh strawberries so readily available on the colony. All Father could manage on his salary was food at bargain prices. A sympathetic Jewish grocer in Winnipeg who ran a small corner store agreed to sell him produce that had outlived its shelf life. The Manitoba Hutterites did much of their business with Jewish wholesalers, and Father knew this gentleman from seeing him in Fairholme. The grocer had struggled to compete with the bigger outlets, so sometimes when he was overwhelmed with produce, he had loaded up his truck and come to Fairholme and sold the entire contents to the colony manager.

We called him the *frucht Jud*, "fruit Jew." Besides selling us outdated bread, meat, and vegetables, he sold us so many boxes of apples, oranges, bananas, and grapes in varying stages of decay that his image became synonymous with fruit. He was small and cheerful, with thick glasses that he didn't seem to need because he was always peering over them to look down an aisle, or resting them on his forehead to read a label. My parents were grateful to him for his help, for they simply could not afford groceries from a regular store.

While my siblings and I worked on getting along, our burdened parents pursued a path of forgiveness. The unresolved years of pain that had expelled them from Fairholme hung like weights around their necks. As difficult as it was, they knew that before they could forge ahead with their new lives, they needed to forgive Jake Maendel. They rose early one morning and wrote him a letter, saying that as followers of Christ, they were required by His admonition to love one another. Father acknowledged that his anger often got the better of him during their arguments and apologized. When the letter was mailed, they both felt a measure of spiritual and emotional relief.

As difficult as letting go of the past was, getting a handle on the present also created some challenges. Mother was excited at the prospect of having her very own telephone. She didn't have anyone to call, but that didn't dampen her enthusiasm. An employee from Manitoba Telephone System arrived to install her phone to the party line, after which he told her cheerfully, "Mrs. Dornn, your ring is two long."

"Too long?" Mother asked. "Please fix it!"

Mother couldn't grasp that two sustained rings would mean she should answer the telephone, and she saw her hopes of owning her own phone slipping away like flour dust between her fingers. She wasn't about to let him leave until the ring was the right length. The installer finally resorted to calling the operator and asked her to call us so Mother would understand what he meant. Even with the lesson, she sometimes confused our ring with the others on our party line, as we all did. Isolated and lonely, we were known to answer the phone before it stopped ringing, hoping it was for us. Sometimes we listened in on other people's conversations just to hear what English people talked about, but we soon learned that sort of thing was not appreciated.

We slowly transitioned to life outside the colony. Though we continued to wear our Hutterite clothing, Mother allowed Rosie and me to abandon our *Mützen*. Mother removed her own polka-dotted *Tiechel* and, as a small symbol of liberation, replaced it with a plain black one for church, special outings, and each morning and evening when she knelt beside her bed to pray.

Despite the adjustments we were making, we stuck out like sore thumbs, even among the Holdeman people, who were a strict religious sect like the Hutterites. They lived in nearby Rosenort, a Mennonite enclave, and their members were deeply traditional, which appealed to my parents. They didn't allow worldly intrusions such as televisions or radios in their homes, and they dressed in a very conservative manner. The men wore beards, but the women fashioned their kerchiefs into small black caps with an extravagant number of hairpins. For Mother, who was still learning to answer a telephone, learning to fasten the kerchief as they did was too complicated. She was not moved by convention and had not left the colony to learn a new way of tying her kerchief.

But I was, and this provoked the first of many of my attempts to conform to the standards of others as I embarked on a journey to reinvent myself. All the young Holdeman girls carried a carefully folded and beautifully embroidered handkerchief with them to church. I reasoned that if I could join the hankie crowd, then I would at least begin to fit in. Mother's handkerchiefs were all industrial-strength nose blowers, and not a single one of them could be mistaken for dainty, even from a reasonable distance.

One day, when Dad stopped to fill the gas tank at the Co-op, I spotted a paper napkin that someone had dropped on the floor by the cash register. It was white with large, yellow daisies. We hadn't used napkins on the colony, and I had never seen one like it, so when no one was looking, I grabbed it. Once home, I ironed the frayed edges on low, carefully folded it, and tucked it under my pillow. Sunday couldn't come quickly enough, and when it finally did, I was the first one ready. The Holdeman women flowed into church in their smart dresses sewn from yards of pastel blue, green, and yellow cotton. I envied the way their skirts flared at the knee and their belts cinched their impossibly small waists.

Our family took up one whole pew, and it felt odd to have my parents sitting together and to be seated next to them or to hear the sound of small children in church. When it was time to pray, I placed my napkin on my seat like the rest of the young girls and knelt, peering over the back of the bench in front of me at a neat row of expertly stitched hankies. I envisioned the girls behind me gasping with delight when they saw the daisy pattern on mine. Instead, I heard the unmistakable sound of snickering.

"It's a napkin," one of the girls whispered to muffled laughter. My neck and cheeks flushed with embarrassment, and I could feel their eyes boring a hole into the back of my head. As soon as the prayer ended, I wadded my hankie into a ball, and when church was over, threw my key to acceptance in the garbage.

After church, we were often invited to some brave family's home for the noon meal. Nine extra mouths to feed was no small undertaking, but the church people tried to make us welcome. Our family had never been to another household for dinner. When we visited another colony, the adults would often eat together in the host home, but we were sent to the *Essenschul* to eat with the children. Every grouping of four children received their own platter, so we never worried about taking too much or helping ourselves to another serving. If we ran out, we simply shouted for more, and the *Essenschul Ankela* would come running.

Here, in a Holdeman family's home, the food was served in breakable glass bowls and fine china, and the amounts were so small compared to the generous quantities we were used to on the colony. The roast beef was no bigger than my father's fist, and I wished Jesus could perform a miracle like he had with the five loaves and two fish in the Bible.

From across the table, one of my brothers grabbed a slice of meat with his hand instead of the serving fork, and another followed suit. I noticed the host family looking at them in a wide-eyed sort of way and remembered the story of an outsider who had come to the colony on business and was invited to eat with the men in the *Essenstuben*. Seated next to the Hutterite member he had been visiting, the businessman asked, "Please pass the buns." He was bluntly informed, "We don't pass around here. I'll lean back, and you take a long-distance reach." Our enthusiastic table manners and generous appetites, considered practical and healthy on the colony, were now a source of embarrassment.

Later, up in the girls' room, as my sister and I struggled to get in a flow in the conversation, I spotted a tiny pink container near my foot. I had seen one just like it for ten cents at Kresge's department store when I still lived on the colony, and I knew there was a plastic rain cap inside. Initially, I didn't mean to take it with me, but when the time came to go home, I found myself in the truck, clutching it in my hand as I watched the scenery go by.

Alone in my room, I opened it. Sure enough, it had a clear, plastic rain cap inside. Wearing it even in the pouring rain seemed unwise in light of the fact that my brothers and sisters would laugh their heads off at me. First, I thought to myself, I would try to get myself a hairdo that would require protection so I could wear it with purpose. I painstakingly refolded it and put it back in the container.

That night I was hit by a powerful sense of guilt and couldn't fall asleep. On the colony we were taught to abide by the Ten Commandments, and I knew perfectly well that stealing was a sin. Among baptized members it was even more serious. I remembered how Annie Stahl had to stand through the entire church service, her head bowed in humiliation, for stealing a bag of marshmallows from the Woolworth store.

I was beginning to understand how different our perspectives were from everyone else's. For example, if Mother received unexpected visitors for *Lunschen*, she would go next door and help herself to one of the neighbors' pies, but English people, we soon learned, considered our version of sharing, stealing. Annie had had a hankering for marshmallows and had taken a package with her to the back of the store to have with her coffee while she waited for her husband to unload some chickens in town. After paying for the coffee in the cafeteria, she spotted the chicken truck out front, with nowhere to park. She got caught when she made a dash for the door, not even attempting to hide the marshmallows.

I felt the flames of hell inching toward my bed, so I climbed out and went downstairs to my parents' bedroom. Waking Mother, I made my confession. She sent me back to bed, saying we would resolve it in the morning. Relieved, I returned to my room and fell fast asleep.

The next morning the verdict seemed unnecessarily harsh. My parents informed me that after church the following Sunday, they would take me back to the family's home, and I was to apologize and give back the rain cap. I was prepared to quietly give it back, as I would have in Fairholme. Instead, I was forced to apologize in front of the entire family, gathered around the dining room table. The embarrassment was too much, and I buried my face in my hands and cried. I missed everything about Fairholme. It seemed as if we had been gone forever.

My siblings and I finally persuaded Dad to take us for a visit one Sunday afternoon, and I felt the tension melt away from my body as we rounded the bend to the colony and pulled up to our old house. I ached to be inside and skate across the polished floors in my socks, to look through the glass of our windows, and to touch the cupboards and counters in our kitchen. I wanted to see my mother hunched over her sewing machine, buried in fabrics, and hear the sound of Father's voice as he sang with us at night.

Oma's face filled with joy when we unexpectedly walked through her front door. She fussed over us and began to prepare *Lunschen* just as Catherine appeared in the hallway, beckoning me to come with her. I jumped up and followed her next door to our old house, where her family now lived. We headed for her bedroom, which had so recently belonged to Rosie and me. Catherine slept with her sister, too, and occupied the same side of the bed as I had. It was covered in a thick feather comforter, just as mine had been, and I melted into her pillow. We had missed each other so much!

The table in our old kitchenette was cluttered with Fat Emma and coconut chocolate bars, and Paul Jr. gave me a big smile when I entered. "We knew the runaways would be back!" he said gleefully, rubbing his hands together. "How can you say something so foolish to an innocent child!" his wife, Katie, scolded. She was serving raspberry pie with homemade ice cream that she had just retrieved from the community kitchen, and it was disappearing as fast as she could dish it out. On the colony, *Lunschen* was a relaxed, lighthearted, and social time, and I preferred a good-natured ribbing to the awkward silences at mealtimes in

English homes. "We stole your house," Paul continued with a grin, "and we're not giving it back!"

"Dad, stop," Catherine jumped in, irritated.

A basket of fresh buns in the corner of the kitchenette made my mouth water, and I helped myself before being asked. Everything was at once so familiar, especially the teasing, and we sat and socialized just like we'd never been gone. After filling up, I ran over to Sandra's house. I let myself in and shouted, "Is Sandra home?"

"Oh, Lord," her sister Rita said wickedly. "It's Ann-Marie!" She came around the corner to look. "What on earth are you doing here? I thought you ran away!" She sighed, hands on her hips.

"I want Sandra." I squirmed.

"Come in. We want to look at you," her sister Dora interjected. "We want to know if you look English already or if you're still a beautiful Fairholmer."

Sandra took my arm and pushed me outside. "Let's go," she instructed. We led each other to our favorite sand hill and began carving out bedrooms in the warm sand for our imaginary families, represented by hairpins, toothpicks, and safety pins we had snatched from our mothers' glass containers long ago. The toothpicks were our fictional "children," which we broke into different sizes according to the child's age. The afternoon sun was suspended like a gleaming lantern above our heads as we played out scenes from our own lives, moving easily from one contrived family crisis to the next, until the supper bell rang and I went to eat at Oma's house, wistfully watching Sandra run to the *Essenschul* with the other children.

∷

We hardly ever saw Father anymore. He was gone most mornings before we awoke and arrived home late in the evenings after everyone was in bed. Mother craved adult companionship, and sometimes I would find her gazing longingly out our kitchen window, watching a single car drive past our lane until it was out of sight. What she would give to share a cup of coffee with Katie Hofer or to sit and fold clothes with Oma, who made every crease vanish and our underwear and towels look as if they had been ironed. A week earlier, Mother had learned of Jake's reaction to her and Father's letter. "I will never forgive them until they return to the colony," he had said.

Mother thought about the dream she'd had after the letter had been sent. In the dream, she was looking out of the kitchen window and watching her brother Jake drive up in a pickup truck, with their brother Hons sitting beside him. Jake stepped out of the vehicle, carrying a large sheaf of wheat to present to her. The grain looked plump and golden, but she could tell that it came from one of Pete Siemens's nearby fields, which had been ruined by an early frost. As tempting as the wheat looked, Mother knew the kernel was hollow.

I sensed her loneliness and started to wait up with her to keep her company. Every night, often until midnight, Mother stroked my hair and told me Bible stories of faith and perseverance while we sat by the picture window, looking out into the darkness. I could tell she was trying to shore up her own faith, and the stories were as much for her benefit as mine. On the colony, a family had no worries about food and shelter, paying the bills, or caring for children. In our new lives, far from the security of Fairholme, Mother had no idea how we would survive if something should happen to Father, or what we would do or where we would go. When we saw the headlights of our truck turning onto our deserted lane, we were both relieved, and I would rush upstairs to my bed before Dad was in the door.

Mother found an unlikely companion in an abandoned house

behind ours. During the course of an innocent exploration, she found a radio. It was a large antique, but she managed to drag it home. Our new church didn't permit radios any more than the old one, but she was quite sure God would forgive her if all she allowed herself were religious programs. The radio cut in and out until Alex, our eleven-year-old electrician, fixed the problem by placing a knife in a strategic spot in the back to stabilize the loose connection. The radio lifted Mother's spirits and became a source of inspiration for her, but she hated having to hide it under a blanket when church members stopped in for a visit.

The long, lonely summer drew to a close, and the school year was about to begin. Our cousin in Deerboine, Katrina, and Dafit Wurtz's daughter Katie, surprised us by mailing a package that contained two pairs of matching Fortrel dresses for Rosie and me. They covered our body from our necks to our ankles, but the few flourishes of lace and ribbon made us feel very English.

We had heard rumors that the teacher in Domain didn't want us in her school because she didn't think we would fit in, but the school board had advised her that she had no choice. Mr. Read, our nearest neighbor, who lived three miles away on impossible roads, turned out to be our "bus driver." He was hired by the school board to transport us in his own car. Mr. Read was old. Bell's palsy had left him with a lip that dangled loosely and that distorted his words when he spoke. On the colony, he would have had his meals brought to him three times a day, enjoyed long afternoon naps, and had his floors washed every Saturday. He certainly would not have been driving children to school on treacherous, muddy roads.

He met us at the end of our lane in a worn, four-door Pontiac Parisienne. We were the only ones on the "bus," and my three brothers piled in the backseat. My sister and I stood outside and argued over who would get the window seat in the front because no one wanted to sit beside Mr. Read. We didn't know what Bell's palsy was, but it frightened us. Mr. Read waited patiently for us to work out our little problem. I managed the window seat that day, but only after we agreed to take turns.

As soon as we entered the school yard, I knew I was wearing the wrong thing. I was shocked by the outfits running around outside. Hot pants and ringlets covered the playground. One girl was wearing a red, satin minidress with a slit that revealed matching red shorts, and I liked it so much I wished someone would hit me over the head and put me out of my misery. I knew it was a sin to like an outfit that insufficient, but with no Sana Basel to prod me, my fears about *Jüngste Tog* had started to fade, although my parents were doing a good job of not letting us forget about hell and the hereafter during our nightly devotions. All the girls were wearing something up-to-date and shiny, and their hair was abounce with perfect curls. On the colony we got new outfits for weddings and *Feiertog* (religious holidays), not for school. School was just like every day, where you dressed for comfort, not to show off.

"You're Hutterites!" said one of the hot pants, wrinkling her nose as if it offended her. She whispered something to two girls with ringlets standing behind her, and they all began to giggle. "Nice granny dress," she scoffed. Tanya Radner, I would soon learn, was the teacher's pet and top student in my grade. The school bell rang and off she dashed, arm and arm with the other girls.

Rosie was in grade four. My brother Alex and I were both in grade five because Alex had failed grade one on the colony. Actually, the colony teacher had failed everyone in first grade, and, typically, nobody thought to ask why. Edwin entered junior high that year, so he transferred onto a bus in Domain to go to Sanford. Five-year-old Eugenie and four-year-old Carl stayed home to keep Mother and her radio company.

Our fifth-grade teacher was Mrs. Erb. She wore nice clothes

and sensible shoes and wasn't as glamorous as Miss Pattimore, Phillip's grade-three teacher who taught the primary grades downstairs. She was young and kind with the most amazing dark hair. Sometimes she startled us by wearing a wig. It was a lighter color and a different style than her own hair, and it gave her a whole new look, which I found fascinating. But more than attractive, Miss Pattimore made a concerted effort to help us fit in and wouldn't tolerate other students sneering at us. Once a week, on Friday afternoons, she came upstairs and taught our grades French. It soon became my favorite subject. "I really like the Frenchman," I once overheard Father telling Mother over *Lunschen* in Fairholme. "I feel myself at home with them." I knew he was referring to the truck driver from Modern Dairies who came each week to collect the milk. He was so affable that the company had kept him on even after he lost his driver's license due to careless driving. They just had someone else drive him.

In school, we collided head-on with popular culture. I knew we were different, terribly different, and I half forgave the teacher for not wanting us in her school. We didn't know how to swim or skate or ride a bicycle. We had never tasted pizza, macaroni and cheese, or a banana split—rites of passage in mainstream society. Our knowledge of the English language was adequate, but we much preferred to speak our own language, which we called *Hutterisch* and which is spoken by all Hutterites in North America. It is a sweet, guttural language that can get to the point with a candor and precision not found in English. Unfortunately, though, our dialect does not require the "th" sound, and at recess, my call for a classmate to "trow da ball to turd base" during a baseball game was met with peals of laughter from the other children.

I also wasn't up to speed on the Department of Education's standards, or quite possibly I had been too busy taking note of Mrs. Phillipot's outfits to pay attention to the lesson, but when

Mrs. Erb asked me, "What country are you from?" I confidently told her "Fairholme Colony" in front of the whole class. Mrs. Erb cleared her throat and changed the subject. It was going to be a long school year.

The ringlets and hot pants wanted little or nothing to do with us. They enjoyed feeling superior, always glancing at us sideways or laughing at our ignorance. On the school grounds, my sister and I never had much trouble finding each other, with our long dresses billowing in the wind. Since none of the girls wanted to play with me at recess, I often headed for the swings. I would swing as high as possible, feeling the wind in my face and my long braids flapping against my back. It made me feel free. I envisioned myself back on the swings in Fairholme, with Catherine and Sandra by my side. During class time, I shadowed the "in crowd," all eyes as to what they wore and all ears as to what they talked about.

I felt hungry all the time. The longing to fit in translated into craving for food, but our school lunches became another lesson in humility. Mother had never made school lunches before. Now she had to make five of them every night while I tried to explain to her what the English kids were eating.

We were complete sandwich novices. On the colony we ate full-course meals daily, and only on special occasions, such as weddings or funerals, were ham sandwiches served as a night snack. Ham was now out of the question. The only luncheon meat we could afford was bologna that was weeks past its "best before" date and mottled with mold. Mother trimmed the green edges from the meat with a knife and tucked an uneven piece between two slices of stale white bread. She included a large carrot, peel still intact, with each sandwich. On the colony, eating a carrot straight from the ground without the benefit of a wash was considered healthy, but I washed them as a precaution. Mother sorted through the box of apples from the grocer and cut out the rotting pieces before adding them to our piles. When we protested, she told us that when children in Africa were starving, it was a sin to complain! Their parents, she noted, would just love the good half of our orange or apple to feed to their kids. Mother was so persuasive, we starting feeling lucky—until we got to school.

She packed our lunches in clear plastic bread bags she had saved over the summer. They had the predictable effect on our classmates, who carried crisp, brown bags filled with fresh food. Our classmates stared at us as though we were the eighth wonder of the world, but I swear I heard beautiful music when Russell Monroe opened his lunch box and pulled out a small thermos with steaming hot soup and cellophane-wrapped soda crackers. Next came a sandwich piled with pale, thin slices of meat topped by a sheet of lettuce. The sandwich was wrapped in wax paper and cut into four even triangles. He brought out carrots the size of french fries and matching celery sticks to dip into a white, creamy mixture. I was determined to dip my finger into it for a taste if ever he looked away, but he never did. Then, just when I thought a lunch couldn't get better, he produced a triangle-shaped Tupperware container with a piece of apple pie and whipped cream. The only thing missing were the servants. I couldn't take my eyes off him or his marvelous lunch.

I watched him take out a napkin and place it on his lap. Adjusting his glasses and running his fingers through his coarse, blond hair, he began to eat in a very civilized sort of way. Russell always drank his water at the end of his meal, not washing it back in between as we did. I was certain that with a lunch of this magnitude, I'd have good manners too. I wondered if his mother's entire day was taken up with the planning and preparation of his lunches, and I began to fantasize about being his sister.

When it came to technical presentation and artistic merit, Russell's food got my vote every time, but my other classmates pulled out delicious-looking assortments too. Their sandwiches were wrapped in some kind of magic plastic, and when I asked what it was, the whole class began to snicker. Tanya Radner's sandwiches oozed with a white substance that was even more curious. On the colony we never used mayonnaise or salad dressing. "What a dummy!" Tanya told everyone within earshot when I worked up the nerve to cautiously ask her what it was. I quickly informed Mother that we had to purchase Saran Wrap and mayonnaise immediately if we were to amount to anything, but when she started in on those African children again, I knew I would get nowhere with her.

Taking matters in my own hands, I discreetly started picking plastic wrap and paper bags out of the garbage can beside Mrs. Erb's desk. One day, when the rest of the class had gone out for recess, I spotted a large gob of excess mayonnaise on Tanya's Saran Wrap. Locking myself in a bathroom stall, I carefully opened the crumpled plastic and licked the creamy paste with my tongue. I expected it to taste like the wonderful *Schmond wacken* (thick dipping cream) often served on the colony, but the flavor was bitter and unpleasant. I was profoundly grateful that Mother hadn't gone out to buy a jar at my foolish insistence, and my heart went out to poor Tanya, whose sandwiches were smothered in mayonnaise every day.

It didn't take long for me to collect enough discarded Saran wrap and paper bags for all five of our lunches, and Mother and I both loved it. We wiped the durable plastic clean every night and used it over and over again. The paper bags gave some measure of privacy to our inferior lunches, and for me, at least, that was a great relief.

The ceaseless rain had now made it impossible for Mr. Read to get anywhere near our muddied lane. It was a quagmire. He resorted to taking us to school on a stoneboat, a wooden slab harnessed to a horse. We met our new "bus" at the lane entrance and climbed onto the open makeshift sleigh. Mud flew up from behind as the poor horse dragged us over miles of gumbo. By the time we reached the school yard, we had mud splats on our clothes, our faces, and in our hair.

Father battled the mud too. After work, he would park his truck three miles from home on an adjoining gravel road, then slog through the quagmire to our house. And every morning, he'd walk back again and drive to work. At night, Mom and I would wait for him by the window and rejoice when we saw his dark, solitary shape in the distance, struggling to lift his boots, heavy with muck. Mother hadn't waited for him like that since she was eighteen years old and still lived at Sana Basel's house. She remembered the drone of his tractor in the fields and how she had longed to be alone with him, to explain her feelings, and tell him that it was her brothers who wanted her to marry Elie. That was so long ago she caught her breath at the thought of it. Once home, Father sank into a chair, often too exhausted to eat the supper Mother had waiting for him. He just took off his boots and collapsed into bed.

Being mud-splattered from head to toe was one thing, but we found the English kids' aversion to dirt equally peculiar. The girls were obsessed with keeping their clothes clean during recess. They acted as if their mothers didn't know how to use a washing machine. Even some of the boys had this unnatural obsession with being tidy. I remember one muddy afternoon when Marty Wilkes came screaming down the far end of the playground, pointing to a large gob of mud on his light-brown corduroy pants. "My mother's gonna kill me! My mother's gonna kill me!" he wailed.

I had never in my life heard such a pronouncement, and I rushed toward him, completely forgetting my inferior status as I faced him friend to friend. I had to know what he had done that would condemn him to death at the hand of his own mother.

His mouthwatering lunches flashed before me as I recalled thick egg-salad sandwiches on soft, white bread and chocolate cake with at least an inch of icing. "What did you do?" I asked, my heart pounding.

"She's gonna kill me because I got my good pants dirty!" he howled, tears streaming down his face.

Mouth agape, I looked down at his soiled pants and back up at him. By now Mrs. Erb had arrived, but I stood there as if I were nailed to the ground. I had no words for a young boy about to be killed by his own mother. How on earth could a mother who packed those wonderful lunches kill him just for that? I asked myself. Quite unexpectedly I felt grateful for my own parents. All our difficulties combined were still better than death over a blotch of mud. Mrs. Erb helped Marty clean some of the dirt off his pants and calmed him down. By the time she finished with him, I thought he was taking his impending death rather well.

I rushed my mud-splattered self into the house after school. Kicking off my boots, I found Mother in the basement, getting ready for her nightly round of laundry. On the colony, when we were young children running around barefoot and playing outdoors, she sometimes would put clean clothes on us up to four times a day, and it was still a point of pride with her that she send us out of the house with clean clothes and boots. I poured Marty's anguished story on her in great detail. She was pretty sure that the worst that would happen to him was a good spanking, but I wasn't swayed. I knew Mother didn't have a clue how those English people carried on. I thought that they probably would rather kill their children than be caught spanking them. I feared for his life, and I knew only God could save him now. All those old Bible stories came back to me, especially the one about Abraham going off to kill his son Isaac. I got on my knees at bedtime and prayed that God would spare Marty's life too.

My eyes searched the room for Marty as I entered the class the next morning. There he was, clean pants and all, chattering away as if nothing ever happened. He didn't look at all relieved to be alive, nor the least bit grateful that I had personally intervened on his behalf before God to spare his life. *Well,* I thought to myself as he cast me a condescending "What are you looking at me for?" glance, *I will never bail you out again!* In light of his obvious ingratitude, I felt sorry that God hadn't allowed him at least a bit of damage.

::

Winter and its predictable cold descended early, and plans for the annual Christmas concert got under way in earnest. I brought home the wonderful news that I would be participating in something called a square dance. It was greeted with a moment of silence from both of my parents. "We did not leave the colony to go dancing," Dad announced as he left the room. Poor Dad. He had been warned before leaving the colony that his children would run wild and go dancing when they grew up. The devil with the dancing shoes had arrived much sooner than expected, and he felt his worst nightmare was coming true. I was devastated. At school we had already spent the previous afternoon practicing in the gym downstairs, and I was completely dazzled. Entirely uncoordinated, I worked double-hard with my two left feet, lest I be expelled from this fantastic opportunity to advance socially. The other girls handled themselves with incredible ease, but I didn't let their giggles interfere with my concentration. Not now; this was too important.

I couldn't believe my parents were out to ruin my chance to fit in with the others. I begged and pleaded to no avail. The next morning, heartsick, I headed for Mrs. Erb's office at the back of the school and announced an end to my dancing career. She pursed her lips and, without commenting, sent me back to the classroom. In the afternoon, Mrs. Erb insisted I join the dance rehearsal. I was so grateful, I forgave her for the cool reception she had given us at the beginning of the school year. I had noticed a shift in her attitude ever since she had assigned our grade an essay about our biggest surprise. While the rest of the class wrote about waking up on Christmas morning to a new toy or bike or puppy, my story recounted the shock of finding out we were leaving the colony. Later that week, when the rest of the class was skating at the nearby community rink, I stood behind the boards, watching, because I didn't have any skates. Mrs. Erb came up and asked me about the essay and what I missed about living on the colony. Our exchange made me feel good as details tumbled out about running to the *Essenschul* for a hot meal every day at noon, living within shouting distance of my best friends, and the sound of Sana Basel's voice when she told us a story. Her face softened, and there was a tenderness in her voice that I had not heard before.

Mrs. Erb decided to take on Father. It wasn't a dance, she told him. It was a drill. Only the girls were participating, and for a dance to really be a dance, boys must be involved. She stressed that it was a vital part of school curriculum. "All the children," she said, "must participate in the Christmas concert." Father scratched his head in bewilderment. Wouldn't he be proud, she added, seeing his daughter on stage, not really dancing?

My outfit was the next challenge. Mother and I worked on it together. We were sent home with instructions to wear white blouses and red square-dancing skirts to the concert. I didn't dare mention the square-dancing part of the skirt to Mother, lest the *dance* word set off more alarm bells. I simply told her I needed a red skirt and a white blouse. Somewhere in her closet, she found a white, frilly blouse, which fit fairly well, but we had to resort to the secondhand store to find the skirt. The store racks bulged with miniskirts of every conceivable size and color, but to Mother, proper length was far more important than style and color. After an extended search, we happened upon a below-the-knee, rusty-red skirt that she bought for seventy-five cents.

The night of the Christmas concert, we rushed through supper, and Mother, Rosie, and I hurried to get the dishes done. Our whole family was going, and the excitement was palpable. It was too cold for anyone to sit in the camper, so all nine of us piled into the cab of the pickup. Six-year-old Phillip sat on the left of Dad, the driver. On Dad's right, Alex occupied Edwin's lap, Eugenie sat on mine, and Rosie sat on Mother's. Carl, the baby, held on to the dashboard and leaned back on the rest of us. It was a tight squeeze, and an elbow scuffle ensued as we all tried to get comfortable.

I rushed into the community hall in Domain as soon as I could propel myself from the pickup. Fighting my way through the frills on Mother's blouse, I arrived at the back of the stage to find myself surrounded by short, red, flared skirts and crisp, white shirts with little red bows at the collar. What had been apparent to the other girls all along suddenly became apparent to me. A square-dancing skirt was no ordinary skirt. I turned crimson with embarrassment. "See," said Father, following my red-faced performance, "dancing is a sin!" Fortunately, one of the mothers took pity on me and created a longer, less-flamboyant version for me to wear in future performances. I still didn't look nearly as cute as the other girls, but if dancing was a sin, it was a risk I was ready to take.

The next day, school let out for the Christmas holidays. We were playing on the high banks of snow in front of the school, waiting for Mr. Read, when Bernie Legit stopped by. He lived in town and walked home like other students, but today he didn't seem to be in much of a hurry. "Hey girls," he announced, "I'd like to sing a song for you." On the colony, singing a song for someone is a way to honor them, and we were all ears as to the nature of this tribute. "Okay," Rosie and I said in unison as we stopped playing and stood at attention in front of him. He opened his mouth and began. "I wish you a merry Christmas, I wish you a merry Christmas, I wish you a merry Christmas, and an awful New Year." Before he could enjoy his own cleverness, Rosie, with a fist to his stomach, had knocked the wind out of him and landed him in a snowbank. As he gasped for air, she pinned his arms behind him and demanded an apology. "Little, but Oh My," is how Father referred to Rosie. Her small stature belied her natural athletic abilities. Even though Bernie was twice her size, I could have told him to not take her on, but, God forgive me, the scene with him begging for forgiveness was altogether enjoyable.

Our Christmas present was another trip back to Fairholme. Catherine loved the Fortrel dress with the lace that Katie Wurtz had made for me and was full of questions about my new "English life." I told her all about the hot pants and the smarty-pants at school. Admittedly, I was economical with the truth when describing the wonderful school lunches Mother made, smartening mine up by including a few of Russell's hot items. Catherine's mouth just watered.

When we made our way over to Suzanna Basel's house, her son Hardi spied us from the back window and quickly pried it open. "Go home. We don't want you!" he yelled mischievously. "Ann-Marie, how come you're so fat?" his brother Ernie bellowed, his dark hair falling in his face as he bent toward the opening to be heard. At school, Mrs. Erb had weighed us with her black bathroom scale, and I came in at 112 pounds. I was eleven years old, and heavier than the boys in class! I could forgive myself for gaining weight on Hutterite food, but to do so on past-due edibles was very discouraging.

"Be quiet, you dumb dogs," my Suzanna Basel shouted to her unruly sons. The table was sagging with cakes and pies and chocolates and nuts from the colony's *Weihnachtsgeschenken*, "Christmas goods." Suzanna Basel pinched my cheeks and dusted the peanut shells off the chairs for Catherine and me to sit down. "Gold remains gold." She smiled as she pressed her cheek against mine. Suzanna Basel asked her daughter Hilda to find the McIntosh toffee bar she had saved for me and hidden in her underwear drawer. It was my favorite treat, and my aunt had not forgotten. Fritz Vetter tumbled in the door from the turkey barn and marched straight to the sink to wash. "Ann-Marie, what are you doing here again?" he teased, splashing his face with soapy water.

"*Ach Stilla Voter*," his wife scolded. "Oh, Father, be quiet."

"Can you dance yet?" he asked cunningly as he reached for the nutcracker and settled into a chair.

"Yes," I countered, knowing he wouldn't believe me.

"You're going to go to hell!" Fritz Vetter teased, and Suzanna Basel bopped him on the head with a flyswatter.

"That's enough, now," she said.

After *Lunschen*, Hilda, Catherine, and I went to the living room to sing. As our voices blended together, I was enveloped by a warmth I could not describe. I wanted to put that moment in a box and take it home with me so that when I was lonely, I could unwrap it and it would comfort me.

Darkness descended before my sister Rosie came to collect me for the trip home. She had spent the afternoon playing with her best friend, Janice, Catherine's sister. Hilda sent us out the door with a generous bag of treats. Catherine's mom and my Oma packed all the leftovers from *Lunschen* and supper in a box and followed us to the pickup where Dad was waiting with Mother and the others. Sana Basel was there, too, with a box of goodies and a round of hugs. Our school lunches cheered for days.

∷

Winter storms that year made it difficult for Mr. Read to get back to school to take us home. The five of us would have to sit and wait for him, sometimes up to an hour and a half, because of unpredictably bad weather. We were hungry and restless, so Mrs. Erb decided to let us watch cartoons on a small, black-and-white television in the library. This was our first foray into the land of TV, and we were captivated by the images on the screen, especially with Mighty Mouse.

The kids in school often discussed what they watched at home. We soon learned that their favorite program was Walt Disney. It aired on Sunday night, and on Monday during lunch hour, that's all they talked about. We couldn't figure out who Walt Disney was, and Alex and I got into a big argument about whether he was a horse, a person, or a dog. Every week the show seemed to change, and it was so frustrating to try and follow the plot. I loved Mighty Mouse for being so clear about himself. He was a mouse and he stayed a mouse.

In the beginning of January, I got whooping cough and had to miss over a month of school. Mrs. Erb sent my schoolwork home with Alex, but I just coughed all over it and didn't get very much done. Every morning, Mother prayed over me before tackling piles of laundry, dirty floors, and a kitchen strewn with boiling pots and dirty dishes. She had taken to praying over everything, including her secondhand appliances, and God mercifully extended the life of her washing machine and stove a number of times.

By Valentine's Day, the cough had begun to subside, and I finally started to feel better, but Mother kept me home a few more days as a precaution. Mrs. Erb gave Alex a box of valentines for me from the class. Up in my room, I sat on the edge of the bed and opened the lid, covered in red tissue and decorated with silver cardboard hearts and pink flowers. I was delighted to find that nearly everyone in my grade had sent me a valentine. I read the sweet little rhymes and greetings on the cards and they almost restored my faith in returning to school. "Be a Cool Cat." "Have a GREAT Valentine's Day." "Smile, You're Fascinating!" read some of the cards. Diane, with the luscious blonde curls, had decorated and sent a heart-shaped gingerbread cookie. Even Russell had thought to send me a card. "You're swell, Valentine," it read. *So are your lunches!* I thought to myself.

I reached for the last card on the bottom of the box, recognizing Tanya Radner's handwriting on the front of the envelope. My heart skipped a beat as I pulled out the card shaped like a duck with a hat pulled over its eyes. Her valentine message was scrawled across the front. "I hope I never see you again—Tanya." I could feel what little bit of confidence I'd gained begin to wash away, despite the talk I'd had with Mrs. Erb about my essay. I was suddenly ashamed of our poor clothes and rotting food and Hutterite accent. I was ashamed that, in spite of my daisy hankie and square-dance skirt and saved Saran Wrap, I was a failure at being English. I ripped up her valentine and threw it under my bed.

Not long after that, Mother called us into the living room when we came home from school. Pale and shaken, she told us Dad had had an accident and was in the hospital. Our eyes grew large as she explained that the two middle fingers on his right hand got caught beneath a truck scale in a freak accident at work and were crushed. The doctors were talking about amputating. Mother asked us to all kneel down and pray for his fingers to be spared. Alone in his hospital bed, Dad was more worried about being out of a job than he was about losing his fingers.

The doctors decided to give him time before resorting to surgery, and they released him later in the week. His hand was tightly wrapped in thick, white bandages and he grimaced and winced when Mother changed them. It was a gruesome sight to see his fingers flapping from his blackened hand, but Mother prayed diligently for their recovery.

My father's primary concern now was his family's survival. As he endured the agonizing wait for his hand to heal, salvation came in the form of adult education. He discovered he could be paid to go to school in Winnipeg, and the prospect excited him. He had only completed grade eight on the colony, but given the opportunity, he would have favored a full and broad education.

Father excelled in school and received top marks. He loved it, but by the end of June, the program ran out of money and the school closed. We were glad to have him back home. During the week he had boarded at Dippety Doo Pete's in Winnipeg and only came home on weekends. Mother had found this especially difficult. Miraculously, though, his fingers were coming back to life. The doctors couldn't believe it, but Mother said she knew all along that they would. On the heels of such good news, Father announced we'd soon be moving. But not before the last day of school.

Everyone referred to field day with some kind of reverence. We didn't know what to expect, but it sounded exciting, and we were hoping it was something like picnic day, the last day of school on the colony. Picnic day always included a rousing game of baseball. Fairholmers took their ball games very seriously, and poor players had to give it their all or risk the disapproval of the senior boys. If the boys were too harsh, saying "*Du bist Zunichts!* You're not worth nothing!" to someone who struck out, the older girls ran interference. With the skill of a sharpshooter, they put the boys in their place, saying, "And you still wet your bed!"

When everyone was dusty and winded from stealing bases and diving for catches, often with bare hands, we all ran to a little valley shaped like a bowl for the bubblegum throw. Peter Vetter stood on one end of the field surrounded by white boxes of *tsutzel* candy ("sucking" candy) and gum. The boys readied their pants pockets, and the girls folded up their aprons to create a pouch as we waited in a long line. "Ready, set, go!" cried Peter Vetter, throwing the treats in the air. For the next ten minutes, it rained candy and gum until our pockets and aprons overflowed.

All the girls at the school in Domain appeared to be wearing new hot pants on field day morning. I envied their outfits, though it hadn't occurred to me that the last day of school would be the sort of day that required new clothing. Mrs. Erb and Miss Pattimore came out of the school wearing sun hats and carrying clipboards. They were both wearing white slacks, and it was the first time I had seen either of them in pants. My sisters and I were the only skirts in the school yard.

The yard was filled with all kinds of athletic challenges that, seemingly, had appeared overnight, and some of the students were practicing their skills in the high jump, the ball throw, and the triple jump pit. Their parents were stationed at various events as volunteer referees. Many of them were so openly affectionate to their children, I just stared at them. Very young children were unabashedly kissed and hugged and squeezed on the colony, but after a child turns six, affection is verbalized rather than demonstrated. Endearments such as "*Du lieba, du bist fein* (My sweet one, you are wonderful)" were spoken by mothers with love in their eyes, but physical affection was more restrained.

We were segregated according to age and gender and given instructions on when and where we would be competing. I followed my group to our first event, which was the hundred-yard dash. I ran as if I were being chased by a herd of wild elephants, my skirt trailing behind me, and caught everyone by surprise, including myself, when I came in third. At the high jump, I hurled myself over the bar for another third-place finish. I lost out on the three-hundred-yard dash but came second in the ball throw. The last event was the triple jump, where I had to hop, step, and jump to the finish. I heaved myself across the sandpit but caught my skirt in my shoe and landed with a thump. It was still enough for third place.

A strong breeze that smelled of dust and hot dogs blew past us. I was hungry. I headed straight for the hot dog stand, pleased with the way my blue and white ribbons fluttered against my face when I walked. The hot dogs were free of charge, so I ordered two and spread them with relish. In the distance, I could see Rosie and Alex covered in red ribbons. They had placed first in all of their events, and Phillip had only to win the triple jump to do the same.

All the parents had been invited to school that day, and as I made my way to the sandpit, I saw my own parents arrive, a moment I had been dreading. Mother's dark-purple, Fortrel English dress was long and shapeless, and she looked so out of place in her black kerchief next to the other mothers in their light-colored shorts and sleeveless blouses. Dad still wore a beard and was hard to miss in the land of the clean shaven. Despite my embarrassment, I ran over and urged them to come quickly and watch Phillip in his last event.

A large group of spectators gathered at the sandpit, and you could feel the tension in the air. Too many red ribbons had gone to our family, and some of the parents whose children had placed first in previous years looked irritated. Phillip's main rival was an athletic boy in his class named Gary. The crowd cheered wildly when Gary's turn came up, and he satisfied them with an excellent jump. Phillip's turn was met with contrasting silence. We kept quiet too—afraid to show any emotion—but the anticipation in our eyes betrayed our lack of composure. My parents stood in the back of the crowd, and Mother's head was slightly bowed. Phillip had grown three inches since the spring, and as he stared straight ahead, practicing the motions mentally before taking the leap, I noticed his pants were too short.

We held our breath as he landed. The referee shook his head and announced it was too close to call. They would have to try again. Gary's turn came up again, and so did the cheers as he landed another crowd-pleasing jump. Phillip took his place once more on the starting line and, with a fiercely determined look on his face, darted straight ahead, hop, step, and jumping his way to a clear victory. The crowd applauded politely, scarcely concealing their disappointment as Phillip was presented with the final red ribbon. We were ecstatic but kept our jubilation to ourselves, to avoid offending anyone.

At the end of it all, we piled into Dad's old pickup. It had been an unexpectedly good day for this band of misfits, and God knows, we needed one. As we drove off, we started cheering and congratulating Phillip and each other for a job well done. Our long and difficult first year had ended on a high note, and we felt a small measure of vindication.

> "Without warning, Sana Basel
> showed up on our doorstep."

Sana Basel,
an extraordinary woman.

TEN

Rogers' Farm

WE MOVED TO Rogers' Farm over the course of our second
summer away from Fairholme Colony. It was three miles from
Dahl's Farm, partway in every direction, and equally isolated. At
the end of a bumpy ride down a series of back roads, the forest
gave way to an enormous house guarding a neglected farmyard.
The home had clearly once belonged to someone of means, but
its deteriorating exterior was marred by gashes of peeling paint
and corroding brickwork. The lawn and flower beds were buried
under tall grass and weeds. Inside, the sheen had long gone from
the hardwood floors, and the air was thick with dust.

We had never seen a house with such big rooms before. The living room and adjacent parlor on the main floor were the size of a small hockey rink—a consideration not lost on my brothers, who would use it to play floor hockey when the weather outside was too wet or too cold. An arched doorway led from the parlor to the kitchen and dining room. Above the kitchen sink, a dirty window filtered a stream of sunlight that fell on withered, green vinyl counters running the length of each wall. The north wall of the dining room had begun to buckle and would have come crashing down were it not for a pigheaded desire to cling to past glories. Father warned us to steer clear of the area.

The basement was a fright. Unlike Fairholme's basement, lined with jars of burgundy beets, red-cheeked apples swimming in syrupy preserve, and the comforting smells of fresh laundry and new potatoes, this room gave us the urge to dash back upstairs. It was dim and musty, with low ceilings and deep cracks in the stone foundation, home to a growing family of mice who thrived in the eerie atmosphere.

At the front entrance, an imposing oak staircase wound its way to spacious bedrooms on the second floor. On the colony, sharing was a way of life, with one bedroom often serving all the male or female children in families until they left home. My two sisters and I claimed a room to the right of the stairs near a long, rectangular bathroom, and my four brothers decided on one on the left. A third bedroom remained empty. Heavy wooden doors off the kitchen opened to the master suite, which my parents chose as their own. Since Mother spent most of her time cooking, she could now all but wake up next to the stove.

Father's employer, Pete Siemens, owned the estate and had offered Dad rent-free accommodations in exchange for repairing the property. The excess rain had ruined Mr. Siemens's crops, so he had invested in cattle. They were housed outside in a lonely feed lot next to a fading red barn that loomed as large as the house, and Mr. Siemens hired my dad to manage them. When not working, Father purchased some used wood at a lumber mart in Winnipeg and began the sober task of making a crumbling mansion inhabitable for his family. Mother scrubbed every inch of the new house and was exhausted before we even began to pack the old one.

After our departure from Dahl's Farm, Dad's brother Christopher; his wife, Susie; and their six children took refuge in it. Dissatisfied with community life and encouraged by my father's bold move to live in the outside world, Uncle Chris had packed up his family and left the colony only a year after his brother. Mother was finally able to enjoy some quality time on her new telephone by talking with Aunt Susie, which helped stave off their loneliness and isolation. Women were not taught to drive on the colony, so personal visits were not an option. But a cup of hot coffee in one hand and the telephone in the other made life bearable for them both.

I felt a constant tug to return to Fairholme. In early July, Mother received word that the colony's strawberry crop had exceeded all expectations and Fairholme was badly in need of help. Calls to other colonies, like James Valley and New Rosedale, were pointless because the women there had their own large gardens to harvest. I begged Mother to let me go help. I behaved like an angel, and the following Sunday, when we went to Fairholme for a visit, my parents left me behind in Oma's care. I slept in her bed and ate all my meals with her, and we resumed our former roles as if we'd never been apart. I was the happy Hutterite girl, free from the dress codes and protocol of the English world, and she was my doting grandmother who loved me unconditionally, braiding my hair or tying bows in the back of my Hutterite dresses with her worn and arthritic hands.

Oma was the only one on the colony allowed to wear a ring. It was made of copper, and she wore it on her right ring finger. The doctor said the metal had a therapeutic effect on the pain and stiffness, and Jake Vetter made an allowance for that. Oltvetter Dornn tried to convince her to use his remedy and go up to the bee house every morning and let twenty bees sting her bare arm, but she would have none of it. I secretly thought she liked the way the ring looked on her hand.

On the first night, when we were lying in bed together, she had me look very closely at her earlobes. They both had pin-sized holes, and she told me that when she was a teenager in Russia, she had pierced ears and real gold earrings. As I lay there in the dark, I thought of her as a young girl before heartache and loss would taint her life with sadness. I tried to imagine her running through a field, being chased by her sisters, her earrings gleaming in the sun. It dawned on me that Oma had been English once, and that maybe one day I would find the joy in being English too. I nestled closer to her and placed my leg against hers, but I knew it could never be. I would never be English enough for earrings.

Catherine was responsible for bringing Oma her food from the community kitchen, and she heaped the already ample servings even higher on my account. Fresh bread was served with most of the meals, and after my daily banquets, I practiced making sandwiches with the leftovers while Oma did the dishes in her little sink. "What are you making?" Oma asked, as I added some jam to a piece of bread that I had spread with cottage cheese. I explained to her that sandwiches were almost all that English people ate and that I needed to experiment with fillings because Mother was always running out of ideas.

I spent most of that week in the strawberry patch with Sandra. The sun had painted her hands and face the color of maple sugar, and her smile warmed me from the inside out. Three times a day, the bell beckoned us to the strawberry patch, and Sandra's dad, my Peter Vetter, promised us a quarter for every turn. I earned seventy-five cents a day, which I rushed straight to Oma, who put the quarters in a canning jar in her dish cupboard so I wouldn't lose them or be tempted to run down to Bambi Gardens and spend them on candy. The weather was hot and the work backbreaking, but Sandra and I were lost in the joy of each other's company. While we picked, I regaled her with stories of the English kids at school, dramatizing Marty Wilkes's theatrical cries for help after he muddied his pants, and demonstrating the length of hot pants by pulling up my skirt as high above my knees as I dared. When I stood up to stretch my back, I saw Peter Vetter hauling irrigation pipes to the tomato fields an acre away. It had been a dry spring, but thanks to his efforts, the garden was as lush as Eden.

I missed seeing my mother working with the other women, hearing her laugh and swap stories with her gardening partner, who was Catherine's mother, Katie Hofer. During our daily ice cream break, the older women patted my head sympathetically and proclaimed me *unshuldig*, "innocent." I knew that they blamed my parents for what had happened, but I was still too attached to let go, not ready to give up the silky sand beneath my feet, the dusty, winding paths, and the sound of the kitchen bell. I ached for the structure of the days, the familiar, lined faces of the women in the kitchen, the smell of the baking buns, and the guttural sound of our language. My heart was not ready to accept that this was no longer home.

We ate strawberries while we worked, plopping juicy red berries into our mouths at will. At *Lunschen*, we savored them in pies and cakes. Whenever the colony had surplus from the garden, it was sold to the public. From early morning until late afternoon, English people came and went, buying the luscious fruit almost as fast as we could pick it.

Galvanized by our family's money troubles, I began offering customers a tour of Fairholme for a quarter. Our first stop was the pig barn, because we knew we could count on Catherine's dad, Paul Jr., the pig man, to provide some humor and entertainment. He was gregarious and didn't let us down. "Come in, come in, and see my beautiful pigs!" he shouted, trying to be heard above the drone of the ventilation fans. Tucking a piglet under his left arm, Paul gave them an animated tour, making no apologies for the pervasive stench. Afterward, we headed for the hatchery to find Michel. He enjoyed strangers and peppered them with questions. By the time they had escaped his interrogations, Michel knew how old they were, when they had started going bald, if they smoked or drank, or if any of their children were in trouble with the law and why. Our tour ended in the main kitchen, where the colony women were transforming crates full of strawberries into a year's supply of freezer jam. Sana Basel and Ankela were sitting on a bench, cutting the stems from a big bowl of berries on their laps, their fingers and corners of their mouths stained red. "What's your name, and what church do you go to?" Sana Basel asked the visitors sweetly. The first thing she wanted to know about anyone was whether they were *geistlich* (spiritual).

I wasn't shy about collecting a wage and requested a quarter for both Sandra and me when we escorted them back to the car. When my parents returned at the end of the week, I had a grand total of nine dollars to my name. On the drive home, the quarters rattled in the jar clutched in my sunburned hands. I had hoped to spend my new wealth on a pair of skates, but when Father told me that skates cost more than nine dollars, my hopes were dashed. I knew that if he helped me buy skates, there would be six other eager siblings in line for a pair, and our financial reality made such an indulgence entirely unaffordable.

I hid my jar of quarters in the drawer beneath my underwear

when we arrived home late that evening. As I climbed into bed, I remembered Mother and Father's late-night whispers about our finances and Oma's fretting that Father needed money to survive now that he was on his own. He was fixing one of the windows in the parlor when I approached him with my treasure. "Dad," I said earnestly, "I think I have more money than you do. You are working so hard, and I feel you should have this money so we don't go broke." Dad studied my young face, tilted his head back, and laughed. Mother stood in the doorway to the kitchen, her hand covering her mouth to keep from laughing too.

"Well," said Father, trying to keep a straight face, "I think you do have more money than I do, and I could sure use an extra nine dollars."

I knew I was doing the right thing, just as I knew that wishing I was back in Fairholme was selfish. Father took the jar from my outstretched hand while Mother watched, shaking her head.

Over the summer holidays, Father would sometimes take all of us along when he went to Winnipeg to buy tractor parts, bags of feed, or medical supplies for the cattle. Other than the occasional visit to Fairholme and going to church on Sunday, these were the only outings we had. We loved every chance to get away, and so did our mother. In the warmer months, my brothers traveled in the camper while the rest of us sat in the cab with our parents. Most of our time was spent in the industrial part of the city, waiting for Dad to finish his business rounds. By late afternoon, we were usually famished. Dad couldn't possibly afford to take us to a restaurant, so he headed straight to his friend, the Jewish grocer.

"Do you have anything for me today, sir?" Dad called out as he entered the small corner store. The fluorescent lights in the high ceilings were bright, and the store smelled of cardboard boxes. "Sure do, Ron, sure do. I've been expecting you." The grocer took

Dad through a door in the back with a sign on it that read No Admittance.

Mother and I wandered around the store, listening to the country music playing on the radio, and gawking at the wonderful things stacked on the shelves. I was keen on anything exciting that could go between two slices of bread, and spotting a plastic container of caramel spread next to a jar of peanut butter, I opened the corner of the lid and dipped my finger into it. It looked and tasted like melted toffee. I quickly closed the lid and went looking for my mother, who was in the next aisle, dangling a bag of buns from each hand. My enthusiasm boiled over as I explained the merits of having caramel spread in our school sandwiches. "No," said Mother firmly. "It probably tastes like honey, and we still have lots left in the jar that Oma gave us." I couldn't very well tell her how much better than honey it tasted without incrimination, but her unwillingness to even consider my request upset me terribly.

Dad and the grocer burst out of the No Admittance door, each carrying two boxes piled one atop the other. They headed outside to the truck, and Dad lifted the camper door and slid them in.

"Is there anything else I can get for you, Ron?" asked the grocer as they came back into the store together. Mother and I were standing at the checkout with two dozen buns and no caramel spread. "Yes, just a minute," said Father, hurrying over to the cooler. He picked up a huge coil of garlic sausage and with his pocketknife cut off about three feet and brought it to the counter. "That's good sausage you have there, Ron. It should last you a while," said the grocer.

"Well, sir, about fifteen minutes!" replied Dad, and they both started to laugh. Father paid his bill and thanked his friend.

Still nursing my grudge, I hopped into the back of the camper with my brothers while my younger siblings climbed into the cab.

Dad cut generous pieces of the garlic sausage for each of us, and Mother passed us a dozen buns while Father opened two of the boxes he bought from the grocer. One contained bananas and the other green grapes, both well past their prime. "Let's pray," Father said as he held the camper door open. No matter where we were or how inconvenient it was, our parents held fast to the Hutterite tradition of praying before we ate, replacing the memorized German prayers we used to say in unison with prayers from the heart. "Thank you for your faithfulness and for your many blessings, O God. Bless these gifts that you have given to us. Amen." He let the camper door down and climbed into the cab to eat with Mother and the younger children.

The sausage was rich and flavorful, and after devouring every morsel, we helped ourselves to salvageable parts of the grapes and bananas. As we were enjoying our feast, the camper door flew open, and a wild-eyed man with torn clothes and long, unkempt hair was glaring at us. My brothers and I froze. "Got something for a starving man?" he asked. His strong body odor mixed with the aromatic haze of garlic sausage and rotting bananas inside the camper. I slowly reached into the box of grapes and tentatively held out a stem. He eyed the shriveled, brown fruit and spewed out a stream of vulgarities, slamming the camper door and storming off in a cloud of profanity. We held our breath before bursting into nervous laughter.

"The kids in Africa would love this stuff!" said Alex, echoing the line Mother frequently used on us. I quickly recovered from my caramel-spread disappointment, and in that moment I was enormously glad to be Ann-Marie Dornn, glad that my Mother prayed to Jesus daily, and despite my standing as a displaced Hutterite, glad to be on my way home to the security of Rogers' Farm.

My eleventh birthday came and went at the end of that July with the same amount of fanfare as any other day: no cake, no card, no presents. On the colony, our parents usually acknowledged our birthdays by reminiscing about the day we were born. Most of us didn't have baby pictures, and we loved hearing those stories. Mother always told me about my delicate features and dainty hands, and that my eyes were like large, shiny marbles when I looked up at her. It made me feel special. But I wished I could have a fabulous party like the girls at school.

I had never actually been to a birthday party, and they sounded like elaborate events. I would listen to the girls in my grade gush about their birthday cakes and new birthday dresses and gifts of Barbie dolls and tea sets and longed to be a part of the fun, but no invitation was ever extended to me. I learned to accept that as I accepted leaving Fairholme. It just was.

Later that summer, we received a box of used clothing from Adele Georg, my dad's cousin who had lived with us at Fairholme for those nine months. We had occasional contact with Adele, Alex, and their children after they had departed Fairholme; and when their parcel arrived from Edmonton, we were elated. Mother cut through the tape with a kitchen knife, and something the color of a sunflower caught my eye. When I plucked it from the pile, a beautiful sleeveless dress with an exquisitely fitted torso and a full pleated skirt unfolded. "That's mine!" I shouted.

"Here's the belt for it," Mother said, tossing me a wide, yellow belt with a plain silver buckle. It was too small to fit around my waist, so I found the scissors and promptly cut the four belt loops off the new dress. "What are you doing?" Mother exclaimed, pulling her head out of the box, clutching a bread bag filled with pink sponge rollers.

"Oh, Mom, those are curlers for our hair!" I blurted, ignoring her question and snatching the bag from her hand. She was like a fish out of water when it came to English clothes and accessories.

My yellow dress filled me with hope. It was strictly a worldly yellow, not something you'd ever see walking around a Hutterite colony, and it begged to be worn on my first day back to school. I locked myself in the bathroom and tried on the dress, studying the girl in the mirror who craved acceptance in this strange, new world. My father's blue eyes stared back at me. "Dornn eyes," the colony women called them. My sturdy nose and good sense of smell, considered valuable on the colony, now seemed like a liability in the land of small, upturned varieties. The heart-shaped face in the mirror was my mother's, a Maendel face, and in that moment, I missed having one of my aunts grab my full cheeks and lovingly pinch them.

Mother still braided our waist-length hair every week, but I yearned for ringlets like the girls at school. Rosie agreed to my suggestion that we set each other's hair with Adele's old rollers, as long as it didn't take too much time. She was more interested in perfecting the cartwheel and climbing trees than in primping in front of a mirror. Her patience for an older sister with stars in her eyes had serious time limits.

When we came downstairs for evening prayers, the boys had a good laugh at our expense, but that didn't dampen my enthusiasm for ringlets, and Rosie didn't care. We endured a rough night of sleep, but early the next morning, as soon as I heard Mother and Dad stirring downstairs, I made my way to the bathroom and took out the rollers one by one. Tight, uneven knots of hair that resembled a ball of prairie tumbleweed stared back at me. I was heartsick. Mother soon had our scalps stooped under the kitchen sink and our hair tamed into braids. There would be no highly anticipated ringlets flowing down my shoulders.

As the first day of school approached, we already knew we no longer had a bus driver. The effort it took to maneuver our lane had taken its toll on poor Mr. Read, and he had made the decision to retire. Father applied for the job, and the school board was more than happy to pay him to transport us. This turned my well-planned first day back into a disaster.

Mother and I took the brown paper bags and Saran wrap we'd saved out of storage. Now that Eugenie was going into grade one, we had six lunches to pack instead of five. Anticipating the extra income he would make as bus driver, Dad had brought home a coil of garlic sausage from the Jewish grocer and we were off on a sandwich-making bonanza.

Up in my room, I laid out my beautiful yellow dress and enlisted Rosie's help with the zipper. "Rosie!" I yelled. She was already outside, climbing a tree, with no thought to our sorry status. "What?" she called back, impatiently. I managed to get her back upstairs to zip the zipper on the dress, but she caught my skin and I screamed. "It doesn't even fit you!" she said, annoyed by the interruption. "Yes, it does. Do it up slowly," I instructed, taking a deep breath as she grappled to separate the metal from my skin. It had not occurred to me to apply restraint in the eating department over the summer holidays. On the colony, women's skirts were held together at the waist by a safety pin. If they gained or lost a little weight, the safety pin was moved to adapt to the change without much fuss or notice. The pleated skirts and fitted jackets suited large and small body types. Being healthy and feeling good were what mattered. We could never understand why English women placed such an excessive focus on their weight, or why overweight women did themselves the indignity of wearing shorts and sleeveless tops, exposing large, floppy arms and dimpled thighs.

By the time I was zipped up, we were both red faced, and Dad was hollering that it was time to go. As I drifted down the stairs, I imagined the reaction of the girls at school, watching me float through the school yard. I knew I would make a good impression and couldn't wait to see the look on Tanya Radner's face. Dad glanced up at the yellow swirl coming down the stairs and asked what I thought I was wearing. "A dress," I answered emphatically.

"You're not going to school without sleeves! Go get dressed," he commanded, as if I were standing there naked. Humiliated, I returned to my room and changed.

At school, we were still treated like outsiders, but the students turned on the charm when it came time to choose sides for a softball game. Alex was the most coveted player and everyone's first choice, but he was increasingly frustrated with the way we were being treated. He became so upset that one day he refused to participate. "The other kids don't want anything to do with us off the field," he told Mrs. Erb, "and we don't want nothin' to do with them on the field." When provoked, Alex could be impossibly stubborn. This took Mrs. Erb by surprise.

"Well, are you just going to quit playing baseball?" she asked incredulously.

"No, we'll take them all on, the entire school, Dornns against the rest!" said Alex defiantly.

"But there's only six of you and thirty-five of them!" argued Mrs. Erb, pointing out the obvious imbalance.

"That's okay," said Alex firmly.

Mrs. Erb could see that the only way to break his resolve was to let him have his way, at least this once. Alex's protest struck a chord with the rest of us, and we stood by his rash decision without bothering to calculate our odds against such a large contingent of players. Minutes later, we found ourselves borrowing gloves from our opponents. Some refused, but others reluctantly parted with their leather goods.

Mrs. Erb retained her position as pitcher. In fairness to both sides, she steered clear of the ball after the pitch, leaving it to others to make the plays. The English kids won the coin flip and the first at bat.

Alex organized and coached us. He assigned Rosie as back-catcher, placed me on first base, Eugenie on third, and he and Phillip took the outfield. Our opponents had their best players bat first. A couple of them hit well and managed to get on base, but Alex and Phillip did a great job of intercepting what could have been home runs. Rosie made some excellent plays, too, and in a weak moment, I felt grateful she was a better athlete than she was a hairdresser.

Two batters were out, and the bases were loaded when Angela Mason stepped up to the plate in her new hot pants and perfect ringlets and struck out. She burst into tears, and we could scarcely conceal our joy.

Alex continued to play a strategic game, using his weaker players first. He had me lead off. I hit well enough to get to first base, and Phillip and Rosie followed with solid ground balls. The bases were loaded when Alex stepped up to the plate. He prepared to bat left, but when the entire outfield simultaneously ran to right field in anticipation of his hitting a home run, Alex saw an opportunity. When Mrs. Erb wound up for the pitch, he swung himself around, batted right, and drove the ball far down the abandoned left field, earning us four runs. Aggravated shouts of "no fair" filled the air, and poor Mrs. Erb didn't know what to do with this new twist on an already awkward situation. After arguing back and forth, Mrs. Erb determined that what Alex had done was fair and square, but he couldn't do it again. She let the score stand at 4–0 and ordered us to play ball. We stuck to our game plan, and when Alex's turn came up again, he batted left. With a loud crack, the ball flew over the heads of all the outfielders and garnered our team another four runs. Our score was well into the double digits by the time we accumulated three outs. The other team played another scoreless inning, and we were again back in the batter's box. At Alex's next at bat, with bases loaded, we were so far ahead he began to relax and tease the out-fielders. "Farther, go out farther," he hollered, motioning with his hand high in the air. "You'd better move back," he taunted. Off they scampered into the outfield, unable to anticipate his next move. Alex bunted the ball, and we all stole home.

We were dusty and bruised but covered in smiles when the game finally came to an end after nine innings. The score was 40–0. We had completely shut out the other team, far exceeding our own expectations. Our classmates refused to ever play against us again, but we had made a point and secured for ourselves a grudging respect.

Throughout the school year, we made bimonthly visits to Fairholme. Catherine and I spent hours in her attic, comparing our lives and imagining how our futures might unfold. The slanting ceilings forced us to stoop over when we walked, and in the warmer weather, it was as hot as a steam bath, but it was the only place we had the least bit of privacy. We reminisced about Mrs. Phillipot, and she kept me posted on the spirited and opinionated *Diene* from Fairholme who had married into other colonies. Every community had its own eccentricities, and sometimes the adjustment after marriage was difficult, especially if the new colony was too strict or old-fashioned.

Catherine represented the cherished life I had left behind, and I was her door to the frightening and fascinating outside world. Only once did we have an argument. Whenever I visited Fairholme, I always spent time alone with both Sandra and Catherine. It never caused any friction, because we respected each other's friendships. During a long walk with Sandra, she told me she knew how babies were born. She said men lie on top of the women "*und nah tut er's einhin* [and he puts it in]." It was at once shocking and self-explanatory. Up in the attic, I anxiously shared Sandra's startling news with Catherine, and a difference of opinion ensued.

Catherine insisted it was complete rubbish, but the damage was done. We could not look our parents in the eye for weeks.

Away from the security of Catherine's attic, I kept to my fixation of improving our image at school and discovered from my classmates that a hamburger was the ultimate lunch. I had tasted a hamburger once before when Alex and I accompanied Miss Pattimore to the Centennial Library in Winnipeg one day after school. By the time we had chosen books and checked them out, Alex and I were fading from hunger. "Let's go to McDonald's," Miss Pattimore said cheerfully.

The only restaurant we had ever been to was Jimmy's Café in Portage la Prairie. It was a little Chinese coffee shop frequented by Hutterites when they came to town on business or for medical appointments. Jimmy was small and friendly, and his English was no better than ours. A haze of cigarette smoke always hung in the air, and the clatter of plates could be heard from behind a set of swinging doors. Everyone on the colony ordered the same dish, shrimp fried rice, because it was the most exotic thing we had ever tasted. Neither shrimp nor rice was ever served in Fairholme, and that one little stop made getting a needle or being sick worthwhile.

At McDonald's, Alex swung open the glass doors and we walked up to the counter, where Miss Pattimore ordered all of us small fries, an orange soft drink, and a hamburger. Sliding into the booth, I lifted the corner of the bun and saw a round pickle and a splash of ketchup on the burger. My brother and I devoured ours, and Alex licked the extra ketchup off his hamburger wrapper. I couldn't really blame him since both of us were still really hungry.

After the meal, Miss Pattimore told us her mother lived in the city and she wanted to stop by and see her for a few minutes. She asked us to wait in the car. We could not understand why her mother wouldn't want to see us too. This was so unlike the colony, where we paraded in and out of each other's homes all the time. The older people, especially, loved to meet someone new, and Alex and I wondered out loud why her mother would be so unsociable. Was she ill, or was her house a mess? We would not have minded. After about twenty minutes, Miss Pattimore bounced down the front steps of her mother's home. I watched the drawn curtains in the living room to see whether curiosity would get the better of her mother, but I waited in vain.

The sun had set when we finally returned home. "We're starving, Mom," I said as we burst through the front door.

"Didn't you have supper?" she asked, surprised.

"No, we didn't," I answered. "All we had was a hamburger and french fries."

"Well, that's called supper, Ann-Marie," Mother replied.

I convinced Mother that we should create our own version of a hamburger since we could not afford ground beef. It was slaughtering season in New Rosedale, and my mother's older brother Eddie had brought us a large pail of chicken gizzards, livers, and hearts. Eddie Vetter was always kind to us, repairing our run-down appliances when God didn't, or replacing them with another secondhand model when death by overuse was confirmed. Mother used a small meat grinder, and the chicken hearts and gizzards were soon ground into "hamburger." We fried it up with some onions and added salt and pepper for taste. The meat was chewy and didn't bind very well, but it tasted surprisingly good. Mother made everyone a hamburger sandwich for their school lunches, and I added a splash of ketchup.

The next day, before I had even taken a bite, Bernie Legit was standing in front of me, holding a large chocolate brownie in the palm of his hand. At almost six feet tall, Bernie looked like an undernourished flagpole. "Trade you this for your hamburger sandwich," he said. My eyes fixed on the thick slab of chocolate. "C'mon," said Alex, with a glint in his eye, "give it to the poor guy.

It'll put some meat on his bones." We traded lunches, and I held my breath. "Wow, this tastes great! It's the best hamburger I've ever had," he said, taking another bite. The whole class was intrigued.

My brother waited until Bernie had swallowed the last meaty morsel before jumping in, unable to contain himself. "Do you know what you just ate?" Alex demanded gleefully.

"What?" gasped Bernie, his eyes filling with fear.

"Those were chicken innards. Ground-up chicken innards! And they taste better than hamburger 'cause they're better for you," he replied smugly. Bernie heaved and ran for the bathroom. It was the last time anyone traded an item of food with one of us.

The leaves turned to red and gold that autumn, and we shivered in the morning cold, anticipating the bone-chilling temperatures that would soon follow. One evening, when frost had cloaked the lawns and fallow fields, Father called me downstairs. "Ann-Marie, come to the kitchen!" he shouted. I was high in the Alps with Heidi, Peter, and the goats, and the budding romance between the goat herder and his alpine sweetheart was just heating up. Borrowed library books were my great escape, and I did not want to be disturbed.

"What do you want, Dad?" I called, leaning over the banister.

"Come right away; you have to come!" he said. Halfway down the stairs, the smell of overripe bananas told me he'd been to Winnipeg to visit his grocer friend. Boxes of fruit and vegetables stood haphazardly around the kitchen, waiting to be sorted and salvaged. Dad was standing there with a broad smile on his face. "Look what I bought for you," he said, holding out a pair of white skates.

"Oh, Dad!" I raced toward him. "Where did you get them?"

"Well," he replied, "remember those nine dollars you gave me so we wouldn't go broke? I found these at a secondhand store in Winnipeg today."

The skates were in good condition, and although I would need to stuff the toes with thick socks until I grew into them, I was absolutely thrilled.

Skating was forbidden on the colony, but every year a handful of the boys in Fairholme secretly acquired a used pair and would take turns with them on the river. If caught, they would be disciplined in the *Essenschul*. Once a year, at Easter, they were allowed to turn the skates over to the *Prediger*, without penalty, to be burned. Easter was a time of soul-searching and renewal, where even children are encouraged to claim a fresh start. But the kind of renewal Oltvetter Dornn undertook that spring would reopen old wounds with Jake Maendel and ignite another controversy.

::

When we left Fairholme, Oltvetter Dornn had wanted to come with us, but Father refused to bend to Oltvetter's one stipulation: that we call Dahl's Farm a Hutterite colony. Still, Oltvetter came once to visit us at Rogers' Farm, and he shuffled around our house in his black hat and gray bedroom slippers, killing flies and conversing with Mother while she worked. At eighty-three, he was out of sorts. Both of his sons had left Fairholme, and he felt alone again, still clinging to the notion that community life was the only way to heaven. Mother had her radio on the religious broadcast channel, where one evangelist gave a compelling sermon in German about salvation. Oltvetter was captivated by the evangelist's urging to make an outward commitment to Jesus, and with tears streaming down his face, he gave his heart to the Lord right in our kitchen. When he returned to Fairholme, he kept quiet about his experience, as Hutterites do not believe in such public declarations of salvation but rather believe in practicing their faith through acts of service.

Back in Fairholme, Oltvetter's soul stirred like a body of *unruhigs Wosser* (restless water). He requested permission for a trip to Ontario to see his three daughters, and while in the province, he also would visit Julius Farm, the community that drew him away from the Hutterites thirty years earlier and the one from which he had been evicted. Oltvetter wanted to return one last time to make peace with the place that had once held so much promise and ended in so much heartbreak.

In the years after my grandfather left Julius Farm, Julius Kubassek's tyranny had eventually been his downfall. Oltvetter's tormentor lost the respect of his followers, and while fleeing the community the previous year, he had died of a heart attack. After his sudden death, his followers learned of his plan to buy himself property with the thousands of dollars he'd squirreled away in a secret bank account.

I remember Oltvetter standing at the train station in Winnipeg, bent over his cane, his trusted flyswatter strangled in the lid of his suitcase, ready to reconcile with his past.

His visit was most agreeable. The people at Julius Farm in Bright, Ontario, were happy to see him. He also enjoyed time with his daughters, who took him wherever he wanted to go, including to local revival meetings. Inspired by his conversion experience via the radio evangelist, he decided to be rebaptized as a way of reconfirming his faith. When news of that filtered back to Fairholme, however, Jake Vetter was furious. Oltvetter's actions were seen as denouncing his Hutterite faith.

Anticipating a period of certain excommunication back in Fairholme, Oltvetter prolonged his return. Then, one night, he went to sleep and never woke up. In the morning he was discovered with his hands in the air and a look of serenity on his face. God had taken him home.

It was left to Father to inform Jake, who unleashed his fury over the phone, telling Dad that his father's rebaptism put his burial on colony ground in question. "He doesn't belong to us anymore. He's no longer a Hutterite," Jake said.

"Well, Jake, that's all I wanted to know," Father said before quietly hanging up the phone. Beneath his bluster, Father knew Jake Maendel wanted more than anything to have Oltvetter laid to rest in Fairholme. He just wanted Father to beg for the privilege, but Father wouldn't.

The Bright community wanted to restore the dignity to my grandfather in death that Julius had stripped away in life, and the people at Julius Farm offered to have Oltvetter's funeral there, with all expenses paid. Christian Dornn's pursuit of security in the realm of community life had left him yearning for something more. In the end he found it within himself, and the lamb lay down with the lion. Oltvetter was laid to rest in the same graveyard as his former nemesis, Julius Kubassek.

After his death, the Bright community decided to honor Grandfather Dornn by giving Father and Uncle Chris, who still resided at Dahl's Farm, four hundred dollars each to buy a cow. This was a most unfortunate turn of events for Tanya Radner, as we ended up with her favorite pet. Tanya's dad owned cattle, and Father put the word out in the spring that he was looking to buy a good milk cow. Mr. Radner had some for sale, and Dad unknowingly chose Tanya's favorite. Edwin and Alex walked the five miles to Tanya's farm to collect Daisy and led the beautiful Jersey cow off her property and home to ours. At school the next day, she begged Alex not to change Daisy's name. "Oh, heavens," said Alex, rolling his eyes. "I'm not sticking with a foolish name like that. We've changed her name to Old Critter," he declared.

"Old Critter!" shouted Tanya. "That's an awful name. How dare you name my cow Old Critter!" she cried.

"She's my cow now, Tanya," said Alex calmly. I knew that finding pleasure in the misfortune of another was sinful, but I hoped God would give me a pass.

Without warning, Sana Basel showed up on our doorstep. She entered the house shouting, "Tank-you, tank-you, tank-you" to the perfect stranger who had dropped her off after confirming her destination. No one could resist her. The driver had dropped by Fairholme to buy some eggs and found himself charmed into giving Sana Basel a ride to her sister's house—destination unknown, but with assurances that it couldn't be far. How they found Rogers' Farm still remains a mystery.

Mother threw her arms around her sister, overjoyed to see her. Sana Basel had a gift for making the mundane seem special, and she soon plunged into the work at hand with both feet, delegating with cheerful gusto. "Oh, my heavens, it smells like cats and rats and mice in here," she said, bursting into my brothers' bedroom and stripping the sheets. She had brought some *Specksaften* with her to help Mother with the spring cleaning.

As they washed walls together, Mother taught Sana Basel the new songs she was learning on the radio, and Sana Basel regaled her with the latest news. At a large funeral in Ibervelle Colony, *die frommer* "the virtuous" Miriam Hofer from Hope Springs had slept with another man, and everyone was talking about it. Miriam's husband had checked into her aunt's guest bedroom early, and at midnight Miriam quietly undressed in the dark and hopped into bed next to him. The next morning, she awoke to find that the man she had spent the night with wasn't her husband. She was in the wrong guest bedroom! The whole colony was aflutter over it, and Miriam was horrified. She just could not believe her foolish mistake.

For a few wonderful days we relished Sana Basel's presence before we reluctantly drove her back to the colony, singing favorite hymns until the old truck rounded the dusty gravel road that led to Fairholme.

There was lots of space at Rogers' Farm, which seemed to have a beneficial effect, and whether by necessity or design, we fared better in our new neck of the woods. With calves in the barn, Edwin and Alex had regular chores to do, which relieved the boredom of the previous summer. When the calves took ill, Mother expanded her prayer constituency to include them, and God turned out to be just as reliable with the livestock as with worn-out appliances. Father saw a future for himself in cattle, but he longed to be independent. He offered Pete Siemens ten thousand dollars for Rogers' Farm. When Mr. Siemens hinted at selling the house and property on the open market, Father upped his bid to fifteen thousand dollars.

While Mother and Dad contemplated their future, along came whirling dervish Terry Miller. He was part evangelist, part comedian and was considered by many Hutterites to be a troublemaker. My parents knew Terry as an outsider who stayed at Forest River Hutterite Colony years ago in North Dakota. Terry promptly evangelized the young people on the colony, causing enough chaos that he was finally expelled. The exile did little to deter him, and wherever there was a soul to be saved, Hutterite or otherwise, he was bound to find them.

By the time he and Mother had consumed their cups of coffee, Terry had her convinced that a free week of Bible camp could do her children no harm, and Edwin, Alex, Rosie, Phillip, and I, with at least one change of clean underwear, were off to Grenfell, Saskatchewan, for a week of deliverance at the Grenfell Bible Camp. As we pulled away in Terry's big, black car, I noticed that Mother and Dad looked bone weary, and I realized they needed a holiday too. They stood at the front door and waved. Carl and Genie cried because they wanted to come as well, but Mother held firm, claiming she couldn't send that many bed wetters at one time; it just wouldn't be right.

Terry's clean vehicle had never been subjected to so many sinners before, but it didn't seem to bother him. We stopped at every fast-food outlet on the expansive Trans-Canada Highway leading to Grenfell and pulled into Bible camp just in time for the evening service. Terry led us to a big, white tent filled with people shouting, "Hallelujah, thank you, Jesus" and "Glory to God." We followed him into the revival meeting, and he led us straight to the front row before proceeding to the stage, his whole body in buoyant motion as he went. The whole place fell under a rapturous spell as he started to sing a familiar hymn. A woman in a large, blue sun hat earnestly played the piano as the throng willingly joined in, hands stretched upward. "I surrender all, I surrender all; all to Thee, my blessed Savior, I surrender all!"

Calls for repentance prompted people to come forward in droves. Brother Miller and two others disembarked from the stage to start praying over people at the front. We tried to push our chairs back to put some distance between the acknowledged sinners and ourselves, but there was no place to go. "Praise God, they're dropping like flies tonight," I heard someone behind me say.

My eyes and mouth hung wide open as more and more people fell backward into a trance and onto the hard ground. I was sure they must have had a heart attack. Someone tried to get me to fall back, too, and applied some pressure to my head, but I pushed forward, grateful for every extra pound of body weight to withstand the force. I could just imagine what the people on the colony would say to the goings-on here. "What insanity!" they would have exclaimed, glad that the good Lord didn't require them to make fools of themselves like this bunch. By the time the three-hour service was over, all of the bodies on the floor had recovered and returned to their seats.

The next morning in the common breakfast area, I took in the full spectrum of mortals attending the Bible camp. There were misfits of every shape and variety: middle-aged women with elaborate beehive hairdos, young women in flowing peasant skirts, and young men with worn blue jeans and outrageous Afros, all desperate to make contact with God.

The second evening's service was as shocking as the first. The focus was on speaking in tongues. After a rousing pep talk from Brother Miller about the utility of such a gift in warding off evil spirits, we were directed to test our linguistic capacity. Everyone went into high gear, grunting and crying out in odd-sounding syllables. A preacher headed toward me, and placing his large hand on my head with a thud, he commanded me to open my mouth and start talking. When my unyielding tongue froze, he shook my head and commanded me to make some verbal contact. Spontaneously, I started reciting a traditional table prayer in German as he jumped up and down, praising God for victory.

Our salvation at Bible camp was not enough to secure our future at Rogers' Farm. When we returned home, Father was in turmoil. Pete Siemens was selling the property out from under him. His renovations were so impressive that Mr. Siemens saw an opportunity to make a profit. Dad found out about other prospective buyers when the strangers knocked on the door and said that Pete Siemens had sent them. Father clenched his jaw as he let them in, and we ate our supper meal in silence while they toured our home.

"God will look after us, Dad. Don't be afraid," murmured Mother, but Father would not rest. The weight of a wife and seven hungry children eating at his table lay heavily on his mind. "*Och*, Mary," he sighed, cupping his face in his hands. "Joining the colony was the worst mistake I ever made. I would be so much further ahead today if—"

"*Votar!* Father!" we cried in unison, blinking and swallowing as we saw our lives flash before our eyes.

"How can you say that? Then you wouldn't have us!" Mother scolded. Father's face melted into a weary smile.

"I didn't mean it that way," he said, chastened.

I thought about the story he'd once told us about coming over from Russia in a great boat. His clearest memory was of his mother sending him to the ship's canteen for some peppermints. The seas were rough, and she was seasick. He was only five years old, but she had pressed some rubles into his hand and told him to get the mints to settle her lurching stomach. On the counter in the store, the steward had a small windup bird that hopped up and down, and Father was so intrigued that he threw his money on the counter and dashed off with it. The steward gave chase, and after wrestling the bird from his hand, offered him a handful of peppermints to take to his mother. Beneath Father's distress lay the heart of that young boy who tried to do the right thing but found that what he wanted was just out of his grasp.

That night we all knelt in a circle in the living room to pray. I caught sight of Father's folded hands. I remembered those hands on the steering wheel of the truck as he and I drove to Deerboine Colony to collect Mother and Renie. They were the hands once fine enough to do delicate calligraphy, the hands that rested on Mother's shoulder in a moment of tenderness, the hands that shook in anger over Jake Vetter's unreasonableness. I saw not just my father, but a man of conviction and principle, willing to do whatever it took to support his family.

Two weeks after we moved out of our beloved mansion, it was completely destroyed by fire. The fire department, we were later told, attributed the blaze to faulty wiring in the basement. But Mother's prediction that God would take care of us turned out to be true.

Miss Winkler in her robe and crown,
with her runners-up.

ELEVEN

A Place of Our Own in Plum Coulee/Winkler

LISTEN TO ME, and I will make you wise," said one of the guests to my father. Our family had been asked to sing at the wedding of Sarah Hofer, one of Sana Basel's runaway daughters. It was the first English wedding we had ever been to. I knew full well that beneath that swirl of white was a Hutterite girl, but everyone said Sarah sure pulled it off. Her husband, Bruce—who chewed nervously on his lower lip—was terribly handsome and ten years younger than the bride. Paul Vetter had let himself be talked into coming, and Sana Basel was holding court with people she had never met, her face aglow beneath her new *Tiechel*. At the reception, over a tray of matrimonial cake, Zacky Waldner, another runaway from Sunnyside Colony, approached my father. "Ron, I know a nice farm for you," he said, leaning in.

The next afternoon we all went to see it. The property was located in the Mennonite heartland of southern Manitoba. A modest three-bedroom house stood on a large yard off the main highway, which led in one direction to Plum Coulee and in the other to Winkler. It had an unfinished basement that Mother imagined would be a good place for teenage boys. Two huge, rectangular chicken barns filled the backyard. It came with ninety-seven acres of land, planted in wheat, as perfect as it was impossible.

Gary Jackman wanted forty thousand dollars for it, and that was a fortune to my father, whose meager savings wouldn't amount to a respectable down payment. Mr. Jackman had anticipated driving by on the highway from town and feeling proud that it was in good hands. He was very attached to his farm and wanted it to go to someone who would realize its potential, but his hopes were fading. He had shown it to so many people he was ready to throw in the towel. Someone had tried to buy it, but the deal fell through.

Father wasn't much of a prospect. "I've got the button, but I don't have the shirt," he said, apologetically. "Well, that's something," Gary Jackman replied. Those words gave Father hope, and when Mr. Jackman offered to apply the two-thousand-dollar down payment from the deal that went sour to Father, his optimism grew.

The manager of the Winkler Credit Union looked into Father's eyes the next afternoon and decided to take a chance on a humble man with a vision. Suddenly Father's dream of owning his own place was a reality, a mere two years after we'd left Fairholme

Colony. Dad's sister Rosie Baer from Ontario loaned him five thousand dollars, and for the third time in three years, we had a new home.

"When you stepped out of your pickup that day, I saw you cast your eyes in prayer toward the heavens, and I knew then that you were the right buyer for my farm," Gary Jackman later told Father.

Father applied the seven years of experience he had acquired as chicken man in New Rosedale Colony, and we were all soon gainfully employed gathering seven thousand eggs a day. An egg contract with Ogilvie Feeds had come with the sale, and a Winnipeg feed company supplied Father with feed and nine thousand Highline chickens each cycle. Father received 10 percent of the profit and all the cracked eggs we could eat.

These were among the happiest times of our parents' lives. The Hutterite colony that had been so central to our being was replaced by the Church of God in Plum Coulee, where Mother became so involved in prayer meetings that some days the breakfast dishes were still on the table when we came home from school.

The people from the nearby village of Plum Coulee and the bigger town of Winkler ten kilometers to the west were conservative, hardworking, and just as keen as my parents to keep their children on the straight and narrow. Consequently we spent most of our spare time in church. Not the solemn and sober Mennonite churches that dotted the landscape, but the loudest and liveliest churches Mother could find.

Mother couldn't get enough of these churches. We eventually became a permanent fixture at the Global Mission's church in Winkler, where an irate neighbor hurled an onion through the window to get the zealous congregation to tone down the "Amens" and "Hallelujahs." The shattered glass and baseball-sized vegetable landed with a thud down the center aisle, and Flower Annie, a mentally challenged woman who helped support herself by making flowers out of crepe paper, put it in her purse to cook in her soup the next day.

Our home was continually crowded with people who needed a place to stay, a hot meal, or a word of encouragement. We never locked our doors, and sometimes when we arrived home late from a revival meeting, our beds were already occupied. No one was ever turned away. "There's always room for one more," was Mother's motto as she spread foam mattresses on the floor of the living room. "When the first shift is asleep, I'll stand them up against the wall and the second shift can go to bed," she teased. Some came and went. Others, like Dave Klassen, a nursing student in need of a family, stayed for years.

When Anna Basel's daughters Rachel and Edna left Deerboine Colony, they, too, became part of our family. Dad helped them get jobs and set up bank accounts, and he insisted they save their money, learn to drive, and eventually buy cars.

My siblings and I were now going to school in Plum Coulee with young people, some of whom were conflicted about their Mennonite roots. Our classmates were having as much of an identity crisis as we were, trying to update their parents and modernize their points of view. They respected their parents but considered them old-fashioned and sometimes embarrassing. Father finally relaxed our dress codes, and we were all soon wearing generic blue jeans while the others strutted around in their Lees and Wranglers.

But I remained most at home with my Hutterite friends. I looked forward to our visits to Fairholme and especially to my letters from Catherine.

Hello, Ann-Marie,

I'm not doing much, just wishing you would be here. We'd have so much fun together. I'm trying to sing, but I'm just a croaking pity. You'd better try to come as quick as possible to ease my loneliness.

Oh, I miss you. I miss your long finger pointing at me. I miss it
terribly . . .

— Catherine

Catherine and I both wanted a bigger life. Even though it
seemed improbable, we had earnestly decided to become world-
famous singers and spent much of our time together practicing
songs we'd heard on the radio, for by now she had her own tran-
sistor under her pillow in the attic in Fairholme. We also got
plenty of practice when we were apart, me in church, and she on
the Hutterite wedding circuit.

Hi, Ann-Marie,

Lots of water has passed under the bridge since we last saw each
other. I've been to so many Hulbas. Practiced up my voice. Linda
from Fairholme had her Hulba last week, and this coming week is
her wedding in Milltown to a guy named Jerry. Then, WONDER
OF WONDERS, Walter is getting married to Betty from Elm River
on Nov. 25th. I think. I was in Oakridge Colony yesterday and sang
my eyeballs out there too! They appreciated it terribly much and
loved it even more so.

— Catherine

Our new home came with a new baby. On New Year's Eve,
Mother gave birth to Brian Perry Dornn. My parents hadn't
wanted any more children, but Brian soon convinced us he was
no accident. With a bright-red rash on each cheek, he was sent to
bring us joy. We took him with us on our last visit to see Oma in
the hospital in Winnipeg. She was in so much pain it hurt us to
look at her, but her lips stretched into a momentary smile when
Mother held out her latest production. "Brine?" she asked rolling
her *r*. "What kind of a name is that?"

Oma had visited our farm in Plum Coulee soon after we'd settled in. Father had gone to Fairholme to fetch her and gave her the grand tour . . . the house, the barns, the chickens, and the crops. His enthusiasm delighted her. "I want to live out my life with my own people," Oma told him, cleaning her glasses with her apron as they drove around looking at the wheat fields. That afternoon she extracted a promise from Father that as soon as he could afford a little trailer, she would come and live next door to us just as she had on the colony. Her face shone with contentment when the two of them returned for supper.

Shortly after her visit, however, she took sick. She had always had a weak heart, but when the doctors insisted on putting in a pacemaker, her body rejected it and she had a stroke. Gangrene set into her left leg, and the doctors had to amputate. When the deadly infection spread, the surgery had to be repeated. For nine months she suffered terribly before a merciful death released her from the incessant pain.

At the funeral in Fairholme, I holed up in the attic at Catherine's house, refusing to go next door to view Oma in her casket. Oma and Opa had filled the empty corridors of missing grandparents. I couldn't bear the thought of never looking into her eyes again or hearing her call my name. "You don't have to," my gentle friend assured me until Mother pulled me inside, and insisted, "*Du musst!*"

In her wooden coffin, Oma's head lay on a soft feather pillow, and her hair, as pale as her skin, was tucked beneath a black *Tiechel*. Oma's hands, once so busy with the daily tasks of life, now rested across her navy *Mieder*. I was struck by her silence. No more gasps and moans; at eighty-two years of age, she was free. Her harrowing, pain-filled life was over.

Mother told me that shortly after moving to Fairholme, a letter from Oma and Opa's two missing sons had arrived from East

Germany into the care of my parents. After the boys had been forced into the German army, their parents never heard from them again, but their sons had been released from prison and had written a letter and enclosed a picture. Father went next door and asked his elderly aunt and uncle if they would know their sons Heinrich and Jacob Georg after so many years.

"Oh, we would know them!" they both cried. "There is no such thing as us not knowing our own children!"

Father pulled out the photograph and asked, "Do you recognize these people?"

Eyeing the picture carefully, they handed it back and forth, finally shaking their heads, sure they had never seen the men before.

"These are your boys," Father gently told them.

Oma and Opa gasped, their eyes widening as they took in their sons' images, absorbing the hardship and the sadness in their faces. "*Mein Gott!*" Oma whispered as she and Opa sank into a chair and wept.

::

At the opposite end of the community, fifty-six-year-old Jake Maendel lay dying of cancer. Mother's attempts to see him one last time had been spurned. She had appealed to his daughter Katya by way of a letter pleading for reconciliation.

> Dear Katya,
>
> This will really be a surprise to you to get a letter from me. But this has been on my mind for so long already. You know, Katya, I am deeply concerned about your dad. It must be so very hard for him and for the family to see him suffer and slowly getting weaker. It bothers me many times that we cannot come to see him, I often think of the saying, blood is no water. It is my brother, and I cannot

help being concerned. The thought might come to you that we didn't seem to care much when we lived in Fairholme, for which you have all rights to say, but that time we had all kinds of hurt feelings and were full of bitterness. It was so hard to carry all that around all the time, so we went on our knees in earnest prayer, and we can really say now we are no longer the same. We can only feel sorry that we have wasted all those years. We all have to search our hearts daily, as we all don't know how soon our end may be. May you accept my humble concern and sincerity. We remain in love.

— Mary, Ronald, and
Family

A week later, my father drove Mother to Jake Vetter's funeral. In full Hutterite apparel, she slipped quietly into the last row of chairs. It was a beautiful September day, and so many people from other colonies had come to pay their respects that the funeral was held outside on the front lawn. Jake Maendel was an icon to many in the Schmiedeleut colonies. In the distance, my mother glimpsed his emaciated corpse. It was all that remained of her estranged brother. While the Hutterite sermon droned on, tears spilled from her eyes onto the dark folds of her skirt.

⁘

Back in Plum Coulee, Father's accumulated years of frustration were being converted into a steely determination. In addition to our daily chores of gathering eggs, summers were spent hoeing half-mile-long rows of sugar beets in the nearby fields with migrant Mexican Mennonites. My brothers tarred and patched roofs during the day in Plum Coulee, and by late afternoons all ten of us could be seen walking hand in hand through Mr. Harder's oat fields, plucking out pesky wild oats. Father taught us how to tell the weeds apart from the grain, and we'd trek through the fields east to west, north to south, and then on the diagonal until he was satisfied that Mr. Harder's oat crop would be number one. Even our baby brother got in on the action. The Hutterite philosophy "*Arbeit macht das Leben Süss*—Work makes life sweet" and the importance of being dutiful were values our parents held dear.

By the time Brian was two years old, he was also my assistant on the top floor of barn number one, gathering sixty eggs a day, points down, into a filler. Brian was a sweet child, alive with happiness. Everything was an adventure, and we all adored him. Once, when he finished gathering his row early, he gleefully threw some of his eggs on Old Critter, who was eating her hay down below. When I caught him, I gave him a couple of whacks on his diapered bottom. Deeply wounded, he threw his arms around my neck and sobbed. Thereafter, influenced by Mother's spiritual fervor, he spent his free time praying over sick chickens Dad had taken out of their cages and put on the barn floor so they could die in peace. Some sprang back to life, and we thought nothing of it as Father happily returned them to their cages.

When we weren't doing farm chores, we were coming or going to church or having church people to our home for prayer meetings. Mother went from being a good-natured Hutterite woman to a firebrand. Her faith was fierce, and she tried to convert everyone she talked to, including the Electrolux salesman who thought he'd come to sell her a necessary household item.

The carpets in our house came in gaudy squares of gold and orange and were impossible to clean. Mother called them *ecklig*, "obscene." She took hot, soapy water and a scrub brush to them every Saturday without any satisfaction. But when the Electrolux salesman stopped by to entice her to buy a vacuum cleaner, she had an even better offer for him and set about convincing him to give his heart to Jesus. By the time we returned from gathering eggs— tired, smelly, and hungry—they were only halfway through their respective sales pitches, so Mother invited him to stay for supper. When he saw what she was serving, he bolted, for piled high on a plate in the center of the table, Mother had placed our weekly feast of "walkers and talkers," boiled chicken feet and necks.

Father steadfastly relied on Mother's prayers when dry weather threatened his crops, because her God was big enough to make it rain. During dry spells he was on edge, his face strained from watching his parched wheat fields withering. I remember being awakened in the night by a breeze blowing the screen door in the living room open. I caught sight of my parents standing in the open field that began at the edge of the garden. In the dark I could see their outlines, Mother in her nightgown and Father in his pajamas. Their hands, clasped together, were raised against a darkened sky as Mother, her voice determined and sure, prayed for rain. A rumble of thunder made me jump, and out of the darkness gusts of wind blew drops of rain against the window- pane. I heard cheers of joy as Mother, still clutching Father's arm, ran toward the house. Her simple faith touched the heart of God. She invited miracles, and they came. And every year, by the grace of God, we inched forward.

In many ways, our inner lives remained similar to what we had on the colony, rich with shared memories and experiences. But it was through Catherine's letters that I was given a keyhole peek into what my life might have been had we stayed.

Dear Ann-Marie,

Hello, how are you still keeping? We're very busy hereabouts, picking, canning, cleaning, weeding etc. . . . No end, it seems. When are you coming around? Next Sunday? I wish you'd make it fast. We just finished weeding the strawberry patch and killing a few crate roosters, and now the bell has rung again. Weeding some more . . . (sigh)

. . . I'm back, made a mistake. It wasn't weeding after all. Was only bringing fruit home from the kitchen. To me it seems they enjoy ring-a-linging that stupid bell!

— Catherine

While Catherine was trying to escape the sound of the bell in Fairholme, I was desperate to flee the daily grind of doing dishes, folding laundry, and gathering eggs. Father had tacked a sign on the side of barn one. It read Jesus Saves, and every time I walked through the front entrance, I wished that Jesus would save me from the rows and rows of eggs waiting to be put in fillers.

My "world-famous singer" side just couldn't bear the constant clatter of work. A 4-H cooking class was being offered at Mrs. Wiebe's house in Plum Coulee every Thursday after school. Mrs. Wiebe was the mother of one of my classmates. She could have taught underwater basket weaving and I would have enlisted, such was my desperation to get off the farm.

Before the ink was dry on my signature, Rosie had signed up too. Mother couldn't understand why we wanted somebody else to teach us how to read a recipe book and bake cookies when we already knew how. Didn't we spend every Saturday baking up a storm just to get us through the week? Besides, who would give us a ride home? We weren't going to tell her that walking the mile and a half would get us out of supper dishes. I missed the regulated summer afternoon naps in Fairholme, where even in peak season everything came to a halt after dinner so adults and children could rest, and Catherine and I would steal away to the bakery for a pickle and a bun and important Secret Flowerpot matters.

Mrs. Weibe's classes gave us a break from farm duties, but the setting was gloomy and sober. Her house, with its drawn curtains, choked off any natural light and felt dark and uninviting. We could see the dust on all the clutter and trinkets that lined her shelves and on the fake plastic flowers on her kitchen table. Rosie and I felt queasy when she took a duster to them, rearranging the dirt. Her four sons avoided coming into the kitchen area, and the teasing and banter so typical of Hutterite homes was missing. The atmosphere felt hollow without the ribbing and smart remarks we would have been subjected to on the colony as we pored over the recipe book on the kitchen table.

All of Mrs. Wiebe's excess weight had accumulated at her waist, which was mounted on two skinny little legs that appeared below a knee-length hem. Because the belts on her dresses didn't fit around her middle, she fastened them in the smaller expanse immediately under her bosom. While we contemplated oven temperature and serving sizes, a loud explosion rocked us to attention. Four more eruptions followed, all coming from the oven. "Oh dear, oh dear!" Mrs. Wiebe whimpered, reaching for her hot pads. Pulling the handle, she was confronted by a mess of white splats all over the inside of her oven. The potatoes she was baking for supper had blown up. This would have caused gales of laughter in Fairholme, and by supper the whole colony would have known about it. Mrs. Wiebe would have earned herself an appropriate nickname, like *Kartoffel Suzie*, "Potato Suzie," by which she would be referred to forevermore. The story would have entertained the women working in the kitchen, garden, and bakery every time it was told. But in Mrs. Wiebe's kitchen, this was no laughing matter, and Rosie and I had to stifle our amusement as our flustered host ended the cooking lesson and engaged us in cleaning up the splatter while she washed and carefully pierced five more potatoes with a fork.

Dear Ann-Marie:

You wouldn't believe it, but Rachel and some others were involved in helping a getaway. For Sue it was. She left the colony. Her Josh Vetter from James Valley Colony and his wife somehow didn't smoothen out things a bit. Her mother told Josh Vetter that Sue was leaving, and naturally he got all excited, because of course he thinks she's aiming straight for hell with her skirts on fire already. Didn't know if it helped him any tho' because Sue was at Peter Vetter's place when her mother told him, so she just took off right away and walked out to the back roads and Rachel came along and picked her up. But getting her satchel out was another thing. One move toward her bedroom would have been a giveaway, so they're sending it by bus to Brandon.

— Catherine

Catherine kept me plugged in to the Hutterite telegraph and all the latest gossip going on back in Fairholme. We were each other's lifeline. I had an unfortunate imagination and made my life sound much more glamorous than it really was. I pretended I had the world by the tail, when I was actually hanging from a string. Then God sent me Charlene Mironuck.

Charlene was my first English friend, and we met at a revival meeting. She was a city girl from Regina, too beautiful and sure of herself for me to ever think we had anything in common; but for reasons I never fully understood and was too afraid to ask, she chose me as her friend. She had shiny brown hair, an upturned nose, and a warm smile that made her popular with the boys, while I was still trying to get girls to like me. We were in an entirely different class. Charlene got the latest fashions every season, while I wore clothes other people had discarded, but she saw potential in this overweight girl with a thirty-six-inch waist and a bad wardrobe.

Charlene cornered me after the church service to ask why I was wearing a light blue dress with white pantyhose in the dead of winter. Her directness was blunted by a glint in her eyes that said, "I can help." From then on we were fast friends and kept in touch through whatever means we could, mostly letters. For one blissful week in the summers, we both attended church camp in North Battleford, Saskatchewan, where we stayed in the girls' dorm together. It was heaven.

Charlene was twelve and I was fourteen, but she tended to me with the devotion of a *Mutterle* (little mother). She staged a fashion intervention and taught me how to curl my hair, what to wear and how to wear it, taking up where Mother, who was too busy praising Jesus, left off. Slowly I began to develop a sense of myself.

I was now in my teens, and I started to rebel against the work-and-revival-meeting routine that dominated our lives. On weekends I was determined that if Rosie and I did the floors, the dishes, the baking, and general cleanup, by which time the boys had nearly succumbed to the fumes of chicken manure while cleaning the barns, we should all be taken to town in the afternoon for an outing.

Mother was relatively easy to convince, but Father was a tougher case. He needed a reason to go to town. He was too tired to wander the stores in Winkler, looking at things he couldn't afford, but he was the only one with a driver's license. Every weekend we had a tug-of-war over the shopping trip. "The cat can look at the king," Mother used to humor him, unsuccessfully. Nothing made farm chores more enjoyable for me than the thought of wandering the spacious Winkler dry goods store on Main Street, fingering crisp new blouses and the stiff cuffs of the latest bell bottoms in the Style-Rite women's department, side by side with the sunburned faces of Mennonite ladies.

The one time Father went without a fuss was when he'd

decided to buy an accordion for Rosie and me. It was the closest thing to a piano he could afford. Our passion for playing a musical instrument began in earnest in Domain, where a piano stood at the back of the classroom. All of the girls except my sister and me took turns playing "O Canada" every morning while the rest stood at attention and sang. I was seized by such jealousy with the way Tanya's hands danced effortlessly on the keys; I could barely sing along.

Father loved music and felt bad that he was unable to provide us with formal lessons. Every evening before bed, we gathered in the living room to sing and pray, and he had promised us that as soon as he could afford it, he would buy us a musical instrument, although lessons were still out of the question. At the Winkler music store, Mr. Riemer showed us how to push and pull our new instrument into submission. It looked easy, but it wasn't. It was a heady experience for my sister and me, who thought we were on our way to accordion greatness. All the excitement at the store came home with us. Rosie and I timed each other for exactly half an hour of practice before we traded off. We were hard at it when Father tried to hush us because he couldn't hear on the phone.

"Are you missing anything?" yelled the manager of the Winkler music store through the commotion.

"No sir, I don't think so," Father replied.

"Well, there's a little boy here who's crying, and he says he belongs to you," shouted Mr. Reimer through a screech of bad notes. In all the flurry we had forgotten Phillip, and no one noticed. We would surely have discovered his absence when it came time for chores.

As a teenager, I craved my own sense of space, a measure of independence. Father agreed that I could get a job and came with me for my interview at the Salem Personal Care Home in Winkler, where my cousin Rachel already worked full-time. "If she gives you any trouble at all, just call me," he told Mrs. Shritt, who agreed to hire me for four hours after school in the dining room. I was thrilled to be earning my own money. After class I reported to the Salem Home kitchen to serve supper and do the dishes for frail and elderly Mennonites.

Mr. Heoppner always took his false teeth out of his pocket and put them beside his plate for moral support when he ate his supper. Most of the time he forgot them on his tray, and I put them through the dishwasher before returning them to him. He was a sizable man with bedsores, who only wanted to eat bread. Eating bread was a source of comfort to him, and if we denied him five slices with his meal, huge tears would stream down his face. "You are starving me to death!" he'd cry accusingly.

I felt sorry for him and many of the others because it seemed so sad that none of their families could look after them anymore. On the Hutterite colony we were taught that it is an honor and a privilege to look after your aging parents and grandparents, but the monetary and time demands on families in the outside world made such a cushioned circle of care difficult to duplicate.

Hello, Ann-Marie:

They told me how disappointed you were when you were told I was in Baker [Colony]. I was so terribly sorry. Especially that birthday cake. We could have had lots of fun. You were too considerate, Ann-Marie, with that John Denver songbook. I don't know exactly what to say. Thanks a billion! But mostly I feel the motive behind it which I appreciate even more than that. What can I say? . . . when I heard you were here I was kind of floored. I thought you'd come the Saturday before at Dafit Vetter's funeral. So I didn't bargain on you coming next weekend. I didn't have much choice. Lisa and I had to clean my Aunt Mary's house. I knew that for four weeks beforehand, but didn't know precisely just when. I can vouch that your cake was delicious. I was wondering if you had baked it. I especially thought those yellow roses were very pretty. When will be the next time you come around? I missed singing with you . . . groan. I could knock someone on the head! Thunk, blam . . . I missed everything! I'm so darn sorry it had to work out that way, you going one way and me going the other. Thanks for the songbook, but mostly thanks for being my friend.

— Love, Catherine

Winkler and Plum Coulee were predominately white societies, and it was through the Global Missions Organization that we made our acquaintance with black people. Each summer the church imported a dash of color from Africa and the West Indies, a handful of brothers and sisters from affiliate churches, to attend church camp in Canada. After a week of sitting on pews, they naturally wanted to stay on and experience some Canadian culture, so the elders in the church asked my parents to take them in for three weeks. We had no room, but my parents said yes.

We could not have been more opposite, from the color of our skin, to the speed with which we moved, to the foods we ate. At a loss for words, Father referred to them as "darkies." They in kind called us "whities," and we hit it off immediately. Summer was our busy season, and we had so much work to do we hurried everywhere we went. Our guests, however, sauntered, slapping at the flies and mosquitoes with one of Mother's dish towels. We gulped down our meat and potatoes while they chewed and savored theirs, wondering out loud if we ever ate curried rice or fish. We had not heard of their dishes, but Mother let the ladies take over her small kitchen and show us how.

They asked to use Mother's washing machine but failed to mention they had never used one before. When we heard loud groans and rattling coming from the basement, Mother discovered that they had stuffed the machine with their entire wardrobe and every color of garment they owned. Our differences in speech became more fodder for humor. We razzed them for the way they said "ax" instead of "ask," and they poked fun at our pitiful "th" sounds, laughing until our sides hurt. Sister Jenny let me touch her hair and roared like thunder when I told her it felt like soft steel wool. Her arms and legs glistened from her daily application of Vaseline. She said it was her best beauty secret, and I immediately started in on the large jar mother used for Brian's diaper rash in the hopes that my skin would look as silky as hers.

It was clear we had the same God. We sang and worked, played and prayed together. They injected our summers with fun. Their laid-back disposition was good for us. They got just as much work done without being as frantic as we were, tearing around at high speed. We held hands and wept when they left for home. None became dearer to us than Rhoney Pryce.

He was a tall, handsome nineteen-year-old from the Caribbean island of Antigua. Mature and resourceful, Rhoney loved hard work, good fun, and playing pranks. He was black as midnight, but he fit in with us like a missing piece of a puzzle. We all fell in love with him. My brothers idolized him; my parents, whom he towered over, adored him; and I without any effort developed a crush on him.

We had a large strawberry patch, which we slaved over in early July when the berries were ripe. Our challenge was to sell them as soon as they were picked, because they perished quickly in the hot weather. Rhoney knew his way around the marketplace at his home in Antigua, and he showed this clueless bunch how it should be done at our home. Piling one crate on top of his head and one in each hand, he walked out to the road. Tall, proud, and statuesque, he created such a spectacle that cars on the highway slowed down for a good look, and then he had them. With his blinding white smile and charming manner, he coerced tight-fisted Mennonites into buying every last strawberry we picked. My brothers swore he cheated and put glue on his head to balance the crates, but he just laughed as they tried desperately to imitate him.

That first summer we became buddies while working in the garden and gathering eggs together during the day, and in the evenings playing soccer and football on our large front lawn. He was full of zest and energy and gave my athletic brothers a work-out to remember. Rhoney didn't seem to mind that he spent his so-called Canadian holiday working on a farm. He was meticulously groomed, his light cotton shirts and pants pressed to professional standards. Mother couldn't believe the way he could wield her iron but insisted on doing his laundry and promised his standards would be upheld.

When he left to go home, we all stood in a row, sniffling. He was like our vacation, and now it was over and the fun was going home. After he'd said his good-bye to the rest of the family, he asked me if I would go on a short walk with him. He took my hand as we walked, and I started to tingle, and my stomach had butterflies. He talked about how much he'd enjoyed himself and how dear my family was to him. When he hugged me and asked if I would be his girlfriend, I said yes, and Rhoney gave me a silver clasp bracelet, promising to return the following summer.

Dear Ann-Marie,

My 16th birthday went by unnoticed by everyone, even myself. Who can remember such a thing on a day the Canadians lost their pants to the Russians? I won't talk about the Canada–Russia series. It's a thorn in my flesh. Oct 8, 1974.

— Catherine

I could not relate to many of the Mennonite girls at school, who seemed content to get a job, marry locally, and have children after high school. I wanted a much bigger life, even though the dangers of such a dream were constantly drilled into me at church. God, marriage, and family were all that was offered to a good Christian girl, but I wasn't sold. Instead, I wrote myself a letter in which I promised to not marry until I was at least twenty-eight years old.

I had Sandra, who was always so happy to see me; I had faithful Catherine, whose letters I lived for; I had Charlene looking out for me; and now I had Rhoney too. But my desire to fit in was broadened to a bigger challenge: the English world at large. With Charlene as a tutor, I was gaining confidence, and I shared everything she taught me with Catherine.

The summer after Rhoney left, I was immersed in our murky dugout, wearing the bracelet that he had given me and a Hutterite dress. My parents took the plunge, too, so to speak. But it was a decision Mother in particular wrestled with.

Adult baptism is one of the tenets of the Hutterite faith. Jacob Hutter was burned at the stake in the town square in Innsbruck, Austria, for insisting on adult baptism, in direct contradiction with the teachings of the Catholic Church. Those sacrifices still meant something to Mother, who had been baptized in New Rosedale as an adult at age nineteen. In preparation for baptism, her behavior had been scrutinized for a full year, and she was required to memorize long excerpts of Hutterite catechism and say them aloud in church. Every Sunday afternoon, for six weeks prior to Easter, she and the other candidates had to attend the homes of all the department heads at the New Rosedale Colony and receive a half hour of admonition and Bible reading. These included the German teacher, John Maendel; Andreas Hofer, the senior minister; Jake Maendel, the assistant minister, and Paul Hofer Sr., the farm boss.

Each candidate confessed his or her sins to the head minister and by doing so became reborn in Christ. Transgressions, such as earning private money, drinking to excess, or physically and verbally abusive behavior, warranted harsher punishments for those who had made baptismal vows, since a higher standard was now expected of them. According to the Hutterite Church, faith in Jesus Christ must be expressed through the love and service of the community.

On Easter Sunday, the baptismal candidates were called to the front, where they knelt down in a row. Andreas Hofer, the senior minister, cupped his hand over each head while Jake Maendel poured water into Andreas's hands. When the water was released, each became full members of the church and received communion for the first time. Father had taken his vows and officially joined the Hutterite church a year before my mother. After much thought, arms locked, my parents were rebaptized together.

It had taken them a long time to let go of the vestiges of their Hutterite life. Their appearance had not been a burden, but one day we arrived home from school to find Mother with her hair cut and Father with his beard shaved off. It was astonishing. Mother looked much younger, and Father didn't seem as stern without his beard. It had really suited him, and I was sorry to see it go.

Dear Ann-Marie:

I wish you'd come around. I'm often wishy for you. We could go for a walk in the rain. You know, nobody would be crazy enough to go for a stroll in the rain except you. Come soon!

— Love, Catherine

Rhoney returned the following July. We were like a bunch of happy puppies, jumping up and down, thrilled to see him. I was a few pounds heavier, but he just shook his head when he saw me, released his suitcase, and stretched out his arms.

We worked hard in the vegetable patch that summer and enjoyed starlit walks in the evenings along the railroad tracks that ran across the far side of Father's fields. Rhoney tore up and down the yard with my spirited brothers and lingered over coffee in the afternoons with my parents, exchanging stories about how faith in God had changed their lives. He had earned their trust, but my father was very uncomfortable with me dating. He didn't have the heart to say anything to Rhoney but sent word through Mother, who discouraged a serious relationship. Rhoney knew I was still very young, but he assured me he would give me time to grow up. In the meantime, he would direct his energies toward immigrating to Canada and getting a job in the hospitality industry.

Our relationship lost its innocence when Rhoney and I went to the Winkler fair. I could feel the stares from the townspeople as we walked by holding hands. Rhoney was so proud, but I wriggled like a kitten trying to escape his clutches. My face grew red as I twisted my fingers out of his grip. I didn't like being gawked at, and I wished the ground would swallow me up. Those awful feelings of inadequacy came rushing back at me like a tidal wave. My own culture was so subject to ridicule that I didn't have the maturity or confidence to defend Rhoney's. I was still that vulnerable ten-year-old trying to make sense of myself and my new world, a tender root trying to push through the ground and become a flower. Hiding behind English clothes and hairstyles wasn't enough. I needed time and space to become, but I could not explain this to Rhoney.

He was devastated when I broke off the relationship by letter after he went back to Antigua, and he tried to change my mind. When he saw that reasoning with me was hopeless, he turned to my parents for comfort. They wrote him a letter, reassuring him of the special place he would always hold in their hearts.

To Mum and Dad . . .

I just cannot find words to express myself to you the way I really want to for your thoughtfulness, kindness, and affection to me at all times. I say these words from deep within my heart. Your letter was very meaningful to me, and I just cannot get over the fact of how personal you were to me. It really shows me you care, which I must honestly say I was aware of. Mum and Dad, your letter drives the stakes of love in my heart for both of you deeper still.

— Love, Rhoney

I went back to dreaming and becoming. I wanted to wear makeup and get my ears pierced, but Father wouldn't allow it. With the money from my job at Salem Home, I bought some light blue Revlon eye shadow, Maybelline mascara, and Bonne Belle strawberry lip gloss. When no one was around, I would hide in the bathroom and try them on, but then one of my brothers or sisters would need the washroom and start pounding on the door, and I had to quickly wash it all off. They were such a nuisance!

Dear Ann-Marie,

On Saturday we went picking string beans at Baker Colony. They have a big garden in comparison to the people they got. Anyways, our girls (silly nuts), decided that the boys from Sunnyside will be coming to our place, as they said they would, but any crazy kook could have told them they would rather go to the Hulba in Bloomfield than come here and have a baseball game. So we rushed back and it was all in vain.

— Catherine

In grade twelve, I got a job as a carhop at A&W. I loved everything about it: the teen burgers, the onion rings, the chubby chicken, and the root beer. It was located next to our high school in Winkler, and I worked an eight-hour shift every day after school. Father insisted that I save my wages and buy a used car. When I had accumulated six hundred dollars, he found me a small blue Mustang. I named it Charlie, and it took me everywhere I needed to go.

One day, our manager, Cornie Blatz, called me into the office. "You're going to represent A&W in the Miss Winkler Queen Pageant, and you're going to win!" he said, slapping his hands on his desk. Entering a pageant was the furthest thing from my mind.

"I'm too fat," I told him.

He grinned. "You make up for it in personality and talent."

"I have nothing to wear," I confessed.

Cornie wrote out a check for one hundred dollars and handed it to me. "Then go get yourself something," he countered.

Cornie Blatz was fun to work for. He was a hard-living man with a soft heart and a mischievous twinkle in his eye. He was involved in the community, but his business had never won the pageant. In a staunchly Mennonite town, he was putting his money on a Hutterite. Catherine couldn't believe it when I told her the news.

I heard rumblings that a non-Mennonite girl shouldn't be in the pageant, and Catherine agreed that I should thank my lucky stars just to have been entered. She had to be there, she told me, she just had to, and we started plotting and planning ways she could attend the Old Time Value Days, the annual summer festival in Winkler, where the pageant was held. Part of the pageant included a talent competition, and she loved my idea of singing Sonny and Cher's hit "I Got You Babe" with my then–five-year-old brother, Brian.

I knew the pageant's penny vote was a lost cause. Families of the other girls were stuffing their boxes with twenty-dollar bills, but Dad refused to put any money in my box because he said it was a people vote, and it would be unethical. When I related this to Catherine, she pressed a handful of nickels and dimes in my hand for the boxes.

The day of the pageant was like a dream. Hutterites from nearby colonies had obviously heard of my entry and came to watch. I was excited to see some polka-dotted heads in the throng around the stage, but my eyes searched the crowd for Catherine. My duet with Brian went very well, and we received lots of applause, but one of the contestants had sewn a number of gorgeous gowns, and I felt sure she had won the competition.

It was a warm, windy night up on the main stage. I had lost a few pounds and was wearing the lime green dress I had bought with Cornie's money. When the judges called my name as the winner, cheers rang out, and I was hugged and robed and crowned. A bouquet of flowers was thrust in the crook of my arm, and I was pushed into center stage, looking like I'd been struck by lightning. Then at the back of the crowd, I saw her—dark eyes shining and a hopeful smile watching me as I stood in the spotlight. Catherine!

"I knew it, I knew it, I knew it!" An elated Cornie Blatz beamed as I came off the stage. "You have made me so proud!" he shouted, as he grabbed and squeezed me till I couldn't breathe.

On the way to the photographer's studio with my runners-up, I saw my parents leaning against a storefront, dumbfounded. "You're supposed to say congratulations," I coached.

Back home, I strutted and clicked my way around the house in my heels and regalia. "*Nitt foll in den Brunn einhin.* Don't fall into the well," Father warned when he returned from checking the chickens. Pride was considered the ultimate flaw in Hutterite culture, and we were taught to diligently guard against it. In my moment of triumph, Father was worried I might get my nose too high in the air and wouldn't see where I was going.

I wrapped myself in the long velvet robe and lay down on the bed. The rabbit skin collar choked my neck, and the combs on my crown pierced my head, but I could not bring myself to take them off. It had taken too long to transform from a Hutterite nobody to an English somebody. I'd finally pushed aside the ridicule and rejection and had swallowed the bitterness of school yard taunts. Even so, longing still plagued my heart.

I thought about the girl from a lifetime ago who had slept in her Hutterite dress the night before she was swept away from the colony, blissfully content with her station in life. Fairholme had been full of hope and promise. By now, I would be a *Diene*, and wearing a *Tiechel*. I would have a cook week, a bake week, and a hope chest filled with cross-stitching and dreams about the future. *Oh, Oma, if I could just lay my head against your bosom and feel you stroke my hair and hear you tell me again that someday I would understand Father's desire to be free.* Why couldn't he have tried harder to fit in like other colony men? Paul Vetter and Paul Jr. had their struggles with the system, too, but they hadn't left.

Like a bird pushed out of its nest, I had been forced out of my cherished existence and thrust into the harsh, cold climate of the outside world, left to fumble my way to a new identity. My turning point came in a letter from Catherine. It was then that I realized, and was able to appreciate, the gift that Father had given to me.

Dear Ann-Marie:

I feel I owe you this letter to sort out my thoughts and mixed feelings, doubts, anxieties, etc. . . . innumerable! The list is endless. I'm beginning to feel doubtful about my leaving and whether I'm making the right decision. Not that I'm saying I'm backing off, yet. The reason is because of countless things, doubts of getting a job—well first of all, as it eventually turns out, I'll be leaving just a week before my cooking week, and it could possibly be the week of the big wedding. You know, George is getting married on July 16. I don't know if I feel pangs because of a sense of duty and consider canceling my leaving hence? Am I crazy? You probably think I am. Well, maybe I don't know what is right anymore. And then the girls are going and practicing singing for the wedding, and there I am, of course, along with them knowing pretty well I could let them down on the wedding when they're counting on me. But the thing is if I leave, I feel I'd first of all want to spend a week at church camp with you to analyze my thinking and get myself going the right direction. I don't know if my mom caught on when I told her I'm going and I don't expect to be back. She didn't say much. I didn't either. So it stands. With my Dad, that's another story. He'd be very sore at my leaving, I'm sure. I've talked around the subject several times before with him and maybe he suspects. The thing is, no amount of talking will soothe my parents' feeling about the matter (my dad's anyway. I told him I see no future here and he couldn't give me any good ideas on how to go on and feel satisfied). I know how he feels, but if I start listening to everybody's opinion I'm sure I'll go crazy.

I told sister Janice I'm leaving, and she honestly thought I'm nuts and couldn't believe it. Well, all she thought about was she'd have nobody to sing with at the wedding, that I was sort of leaving her stranded. Well I think that's very selfish thinking, and why shouldn't I do what I feel is right? In a way I can't really blame her. You know we were a big part of wedding entertainment, and weddings don't come every day. I know my lazy self would really like to sit back and indulge in this living. It's really very easy. That's the whole trouble about it. It's so easy to slide back into comfort and security . . . you know I'm so green in life outside the colony, so "wet behind the ears." I get scared. That's why I'd like to get off my easy chair and start living, start giving the most of my ability, making myself a better person.

— Catherine

As Catherine bared her soul, I understood for the first time that freedom is not found on a Hutterite colony any more than it is found off the colony. True freedom is an inside job—it is taking responsibility for ourselves and daring to confront and release the anger and resentment that keeps us from leading meaningful lives. My parents had wanted us to have that freedom by not saddling us with their baggage, but most of all, by pursuing the path of forgiveness themselves. Now, it was up to us to rise to the challenge.

Epilogue

To my Son, Levi,

I can still see your sweet face waiting for an answer as we stood at the edge of the cemetery, a gentle breeze blowing the long prairie grasses around Renie's grave.

After our family left Fairholme, I discovered very quickly that my culture didn't have any value in my new life. Overnight, it became a handicap, and I had to reinvent myself to be accepted. I didn't have a skin color, like Rhoney, to give me away, so I hid my Hutterite self in English clothing, melting into the mainstream and cringing at the word *Hutterite* because of people's harsh and misinformed opinions.

After high school, I wanted to become a professional singer. Your grandpa Dornn was worried about such a worldly career choice, because he knew I wouldn't be satisfied singing only religious songs. It was he who suggested I become a news reporter. Reporting is a form of storytelling, and the Maendels are particularly good at that. I took my training in Winnipeg, and it was there that I reclaimed my "Indian" name, Mary-Ann.

Over the coming years, when someone spoke unkindly about my culture, I had remained quiet, although sometimes, on impulse, my voice cried out, "That's not true!" Ignorance and misperceptions had wounded my soul, and I wanted to rise up and openly take my rightful place in society.

Your grandma and grandpa taught me that liberty from our past begins with forgiveness. When Grandpa brought Grandma to Jake Vetter's funeral, he thought about all the times he had been in conflict with Jake Maendel. As he waited for her, he felt so relieved that he had written the letter asking for forgiveness two years earlier. The pain was raw then, and the memories fresh, but Grandpa had consciously chosen the path of forgiveness.

Levi, you are the great-grandson of Joseph and Katrina Maendel from Old Rosedale Colony. If their bones could speak, they would claim you as their own. Nothing will ever change that. So be proud of it, my son, for it is only when we embrace our past that we can find true fulfillment in our future. The dream I used to have about losing my mother in the fabric store because I was distracted by the glitz of beautiful buttons came true. It was the sight of Grandma's skirt and the sound of our own language that led me back to safety. Today, I am filled with a deep appreciation of where I have come from and a better sense of where I'm going. The Hutterite culture has defined me in ways that can never be erased. In my heart, I will always remain a Hutterite.

So now you know, Levi. Now you know.

Afterword

CATHERINE HOFER LEFT Fairholme Colony in 1981, together with her sister, Janice. They both went back to school and became registered nurses. Their parents, Paul Jr. and Katie Hofer, left Fairholme five years later and moved to Winnipeg.

In 1986, Sana Basel and Paul Vetter left Fairholme too. They were lovingly cared for in Winnipeg by their daughter, Sarah, and her husband, Bruce Nordin. Sana Basel died in 2004 at age ninety-four.

In 1977, Ronald and Mary Dornn bought land near Sidney, Manitoba, built a new home, and continued to farm. The following year, they sold a parcel of that land to Katrina Basel's family, who had left Deerboine Colony. Anna Basel also left Deerboine and lived with the Dornn family for several years before joining her children, who had settled in Winnipeg. The four sisters remained deeply devoted to each other. Katrina Basel died in 1987, and Anna Basel in 1999. In 2004, Ronald and Mary sold their farm and retired to Brandon, Manitoba, where they live today. Mary continues to cherish her three surviving brothers, Eddie Maendel of New Rosedale Colony, and Peter and Hons Maendel of Fairholme Colony.

In 1989, Mary-Ann Dornn married Gordon Kirkby. Their son, Levi, was born in 1996.

••

Many years after Jake Maendel's death, Mary Dornn would learn that the last words he uttered before he died were "*Verzeich's mir.*"

"Whom do you want to forgive you?" his daughter had asked, lowering her head over his frail body, but her father was too weak to reply. "Is it Ronald and Mary?" she ventured softly.

He nodded his head and slipped into eternity.

Acknowledgments

I AM FILLED with gratitude to my people, who have always received me with kindness, from the Rockport Colony in Alberta, where we were gently led to our grandmother's grave, and to our friends at the Leask Hutterite Colony near Prince Albert, where I go to reconnect, to my home colonies of Fairholme and New Rosedale that I still love to visit, and all the stops in between.

Thank you, Susie Basel from New Rosedale, for giving me the dress I wore on the book cover, and thank you, Cousin Helen, for being flattered that I wanted it. Mothers have special "giving away" privileges.

Thank you to those who have surprised me with an old photograph or had me into their homes for *Lunschen*. Your stories and anecdotes have found their way into this book to give the reader an honest helping of our humor, our way of looking at the world, and our unmistakable candor.

Some names and places have been changed to maintain privacy, but the sweet and enduring essence of our culture has remained untouched.

A million thanks to Arvel Gray, the spiritual guardian of this book. Thank you for the many hours you spent weeding, watering, and nurturing my manuscript. Thank you for your sense of excellence, for your generosity, and for knowing that writer's block is cured with a sizable piece of pie. Most especially, thank you for the skillful way you helped knit this story together!

Thank you, Catherine Hofer, for revisiting the memories of our childhood with me, for permitting me to use excerpts of the letters you wrote, and for your continued friendship. I cherish you and them, always.

Thank you, Darius Vetter of New Rosedale Colony, for access to your recollections and writings and for letting me sift through your old photographs. I know how much you wanted to read this book, and I hope it makes the library in heaven.

Thank you, Dora Maendel of Fairholme Colony, schoolteacher and daughter of Peter and Sara Maendel, for translating the Carinthian dialect and High German for me. It was a joy to work with you, especially in our own language!

It is with love that I acknowledge my brothers and sisters who took this journey with me, and Mother and Father for trusting me with their deepest secrets.

Thank you to my mother-in-law, Gwen Kirkby, a registered nurse, for guidance on medical protocol; to my husband, Gordon, for your support along the way; and most especially to my treasure Levi, for continuing to ask important questions.

I am indebted to Matt Baugher, who came to Canada to convince me to sign with Thomas Nelson. After so many years of rejection, my book has finally found a wonderful home. Jenny Baumgartner, you're a gem. Thank you and everyone else at Thomas Nelson for helping me ready my manuscript for the rest of the world.

:: FAMILY TREE

Maternal

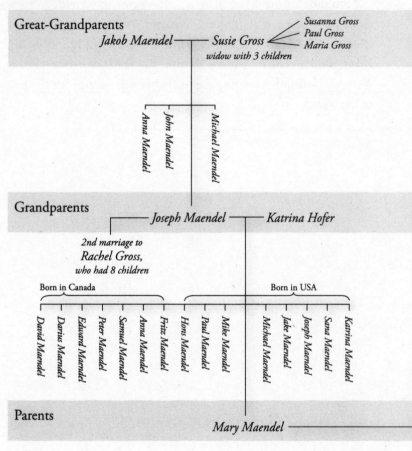

Great-Grandparents

Jakob Maendel —— Susie Gross
widow with 3 children

- Susanna Gross
- Paul Gross
- Maria Gross

Anna Maendel
John Maendel

Michael Maendel

Grandparents

Joseph Maendel —— Katrina Hofer

*2nd marriage to
Rachel Gross,
who had 8 children*

Born in Canada

David Maendel
Darius Maendel
Edward Maendel
Peter Maendel
Samuel Maendel
Anna Maendel
Fritz Maendel
Hans Maendel

Born in USA

Paul Maendel
Mike Maendel
Michael Maendel
Jake Maendel
Joseph Maendel
Sana Maendel
Katrina Maendel

Parents

Mary Maendel ——

Paternal

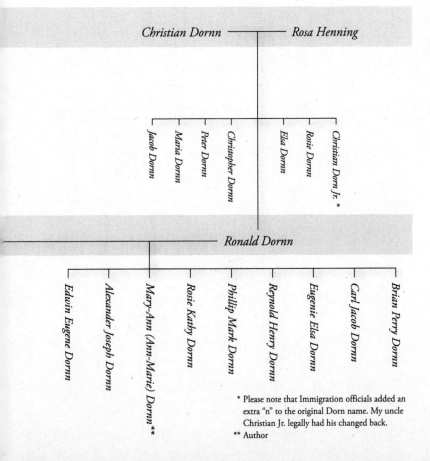

Christian Dornn —— Rosa Henning

Jacob Dornn

Maria Dornn

Peter Dornn

Christopher Dornn

Elsa Dornn

Rosie Dornn

Christian Dorn Jr. *

Ronald Dornn

Edwin Eugene Dornn

Alexander Joseph Dornn

Mary-Ann (Ann-Marie) Dornn **

Rosie Kathy Dornn

Philip Mark Dornn

Reynold Henry Dornn

Eugenie Elsa Dornn

Carl Jacob Dornn

Brian Perry Dornn

* Please note that Immigration officials added an
extra "n" to the original Dorn name. My uncle
Christian Jr. legally had his changed back.

** Author

HUTTERISCH:
Hutterite Language Glossary

Abwärterin, "one who waits on you." A woman who looks after a new mother during the first six weeks after a baby's birth.

Ankela, grandmother

Basel, aunt

Boa, young man

Brot, bread

Buben, young men

bubisch, boy crazy

Diene, a young woman

Dienen, young women

die Wuchen, a six-week period of special treatment extended to women after the birth of each child

drah, twist

Essenschul, children's eating school

Essenschul Ankela, eating school grandmother

Essenstuben, dining room

Federschleiss, feather stripping

Federsock, feather sack

Fittig, pleated apron

Gebet, the evening church service

geistlich, spiritual

Gemeinshaft ist der einzege Weg. Community life is the only way to heaven.

Gerstel, soup

Gonsstoll, goose barn

Gostfrei, beguiling

Gott, God

Henna Hüttel, henhouse

Hochzeit G'schirr, special dishes used only for weddings

Hulba, engagement party

Irdisch, carnal

Jüngste Tog, Judgment Day

Kellerlein, an underground crawl space where store-bought treats are stowed

Kittel, ankle-length, gathered skirt

Korb, basket

Luckela, "baby holder." A young girl between the ages of eleven and fourteen chosen to be the mother's apprentice.

Lunschen, three o'clock lunch

lustig, irresistible

mächtig gut, incredibly good

Mieder, vest

Milch, milk

Mittog, the noon meal

Muetter, mother

Mutterle, little mother

Mütz, bonnet

Mützen, plural of Mütz

Oltvetter, grandfather

Oma, grandma

Opa, grandpa

Ordnung, order

Pfaht, cropped white shirt

Prediger, preacher

Rechnung, accounts

reiche Leut, rich people

Rescha Zwieboch, crisp buns

Schenken, toasts

Schlofbänk, sleeping benches

Schmondengela, creamy angel

Schmond wacken, thick dipping cream

Schmuggi, soft, homemade cheese sprinkled with caraway seeds

Schronk, a fabric storage cupboard

Schutten, cottage cheese

Specksaften, homemade lard soap

stoltz sie, pride

Stonter, trash barrel

Strof, punishment

Stübel, a council of the married men on a colony, who all have a vote on the decision being made

stuck, piece

Teacherin, teacher

Tiechel, a black kerchief with white polka dots

Tiechlen, plural of Tiechel

Tüpfel, dot

unruhigs Wosser, restless water

vermohn, warn

Vetter, uncle

Votar, father

Waiselein, orphan

Wannick, jacket

Weglaufen, running away

Weib, a wife

Weihnachtsgeschenken, Christmas goods

Bibliography

Fairholme Focus. Published by Fairholme Colony.

Hofer, Samuel. *The Hutterites, Lives and Images of a Communal People.* Saskatoon, Saskatchewan: Hofer Publishers

Hostetler, John A. *Hutterite Life.* Scottdale, PA: Herald Press.

The Hutterian Brethren, *Treasures of Time, XVIII.* Published by R. M. of Cartier.

Credits

Photo of Catherine Hofer, courtesy Winnipeg Tribune Photographic Collection, University of Manitoba Archives

Pauline Johnson's poem "The Song My Paddle Sings," courtesy of McMaster University Library.

Hutterite Sucre Pie

1   cup heavy cream
1   egg
$2/3$ cup sugar
2   tbsp. corn starch

Beat together above ingredients and pour into a cooled pie crust that has been baked for 10 minutes at 350 degrees F.

Sprinkle with cinnamon and bake for another 35–40 minutes. Serve warm.

As a young girl growing up at Fairholme Colony in southern Manitoba, this was my very favorite dessert and remains at the top of my list today. This pie is as simple as it is sensational. It will make you happy and possibly fat because you will not be able to stop eating it until it is gone. This pie is the reason I will never be skinny.

Enjoy!

—Mary-Ann Kirkby

*Father and Mother with
Ann-Marie, Alex, Edwin, Rosie*

Mother with Edwin

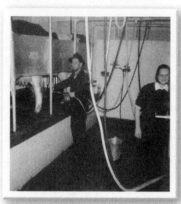

*Mother and Father cleaning the
milk machines*

*We loved visiting Father at the
cow barn*

*Ann-Marie and Rosie
in photo booth*

*Ann-Marie and Sandra
picking feathers*

*Rosie, Ann-Marie with Genie,
cousin Elaine, and Oltvetter*

Brian, our adorable final addition